1

WAR STORIES

WAR STORIES

D-DAY TO THE LIBERATION OF PARIS

ROBERT O. BABCOCK

DEEDS PUBLISHING | ATLANTA, GEORGIA

Most of the material in this book is a subset of stories previously published in 2006 by Deeds Publishing in *War Stories: Utah Beach to Pleiku* by Robert O. Babcock.

Disclaimer - No claim is made as to the historical accuracy of the stories in this book. They are as accurate as memories faded by thirty to thirty-five years can make them, but this is not intended to be a history book that will stand the test of historical scholars. It is the military experiences of 4th Infantry Division veterans as each GI remembers it.

Published by Deeds Publishing
Marietta, GA
www.deedspublishing.com

Printed in the United States of America

Library of Congress Cataloging-in-Publications Data is available upon request

ISBN 978-1-941165-00-3

Books are available in quantity for promotional or premium use. For information, write Deeds Publishing, PO Box 682212, Marietta, GA 30068 or info@deedspublishing.com.

Design and layout by Mark Babcock

First edition 2014

10 9 8 7 6 5 4 3 2 1

This book is dedicated to all past, present, and future veterans of the 4th Infantry Division, especially those who made the supreme sacrifice in defense of our American way of life, and their families.

TABLE OF CONTENTS

Liberation of Paris, August 25, 1944   263

Introduction

This book is one of a series of three that are subsets of the book, *War Stories: Utah Beach to Pleiku,* first published in 2001. That book was my effort to preserve the stories of 4th Infantry Division veterans who had served in World War II, the Cold War, and in Vietnam. Thanks to the input of the 4ID veterans and their family members, that book turned out to be over 725 pages long—much larger than most people want to buy and read.

In this 70th anniversary year of D-Day, the liberation of Paris, the Battle of the Hurtgen Forest, and the Battle of the Bulge in World War II, we decided to republish that book into two World War II and one Vietnam volumes—available in both paperback and e-book. Although the large version is still available in paperback format, we believe our readers will enjoy these smaller volumes as they read or re-read the exploits of Soldiers of the 4th Infantry Division.

As you read the stories, you will see that some stories show the author as deceased. That was the status as of 2000 when the book was first written. Since then, sadly, many more, if not most, of the WWII contributors to these stories are now gone—but their stories live on.

When I first started attending annual reunions of the National 4th Infantry Division Association in 1990, the highlight of each reunion was sitting with WWII vets and listening for hours to the stories of their exploits in Europe. As I anticipated each year sitting down again with a specific veteran whose stories had captivated me the year before, I found that all too often I would ask about where he was, only to find out that he had died, and his stories died with him.

When I became president of the National 4th Infantry Division Association in 1998-2000, one of my primary missions I set for myself was to preserve the stories of 4ID veterans so they would be available long past the time that our veterans went on to their heavenly rewards.

I am currently working on *War Stories II,* adding more World War II, Cold War, and Vietnam stories, and including sections on the 4th Infantry Division's actions in Iraq and Afghanistan. That book will be published once I have enough stories to make it viable. All who served in any capacity with the 4th Infantry Division are encouraged to send me their stories.

As you read this 70th anniversary commemorative edition, reflect back on those members of "the greatest generation" who cared enough to not only fight and defeat the Nazi threat to the world, but also cared enough to write down their memories so future generations could learn from their experiences. I challenge all veterans of all eras to do the same—and make sure your family, your unit, and others you care about have access to your stories. If you need help doing that, feel free to contact this author at info@deedspublishing.com.

Ten percent of all profits of this book will be donated to the National 4th Infantry Division Association to help perpetuate its almost 100 years helping the veterans and family members of those who served in that great division—Steadfast and Loyal,

Bob Babcock, January 2014
President and Historian, National 4th Infantry Division Association
Company B, 1st Battalion, 22nd Infantry Regiment
4th Infantry Division, Vietnam 1966-1967

D-Day
June 6, 1944

"We will start the war from here," was the decision made by Brigadier General Teddy Roosevelt, Jr. and Colonel James Van Fleet when they found the lead elements of the 4th Infantry Division had been landed 2,000 yards off their assigned beach. The first Allied seaborne troops to land on D-Day were men of the 4th Infantry Division who landed on Utah Beach at HHour (0630 hours) on June 6, 1944. From that "Longest Day," the 4th Infantry Division continued the fight across Europe for the next eleven months until finally achieving total victory over the German war machine.

This section is the longest in our book. The D-Day stories included here are part of a presentation made by our veterans to the National D-Day Museum at its Grand Opening in New Orleans, LA, on June 6, 2000. Over one hundred 4th Infantry Division D-Day veterans made up the largest organized veterans group at that significant event, paying tribute to all veterans of D-Day. Here are their stories.

A Chronology of the 4th Infantry Division, 6 June 1944

Extracted from Chronology 1941-1945, Special Studies, U.S. Army in World War II, by Mary H. Williams, Washington, DC; GPO, 1971. Courtesy of Dr. Robert Sterling Rush, 22nd Regiment Society Historian and former Command Sergeant Major of First U.S. Army and 1st Battalion, 22nd Infantry Regiment.

For further studies on the 22nd Infantry Regiment in WW II and the Hürtgen Forest campaign, read: Hell in Hürtgen Forest: The Ordeal and triumph of an American Infantry Regiment. Robert S. Rush, Ph.D. ISBN 0-7006-1128-2. Publication date (tentative) October 2001. University Press of Kansas.

6 June 1944: Utah Beach

The 4th Div, reinforced by 359th Inf of 90th Div, lands at H Hour, 8th Inf leading and against relatively light opposition secures beachhead; 8th Inf gets some elements to Les Forges crossroads and others to Turqueville area, but enemy retains salient between these and 82nd A/B Div units at St. Mére Eglise. 12th Inf, 4th Div, reaches Beuzeville au Plain area to left of 101st A/B Div and 22nd advances along coast to general line Hamel-deCruttes-St. Germain-de-Varreville.

B.P. "Hank" Henderson, Knoxville, TN
Medic, 22nd Infantry Regiment

Looked Like Coney Island

They had a large tent they called the "Blue Room" where they took us in small groups and briefed us on our mission for D-Day. The 3rd Battalion commander was LTC Arthur S. Teague, one of the finest officers in the army. On June 1, I loaded onto the supply ship for the 3rd Battalion. I was in charge of medical supplies for the assault battalion. My jeep driver, Dago Oliver and I were the only two 22nd Infantry medics on the ship. We spent five days on the English Channel, one of the roughest bodies of water in the world. The last three days I was so sick I hardly knew I was alive.

On the morning of D-Day, June 6, I began to come around at daybreak. We had an English crew manning the ship and one of them came over with some of that British tea in a canteen cup. I drank a little of it. He went back over to one of the other Englishmen and I heard him say, "that big old tall boy is not going to make it." (How wrong he was; I made it through the whole eleven months.)

We had to wait until the first and second waves cleared the beach before we got the signal to bring in the supplies. As we started in and could see the beach, one of the guys from New York said it looked just like Coney Island on a Sunday afternoon. When we got closer, the coastal guns were firing down the beach—that killed the Coney Island ideas real fast.

When the ramp dropped, the lead jeep would not start. It had to come off before the rest of the trucks and jeeps could make it off. I decided I was not staying on that ship loaded with ammunition so I was the first man off the ship. I went up to the sea wall, which was about three or four feet high, and dug a squatting foxhole where I stayed until all of the vehicles were off the ship. I got out of my hole and started up the farm lane that the trucks and jeeps took. About 100 yards up the lane, a buck sergeant was leaning on his antitank gun. I stopped to chat with him. As we were talking, a sniper shot him in the leg.

"Holy mackerel, I got me a million dollar wound!" he said.

I left him a bandage and continued up the farm lane and came to a farmhouse. I had been there less than ten minutes when a woman came out with two young boys, about seven and nine years old. Both of them had real bad forearm burns. I used a whole tube of Unguentine (antiseptic salve) on those two fellows' arms. I put gauze on the arms and then wrapped and taped them real good.

When I finished with the boys, one of our guys came up and said, "Hank, you haven't had anything to eat in a long time."

I said, "This is my fourth day without food."

He had some cheese and crackers left over from a ten-in-one ration. He took my canteen cup around by the barn and got me some cider. My first meal in France was cheese, crackers, and French cider.

Later that evening, I was lying by the side of my foxhole as the glider troops were being towed over. I heard later that most of them were casualties. The Germans had the French people plant big poles in the landing fields and that played hell with the glider troops. The next day, a lone plane strafed our ammunition and blew it all to hell and back. I lay in a foxhole with two men on top of me for 47 minutes—as timed by one of our medical officers.

Harry Bailey, Columbia, SC
Company E, 2nd Battalion, 8th Infantry Regiment

Night of June 5, 1944

Early morning hours of June 6, 1944, found me on a troop ship with the rest of my company headed for the beaches of Normandy, France. I was a twenty-year old platoon sergeant trying to lead a platoon that had thirty-eight men plus two medics. We had boarded a Coast Guard troop carrier, the APA Barnett, somewhere close to Plymouth, England. We set sail with thousands of other ships including big battle-wagons, cruisers, and hundreds of destroyers. The night of June 5, we moved all night getting into position at 0200 hours for the invasion. We had a breakfast of beans and bacon and got seasick pills. Then we prepared to go over the side of the ship on rope latticework, which was very hard to do with all the equipment we had to take, plus weapons, ammunition, K rations, and water. Some carried bangalore torpedoes to blow holes in the barbed wire.

The waves were about ten feet high and the LCVPs were bouncing up and down. Some men got hurt getting into the assault boats. We got loaded and shoved off, joining many assault boats. We circled for about one hour, and then in a line we headed for the beach, which was about twelve miles away. At about 0545 hours we passed the rocket boats that were firing thousands of rockets on the beach that burst like artillery. Just then, the B-26 bombers bombed where we were heading. Our battalion, 2nd Battalion, 8th Infantry Regiment, was the first wave of seaborne troops to land on Utah Beach.

Everything happened very fast for this twenty-year-old soldier who felt "like I was in a fog." Then the sailor on the assault boat dropped the ramp and we hit the water, which was about waist deep, and headed for shore. Artillery and small arms fire were all about the beach. My first scout, Douglas Mason, from Michigan, was the first to reach the sand dunes and I ran and dropped down beside him to look to see which way to go. He was immediately killed with a hit to the head by a sniper's bullet. I knew I had to move fast or I would be next so I ran forward as fast as I could go. The rest of the platoon followed. The lieutenant, who was platoon leader, when I last saw him, was pointing inland but would not go with us. He left my squad leaders and me to fend for ourselves. Colonel McNeely relieved him and sent him to another company. I was told he was killed on D+2.

We tried to move to where we thought the causeway was but got pinned down by machine gun fire. We finally got moving and had to cross a minefield. I lost two or three men. My medic got his foot blown off. We made it to the causeway at a dead run and started to get fire from a "knee" mortar. A round hit close and I got shrapnel in my right leg. I didn't know I was hit until a medic saw blood. He gave me a shot and a band-aid.

E Company, 2nd Battalion, 8th Infantry Regiment kept attacking toward St. Marie du Mont. The tanks from the 70th Tank Battalion joined in the fight. One hit a mine and was knocked out. Airborne troopers took twelve prisoners from my company commander. They weren't playing any games. Airborne was called "Big Pockets." The Airborne was in St. Marie du Mont, but we didn't know it. We had the 70th Tank Bat-

talion fire at a belfry, which was visible in the town. We moved i....
Marie du Mont and toward St. Mére Eglise where the Airborne were cut
off by enemy forces.

On D+2, we fought our way into St. Mére Eglise under very heavy
artillery fire, losing our company commander, Howard Lees, for the rest
of the war as well as three or four more men. On the evening of D+2,
the 8th Infantry Regiment and the 505th Parachute Regiment caught
two battalions of German troops trying to relieve each other and demolished both battalions, killing approximately five hundred men. After the
attack, we tried to get some sleep. We had been attacking for almost 72
hours. D+3 found us attacking toward Cherbourg. The count of men at
the end of D+3 was fifteen left of our original forty.

When Brigadier General Teddy Roosevelt Jr. died on July 12, 1944,
I was picked for his Honor Guard as well as Captain George Mabry and
other men of the 8th Infantry Regiment. In late November 1944, George
Mabry earned the Medal of Honor during fighting in the Hürtgen For-
est to become one of four men of the 4th Infantry Division to earn the
Medal of Honor in World War II: BG Teddy Roosevelt Jr., LTC George
Mabry, 1LT Bernard Ray, and PFC Marcario Garcia.

Martin King (Deceased), Wills Point, TX
Company H, 2nd Battalion, 22nd Infantry Regiment

Help Us, Lord

On June 3, 1944, at about 1100 hours, Lieutenant Tommy Harrison
and I went into a quonset building with Sergeants Guinn and Pike.
What we viewed was an amazing sight for me. There, on a sand display
table, was a replica of the French coastline (the landing area) with many,
many "to-scale" duplications of every building or bluff. These recognizable coastal features were to be used as landmark references to guide each
landing party to their proper section of action.

As Lieutenant Harrison pointed out all the details given to him, I
learned that my platoon would be loaded into small landing craft (LCPs)
and put ashore at about H-Hour minus 1. Our land reference, an abandoned windmill or silo type structure on the French mainland, would
be to our left as we approached the assault area. Our mission was to get

ashore, locate two causeways, and, if possible, secure them in order to allow the faster advance of the first and second wave of assault troops to cross over the inundated area. This swamp-like area was about a mile and a half long, up to a mile wide, and five feet deep in places. It was both an excellent antipersonnel and tank barrier. It was subject to being covered with flammable liquid and set afire. It was very important to capture the enemy causeway positions.

At this point, viewing the shoreline replica and reference marks that were to be very important to the whole landing operation, Lieutenant Harrison became very serious in his briefing. He asked for questions and said that this was the time to ask; however, it seemed all we wanted to do was gaze at this table of small scaled-down models and memorize the sight that we would face if the operation was to be a success. "Help us, Lord, help us," Lieutenant Harrison said to us, with an intense stare into my eyes. "Now remember, the landmark structure is to be positioned to your left flank." He repeated this several times. Of course, we would get to review the situation table again the next morning. Thoughts of things past and things yet to come flashed through my mind. Then there were some mini-prayers, I'm sure.

That afternoon, Chaplain Bill Boice arrived in our area and men who wished to do so were gathered for a religious service. We sang hymns while Chaplain Boice played a field organ. I seemed to lead out on the hymns since I had had chaplain's assistant experience, stateside. I was loud with it, to say the least. We listened to his message and blessing with an uplifting prayer for God's strength and protection for us in the times ahead. I remember that service to this very day. It is still a memorable experience that I have relived over and over.

By this time, we were equipping ourselves for the events to come. Each man, except the machine gun operators, prepared a backpack with four boxes of .30- caliber ammunition (eighty pounds) to be carried in on the landing. I, too, bore one of these, as did the men, plus all our other equipment.

At dawn on June 6, 1944, H-Hour minus 1 hour or so (about 0530 hours), my platoon and I went over the side and down a rope-net ladder into a smaller landing craft (LCP). The sea was rough and it took a few attempts for all of us to get aboard. When Sergeant Guinn, the coxswain, and I decided that all were accounted for, we pulled away into a circling rendezvous pattern waiting for the "go ahead" signal. This lasted a few minutes and it was a very impressive sight.

Some rocket launching barges nearby were shooting off their many rockets, sometimes overhead and always toward the shoreline. The coxswain seemed to be very observant and cautious, maybe anxious, but we were all scared and quiet. Suddenly he opened the throttle and sped toward the beach. Gazing ahead, we soon sighted a recognizable feature that resembled our landmark reference. It also appeared to be off to our left flank.

Anxious moments followed. We agreed that this was our action sector, and the coxswain opened the throttle wide open. The windmill silo structure was then very visible to our left. When we were within a hundred yards or so of the beach, he de-throttled, let down the ramp, and shouted, "Get out, get out!" We did. I was first into the water, waist high to me (a six footer) and the rest of the men followed. It was quite a burden fighting to stand up while wading through rough waves with eighty pounds of ammunition on our backs, but each of us made it. This was about 0550 hours. Being on land now, we located one causeway but couldn't tell if the other one was to our right or left. A little confusion to say the least, what with some small arms fire directed at us. Alone on a strange beach was never like what we experienced before on our practice runs; however, the firing was going over us and into the water.

We dug in two machine guns and fell in behind a sand dune. If you have ever prayed with your eyes open wide while scanning the horizon, you can imagine what this was like. We waited and waited. The time was getting closer to H-hour, 0630 hours. It seemed like an eternity because no wave of our troops came in behind us.

You know something? I can't remember hearing a single prayer of repentance, just ones of deliverance like, "Lord, please let me get back home." A joking remark that I had heard many times before surfaced in my mind: "Second lieutenants and mop handles are expendable in this man's army." This seemed accurate. Still, there was no wave of friendly troops.

After about an hour and a half, all kinds and sizes of firepower began coming in and going out. We could tell that a real war was happening down the beach to our left. Sergeant Guinn and two men had gone out to scout our position for a causeway to our right. Surprisingly, someone said to look there on the causeway, since coming toward us were six or eight men in uniform, one of them walking with a limp. We thought this to be very strange for the situation we expected at the time. We had been schooled to be very careful of every move, that it might be a trap. Then someone said, "They're paratroopers." They soon met us and told us that this road was clear for a way inland...only some small arms fire in the distance. These troopers were supposed to have been dropped at St. Mére Eglise but missed their target by seven or eight miles. They had heard the action and came to it thinking it might be some of their outfit. They disappeared down the beach to our right.

We had begun to return fire on two pillboxes as there was more light of day, but all we could do was hold our position and wonder where in the world everybody else was. Near midday, we made contact with men of the 3rd Battalion and learned they had made land to our left, and well out of their proper assault sector.

We would soon find out what a real war was like now that the third battalion had to clear the beach ahead of them.

The 2nd Battalion Commander, Major Lum Edwards, was to have landed behind us as the second wave following the 3rd Battalion (depending on the amount of success), but they did not come in. The 2nd Battalion, which was my battalion, had landed quite a distance to my left.

Years later, reading Chaplain Boice's book, *History of the 22nd Infantry Regiment in WWII*, the thought came to me that I had taken a fighting unit to war and no one came. I dislike saying it, but it seems that we learned the meaning of SNAFU, what with bad seas and questionable navigation. Somehow, we got together and soon got into the fight in support of Item and/or King Company.

They hit the first causeway and cleared it. It was a slow go, but we did cross on the causeway and fell in to support the rifle company. Ahead of us, a small tank had hit a mine and was disabled off on the right bank of the road. We looked at them and traveled on into the hedgerows.

Later, in the hedgerow fighting, Martin King was wounded and on June 22, lost his right eye. After recovering in a hospital in England, he led a provisional truck unit and spent until February 1945, convoying supplies

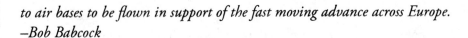

to air bases to be flown in support of the fast moving advance across Europe.
—Bob Babcock

William C. Montgomery, Long Beach, CA
Company A, 4th Medical Battalion

Landing Aborted

After having been in training in Devon for the invasion since January 1944, including participation in the infamous Exercise Tiger, my medical company was shipped about the first of June, to a very large gymn asium or field house type of building. I can't remember how we got there or where it was, but it was doubtless near Plymouth.

We were sequestered there with a very large number of other troops, sleeping in wooden bunks. There was a great deal of speculation about what was going on, but I'm sure we all knew it was the invasion.

In small groups, we were told about what was to happen. We were shown landmarks and given instructions about what to do on landing—plus we were issued complete gas-proof clothing (from the skin out) and invasion money.

The money was in the form of small paper bills in francs. We got four dollars apiece, as I recall. We called them "cigar coupons," or "Raleigh coupons," after the coupons found in those days in packages of Raleigh cigarettes. It seemed like toy money to us, and I was cynical about how the French would receive it. I think I had read about German invasion money earlier in the war.

Gambling started immediately in the vast "blimp-hanger" of a room, and within a few hours, most of the money in the place ended up in two or three very big poker or crap games.

My recollection is that somebody there was said to have sent home a money order for upwards of ten thousand dollars when it was over. And it was over fairly quickly. It took perhaps less than a day for most of the money that was gambled to filter down into a few hands.

I do not remember loading onto ships for the invasion, but I remember being aboard an LSI tied up very close to shore. It must have been Plymouth Harbor, on what must have been the afternoon of June 4.

A large number of LSIs were tied up side by side. An LSI load of combat engineers with rainbow markings arching from temple to temple on their helmets was immediately to the left of our boat. We understood they had already been in several landings in the Mediterranean. We were boisterous and brash—green troops with no idea of what was coming. The engineers knew, and they sat quietly around the deck on their boat, smoking—not talking.

Our trip across the channel almost didn't take place. In a very long line of LSIs snaking out of Plymouth harbor the afternoon of June 4, we followed a winding path that was said to have been laid out so we would not hit any harbor mines. After a little while, I noticed our boat was beginning to drift out of line to the left. I couldn't believe the skipper didn't know what he was doing, but in a few minutes, there was a heavy thump and we ground to a halt. We learned later that the boat's propeller had hit bottom and bent the shaft. We had to return to Plymouth.

Shortly, our boat was nosing up to a long sloping brick embankment between two lines of Bobbies, arm in arm, clear down into the water, chest deep on both sides of the boat. We debarked down the steel steps on either side of the LSI, into the water, up the embankment between the two lines of Bobbies, and into waiting trucks. No one would say a word to us. They realized how dangerous we were. We also knew what was about to happen.

About dark, we were unloaded on a hill high above Plymouth at some abandoned barracks, said to have been a former WLA or WREN camp. Food was arranged for, and I remember an officer bringing us a small portable Victrola.

As we all know now, the June 5 landing was aborted. How we slept that night and how we were brought back to Plymouth, loaded aboard another LSI to make the June 6 landing, I do not remember. Nor do I remember much about the crossing on June 5 and 6. What I remember vividly was that we were offshore of Normandy early in the morning, when we crawled down cargo nets into an LCVP. We joined a large group of identical open boats, circled briefly (pitching and rolling), and then headed for the beach.

I was in front, up against the ramp. We were cautioned not to climb up the ramp to look at the beach for fear of being wounded, but I heard a loud explosion and I couldn't resist. I clambered up, looked over the top, and saw a 4x4 truck on the beach somewhat off to my left. It was burning and exploding. It must have been full of ammunition. As I climbed up the LCVP ramp to see the beach and the burning truck, I heard a voice from the right and above me shout: "Get your f---ing head down, you stupid son of a b---!" I whirled around and looked up to see a Coast Guardsman, hunched on the rail, preparing to operate the mechanism that lowered the ramp. I thought, What is that kid doing here? He sounded salty but looked all of fourteen. I was just nineteen.

The beach was long and straight and not as wide as what I remembered of Jones Beach on Long Island, when I was a kid, or of the Florida beach at Camp Gordon Johnston. There was a low concrete seawall running across the full distance; I could see from left to right, and it had a long dune rising behind it. Off to the right there I caught a glimpse of French farmhouse buildings. We hit the beach at what I recall was 0800 hours on June 6, although why I say 0800 hours, I do not know. It was in the morning, however. The ramp went down and we piled off, to find ourselves up to our chests in water. I think the coast guard guys running the LCVP may have been in to the beach once before and were anxious to get in and out fast.

I waded ashore and ran across the beach to the concrete seawall. There the engineers had blown a big gap and installed a segmented metal ramp up over the dune for trucks and tanks. We had landed at a spot a couple of hundred yards west of the present Combat Engineers monument at Utah Beach. I was able to identify it years later by locating what I remember as the gap the engineers had blown in the seawall in the initial assault. In 1989, I found a cottage complex a couple of hundred yards to the west of where I think we landed, and that may have been what I saw in 1944.

In the landing craft as we went in, were dozens of troops. I had the front end of the folded litter on my shoulder and Bill Rohloff had the back. We went down the landing craft ramp into chest deep water, waded ashore, and ran across the beach and up the metal ramp. Almost at the top of the ramp, what sounded like machine gun fire caused us to hit the ground. I believed it was German planes strafing. More likely it was that truck I saw burning and exploding on the beach as we came in to land.

I hit the deck and immediately began to breathe something very unpleasant and choking. I shouted "Gas!" because of all the warnings we had and all the gasproof clothing we had been forced to wear. I began to fumble for my gas mask. In doing so, I discovered I was lying on the ramp with my face inches from the tailpipe of a jeep, which the driver had temporarily abandoned to take cover. I was breathing exhaust fumes. I got up hoping nobody had heard me and looked back at the astonishing sight of the fleet solidly covering the water to the horizon. Then, going over the dune, I saw a monumental traffic jam of vehicles on a sandy lane below, and a T-junction where vehicles struggled up a wide, pot-holed, sandy track, heading inland.None of us in my four-man squad saw any of the landmarks we were supposed to follow. We regrouped in a ditch along the lane, near the intersection, and tried to figure out what to do. We were puzzling over it, there in the sun, when there was a big explosion and a jeep that was part of the way up the track leading inland was blown into the air. I've never been able to figure out how the preceding hours of heavy traffic moved up that sandy track and over that mine before it finally went off.

We decided to head inland ourselves. Somewhere during this trek the glider troops flew over. It reminded me of the sea I had looked back at earlier, only this time it was the sky that was filled. The horizon was black with tow planes and gliders. Some planes were towing two gliders. Later, when we began to catch up with them, I realized I did not see a single undamaged glider. It appeared to me they had all cracked up on landing. It was like going over Niagara Falls in a barrel.

We saw no other Company A medics near us. We had been given certain landmarks to find that would lead us to our company, but they were not to be found.

We didn't know that the 4th Infantry Division had been put ashore well off target, and that on the beach our General Teddy Roosevelt had said to 8th Regiment Commander, Colonel Van Fleet, several hours before: "OK, we'll start the war from here."

We moved inland during the day, caught up with some paratroopers and worked with them around St. Marie du Mont through the night, still looking for our company. We worked late, and at one point, we ran across a comrade from another medical company who was tending a small circle of wounded. They were on stretchers beside a hedgerow road. He was waiting for others from his company to evacuate them. He whispered a warning to us not to go farther down the road, that these men had been wounded in an ambush just around the bend.

We finally drifted into a cobblestone courtyard, in front of a French farmhouse at the intersection of two rural Norman roads. We fell asleep near the well pump, sitting propped up against the house. We woke up at dawn as paratroopers began to pass through the intersection in what looked like purposeful combat order, unlike the previous night. Some of them came to get water from "our" pump, and we tried to get them to use halogen tablets, like good little medics. They disdained the tablets, like macho troopers. It must have been here that we got information about where the 4th Infantry Division was, and I believe we rejoined our company that morning around St. Mére Eglise.

Joseph Owen, Arlington, VA
HQ, 4th Infantry Division

Admiral Moon

In early April 1944, I was transferred to Division HQ and was assigned as Liaison Officer to Admiral Moon's headquarters in Plymouth. In Exercise Tiger, I was constantly in the command center on the USS Bayfield. My vivid recollection was of going to the observation deck to talk with the junior naval officer on watch and to see in the distance explosions from three sinking ships.

From that night on, Admiral Moon never got much sleep. He took over the job of the (relieved-from-duty) Chief of Staff. He was very much burdened and I stayed near him from early morning to late at night. I was to hear later that the admiral had committed suicide after the Southern France invasion.

On June 4, 1944, we headed for sea—the Bayfield being in the midst of a gigantic fleet of a vast assortment of ships of all sizes and purposes. My station was in the main operations area where I was to see the operation of the radar screen for my first time.

At about 0200 hours, June 5, Admiral Moon dispatched me to inform General Barton of the decision to invade on June 6. Using the message book, I wrote: "General Barton, the invasion is set for June 6." This I delivered to General Barton in his stateroom after awakening him. At this time, the General said, "Owen, come in and let's talk." For about fifteen minutes we both sat on his bunk and talked—about what, I am unable to remember.

The next time I saw the General was the morning after, at about 1000 hours, when we met a boatload of 3rd Battalion, 8th Infantry Regiment cooks and he asked me to escort them to their company. A Company L lieutenant soon relieved me of these frightened men who were walking slowly inland. At about 1100 hours, General Barton sent me toward St. Mére Eglise to ascertain the exact location of the 8th Infantry Regiment. On my way, I was met by General Theodore Roosevelt Jr. who slowed down his jeep to yell out, "Hey boy, they're shooting up there," followed by a big "Haw Haw." At that, I proceeded to the 8th Infantry Regiment Command Post where Colonel Van Fleet instructed Captain Gilby to properly mark their exact front locations on my map for a quick return to General Barton on the beach.

Marvin A. Simpson, (Deceased) Baton Rouge, LA
Company D, 4th Medical Battalion

Aftermath is Truly Fascinating

My memory has faded, but I can still see the tracer bullets streaking through the sky on the night and early morning of D-Day. I can still hear the drone of hundreds of aircraft overhead, flying toward their targets on Normandy beaches. I can still hear the sound of the guns from the big battleships blasting the coastline and the German pillboxes on the beaches, and I can see the results as big explosions lit up the sky.

Through all of this, I was in the English Channel off Utah Beach, standing or sitting (because I couldn't sleep) in a landing craft waiting to disembark. In a way, it was fascinating. At times, the sky would look like a gigantic Fourth of July celebration. I must have been, but I do not recall being scared. It was more like edgy, and—let's get on with it. Then it was daylight and our landing craft was heading toward shore.

I was in Company D, 4th Medical Battalion, 4th Infantry Division. We landed shortly after the first wave of soldiers and immediately set up a hospital camp about five hundred yards from shore. That was the beginning: The entire company, from privates to doctors, went seventytwo plus hours without sleep, taking care of the wounded and the dead who were lined in columns of three, starting from our camp back to the shore. These wounded included not only 4th Infantry Division soldiers but also paratroopers from the 82nd and 101st Airborne, and even some German soldiers. The medics went up and down the lines giving first aid and shots for pain. Most survived and were evacuated on the same landing crafts that brought us in; however, some died before the doctors could get to them.

It was no longer fascinating—it was just plain hell.

Thirty-two years later, in 1976, my son, James Simpson, married Claudia Gaab, a beautiful girl of German descent. Their wedding took place at sunrise on a mountaintop in Colorado. Two days earlier, the parents of the bride and groom met each other for the first time while sitting on a motel porch, having a cocktail and getting acquainted.

I said to Joe, her father, "Were you in World War II?"

Joe, from Detroit, replied, "Yes, I was a German soldier stationed in Normandy at the time of the invasion."

As we continued to compare notes, we were both stunned to discover that Joe had been defending Utah Beach when I landed there on D-Day. Jokingly, we said, "Hey, we were shooting at each other, and now, here we are, sitting together with our families toasting the marriage of our son and daughter." It was a beautiful wedding, and since then we have become best friends with Joe and Henny Gaab. That aftermath of my D-Day experience is truly fascinating.

Malvin Pike, Baton Rouge, LA
Company E, 2nd Battalion, 8th Infantry Regiment

Hit Four Times

As we prepared for D-Day, we boarded "Higgins" boats that were equipped with bangalore torpedoes, satchel charges, and wire cutters. About twelve miles off the French coast, the boats were to rendezvous in a circle and wait until time to go ashore at 0630 hours. As we were going in (first wave), our boat hit a sandbar so we had to jump over the sides into water about waist deep. This was not easy, as we had full packs, rifles, and all of our clothes and boots on, so all we could do was just push forward to get to the beach.

Somehow, Captain George Mabry and I were separated from our Company E. We crossed the causeway under enemy fire. Rommel had flooded the area and two Germans were hiding in the water under the bridge. They had placed mines there to blow up the bridge. Captain Mabry (later General and Medal of Honor recipient) forced the Germans to get the mines out.

I did not get hit until the third day on the beach, but I was near my friend, Michael Baronne, when an 88mm shell hit him in the head and killed him. I was hit four times during the war, sent back to the hospital, patched up, and sent back to the front lines as soon as I was able.

Donald Ellis, Richmond, ME
Company G, 2nd Battalion, 8th Infantry Regiment

From Horizon to Horizon

In the early part of June, we were restricted to camp and spent every day studying a sand table model, set up to exactly resemble the area where we were to land in Normandy. Along with the sand table, we studied maps of the area and were told what we could expect for resistance. Every day these items were updated from photographs taken by the Army Air Corp, and delivered to each unit. On June 4, 1944, everyone was loaded up and sent to different embarkation points throughout England. The 8th Infantry Regiment was sent to Torquey, England.

On June 5, we were told we might be landing on June 6. On the morning of June 6, we were awakened around 0300 hours, told to get our gear together and get ready to go up on deck. When we were on deck waiting our turn to go down the net to our boat, I remembered I'd left my shaving gear down below, so I told my buddy and I went back down and got it. When we got on the top deck, you could hear a steady roar of airplane engines overhead that never seemed to let up. We learned later that they were the 101st Airborne and 82nd Airborne troops going over.

As daylight started to break, all you could see from horizon to horizon were ships of all sizes, flying "barrage" balloons from long cables attached to some ships. They were used to keep planes from diving in to strafe us. When the sun broke through, I can't remember ever seeing such a bright red sun. As we climbed down the net into our landing craft, all of the naval destroyers and battleships began a rolling fire. Each boat was loaded and then we circled until each wave was in the right location for landing. Ours was in the line of the first wave to land on Utah Beach. Some of the men suffered broken bones and were crushed between the ship and landing craft as they were loading.

As the craft approached the beach, the coxswain, anxious to land, dropped the ramp as soon as the keel would hit anything. The noise of the naval guns, the machine guns, and artillery from the Germans was unnerving. Everybody was praying and hollering as well as being seasick. Due to the wind and the waves, the boats were mixed up as the ramp dropped and we hit the beach amid heavy firing. Everyone dropped and tried to orient himself. I landed in a great big puddle, and the barrel of my rifle dug into the sand. Being afraid that my rifle had been plugged, I started to disassemble it and I was fired upon. I shoved the pieces into my pocket and rolled over, but was still receiving fire. So, I jumped up and rushed to the sea wall with some other people.

Men were getting hit all around and General Teddy Roosevelt came by with a .45-caliber pistol in one hand and a riding crop in the other. He told us to get off the beach before we were killed. We did get up and charged forward toward the trenches. Clearing the beach, we finally were reassembled with our own group and proceeded to fight on. The naval gunfire had set several fires and a cloud of smoke began to stream down the beach. Then the cry, "Gas!" was heard, and we were all shook up because most of us had dropped our gas masks on the beach and just kept the carrier as a receptacle to carry rations and ammo.

After penetrating beyond the beach, one lieutenant (I can't remember his name) got four or five of us together to go on a patrol. This was late afternoon and we came to an orchard surrounded by a stone wall. Arriving in one corner of the wall, we halted and spread out. The lieutenant, with a couple of us, knelt down to look at the map. As soon as we did, an automatic rifle opened up on us and killed the lieutenant as well as two others. We dug in and returned fire, while someone went back to try to get a tank to come to assist us. But the enemy pulled out before the tank got there.

Kenneth E. Lay, Ripon, WI
HQ, 12th Infantry Regiment

How Some French Dairy Cows Helped the Allies Defeat the Germans

My job that fateful day was "Beach Control Officer" for our Regiment, the 12th Infantry Regiment. A critical part of the job was guiding our vehicles into an assembly area beyond the enemy beach fortifications. Back in England, a location had been selected and marked on our maps. But when we came ashore, what I saw on the ground did not match at all the features on the map. We had been put ashore about a mile off the mark. What to do now?

Our vehicles were starting to come ashore. Soon they would be blocking others, and German artillery could take its toll. As part of their defensive strategy, the Germans had closed the drainage gates of the lowlands behind the beach, leaving little dry land in between. Then I spotted a cow pasture and I ran to the gate thinking this could be our salvation. But just as quickly, my heart sank. Signs on the gate warned, "ACHTUNG MINEN." (Beware, Mines.)

Wait a minute, I thought. Cows are grazing in this field and they passed through this gate. This could be a ruse, or they ran out of mines, or French labor had thwarted the German occupiers. Whatever... it was worth a shot.

So, I gingerly walked to the gate, swung it open and waved the vehicle column in, still half expecting to be blown to bits in the process.

The cow pasture proved to be a fine assembly area, where vehicles could be stripped of their waterproofing and readied for delivery of much needed ammo and supplies to our fighting units already engaged with the enemy.

Later, I was awarded the Legion of Merit by our Regimental Commander, Colonel Russell P. Reeder, for my work that day. But I'm sure he didn't know how much I owed to a few cows for our success.

James Conway, Jemison, AL
Company G, 2nd Battalion, 8th Infantry Regiment

Grains of Sand

We sailed from England on June 5, 1944, into the English Channel. We had breakfast on the ship about midnight—navy beans and coffee. At about 0200 hours, we loaded into landing boats and circled in the Channel until about 0600 hours, and then we headed for shore.

We landed on Utah Beach—the first wave at 0630 hours, and the second wave at 0635 hours. The landing boats each carried about thirty men with full equipment. The boat I was on leaked and the pumps would not work. So we went in while standing in knee-deep water. The boat hit a sand bar and the ramp went down. We got out in shoulder-deep water and headed for the beach. We lost our first sergeant during the landing. He drowned there in the English Channel.

What was it like on D-Day for a "farm boy" from Alabama, or for any of us? We were all scared, seasick, cold, wet, crowded into the boats in an artillery barrage (mixed with machine gun and rifle fire), and dodging shells from a new weapon we called "screaming meemies" (rocket-propelled shells fired in clusters of twelve). If they didn't hit you, they sure scared you with their noises. There were explosions all around us, the sights and smells of death, and the cries of the wounded. We had the English Channel behind us, the German Army in front of us, and nothing to hide behind but grains of sand.

Our mission on the beach was to turn left and clear out the area to a peninsula (approximately a quarter to a half mile) consisting of six or seven pillboxes built along a sea wall. We got on their blind side since they were set to shoot toward the sea. Only two of these pillboxes gave us trouble. One pillbox was burned by a flamethrower. The other had a tank turret mounted on top that could turn 360 degrees. An American tank came up behind us. The signal for tanks to fire was purple smoke. Someone sent up purple smoke. When they did, the tank fired on the second pillbox, hitting it where the turret turned. The turret went about six feet high, a white flag came out of the banker, and we took the men inside prisoner.

We then assembled and moved inland after going around a minefield. We met up with the paratroopers who had landed earlier in the day.

Glenn Warren, Hardin, KY
Battery C, 29th Field Artillery Battalion

Glad To See You

On or about June 5, we boarded the ship, which later I learned was the flagship. Lieutenant Winters and I were assigned to K Company, 8th Infantry Regiment. He and I were the forward observer and radio operator from Battery C, 29th Field Artillery.

The morning of June 6, we assembled on the deck of the flagship and after a few words from Major General Raymond Barton, Commanding General of the 4th Infantry Division, we proceeded to climb down the rope netting to a LCI. The waves were about ten feet high, which made it difficult to get the timing of the waves with the bottom of the LCI.

As we headed for Utah Beach and the unknown, it was light enough to see the beach and the troops and trucks. I assumed the troops were 4th Infantry Division engineers clearing a path through the minefield just off the beach. The Germans had buried mines and our engineers laid a white tape in the area that had been cleared so we could walk safely. Immediately after we got off the beach, an Infantryman stepped off the tape, onto a mine, and was seriously wounded. He was our first casualty.

As we proceeded inland on the main road, there was a body of water on each side of it. The Germans had flooded the area for defensive purposes. We went inland for about two miles and by mid-afternoon, C-47s came in towing gliders that were bringing supplies to the troops. The fields were so small the gliders had difficulty landing; one came through a hedgerow, stopping about ten feet from where I was lying in a roadside ditch.

We were the first ground troops to make contact with the paratroopers who had jumped into Normandy, prior to the invasion. One of them said to us, "We are so glad to see you."

We were the first ground troops to make contact with the paratroopers who had jumped into Normandy.

One of them said, "We are so glad to see you."

The following morning, the infantry colonel (I can't remember his name) was killed by a German sniper. Later, two Germans jumped out in the road we were on and killed two of our infantrymen. Immediately, one German was killed, the other captured. He said over and over, "Me Polish."

This is as complete as I can remember about the landing and into the next morning. Every June 6, for fifty-six years, I invade Utah Beach. All memories from that date until December 29, 1944, at 0100 hours (the time I was wounded in Luxembourg) are as vivid as if they happened yesterday. There are memories that are more vivid after D-Day that I often reflect on.

Emile Troxclair, White Castle, LA
HQ Company, 22nd Infantry Regiment

Squad Leader

I am 82 years old, and D-Day was so long ago that I can't really remember all that happened that day. I was in Headquarters and Headquarters Company, then in the I&R platoon. I was a squad leader and my squad was attached to the 3rd Battalion for the landing. I was the first one to go down the rope ladder, off the troop carrier, and into the landing craft. I had taken my full field pack off and laid it and my rifle in the far corner so I could hold the net for the rest of the men to come down. After we were all in the landing craft, I wound up next to the landing ramp. I repeatedly asked some of the men to pass over my pack but no one did. I finally succeeded in having someone hand over my rifle. I landed on the beach in the 7th wave with only my rifle and rifle belt. It was two weeks later before I was supplied with some more clothes. (Phew!)

We did not meet much resistance the first day because of the bombings and shelling. The paratroopers had pretty well taken care of the enemy beforehand. Things got pretty hectic afterwards, however. On August 28, I was wounded while on a patrol just outside of Paris. I returned to my Company on November 14, in the Hürtgen Forest, in the thick of one of the worst battles the Regiment was ever in. I was later transferred to Service Company, staying there until I was discharged.

Orval H. Mullen, Bradenton, FL
HQ Company, 1st Battalion, 8th Infantry Regiment

As we were crossing the channel, getting ready to go ashore, I said to one of my buddies, Norman Day, "There goes a craft that would be very good to be on, number 777." It was to go in ahead of us. As we got ready to proceed, there lay pieces with the number 777 in the water as it had taken a direct hit....lucky again.

I went in on the third wave about twenty minutes after the first wave hit. When the ramp went down, the first man off went in over his head. For a short guy like me, I didn't know what to do with all the things I had to carry. There was a half-track and antitank gun on this craft, so as it started to go off the ramp, I wrapped my arm around the barrel. It dragged me into water where I could wade in to shore. On the beach it was not a very nice thing to see—bodies in the water, some wounded, some dead. The medics worked on some—you wouldn't think that could happen so fast. There was a lot of shelling and small arms fire going on—many men were lined up behind the sea wall waiting to move inland.

We moved up the road across the swamp area (being sniped at from several areas, along with the shelling), heading for whatever was ahead, toward the hedgerows and a small town. Even some females had joined with the German troops and would shoot at us. Also, we took care of that.

John H. Sears, Plymouth, MA
Company A, 87th Chemical Mortar Battalion

The Best Outfit

My outfit, the 87th Chemical Mortar Battalion, was attached to the 4th Infantry Division at Tiverton, England. We practiced with the 4th at Exercise Tiger. We turned in ninety jeeps as they bogged down in the oily sand, as did the 4th Infantry Division. I drove my captain all over England and finally came up with ninety M-29 Cargo Carriers. These M-29s were called "Mud Hens," "Weasels," and "Purple Heart Wagons," since they flipped over.

My Colonel, James Battle, transferred me to the 4th Infantry Division to drive Brigadier General Barber. He became ill and did not show on D-Day. Instead, I drove two majors and landed on Utah Beach at 0630 hours on June 6. I was asked by the aide of Major General Barton to go back and tow the M-29 that they had landed in, as it was stuck in the sand. I found the M-29 and saw it had a broken track, so I transferred Major General Barton's gear and maps to the CP (Command Post) on Utah Beach. I was asked to drive Major General Barton and his aide the first day. I did, and we went forward to the 4th Infantry Division advanced CP and then to the Division Artillery CP. As it was getting dark, I drove them to the "Jayhawk" forward CP for the night. The aide held me two more days, but MG Barton went back to his jeep. I was released and reported to my unit,

Company A, 87th Chemical Mortar Battalion. We were attached to twenty different outfits for 326 days of combat action. We fired 184,010 rounds of 4.2-inch mortar ammo (high explosive and white phosphorous). The 4th Infantry Division was the best outfit to fight with.

Joe Blaylock, New Orleans, LA
Battery B, 20th Field Artillery Battalion

Treading Water

We were given orders that we would be in the first wave landing on Utah Beach on D-Day.

I was on LST 399 coming from England. We were given orders that we would be in the first wave landing on Utah Beach on D-Day. We climbed down a rope ladder at 0230 hours on the morning of June 6, into an LCP with two jeeps and twenty-five men from the 101st Airborne Assault Troops. We circled around until we all came together for the first wave going into Utah Beach. As we were coming in, one of our bombers was shot down near us. We approached the area and yelled that we would pick them up. We picked up three guys from a raft and took them with us on to the beach. As we neared the beach and they let the front gate down for us to go ashore, Lieutenant Fitzpatrick gave me orders to get out and check for mines. I followed orders and told him to come out; there were no mines. As I had treaded water in the creeks of Mississippi all my life, I treaded water checking for mines. Later, I thought he must have thought I was one brick short of a full load.

I trained with the 4th Infantry Division as a forward observer for the 20th Field Artillery Battalion. Our mission was to find the right bivouac area for the guns. I was with Lieutenant Fitzpatrick, Lieutenant Berganovki, Warrant Officer Manning, and our driver, Sterling. As we all ran for the beaches from our landing craft, there was mortar fire and 88s firing at us. When we reached the beachhead, our driver picked us up and we went to the area where General Teddy Roosevelt told us we had landed off course, above our original landing site. He gave us our new location and told us that the war would "start from here."

As we started to our location, we were fired upon by German bombers. I dived into a shallow ditch or foxhole. In a few minutes, two more guys jumped in on top of me and asked if it was OK. I said, "Yes, the more the merrier." After saying a prayer and after the firing stopped, we started on our way to find an area to set up our guns and bivouac. As we rounded a curve, we ran into a machine gun nest that was manned by Polish soldiers. They started telling us something in Polish. As Lieutenant Berganovki was Polish, he answered, and it wasn't long before they surrendered and gave us three Clydesdale horses. We all went to a nearby farmhouse and swapped the horses for a dozen eggs that we cooked and ate. We then drove on and found our designated area to set up our guns and our bivouac area. Later we went back to the beach area to meet the 20th Field Artillery when they landed. We took them back to our bivouac area.

This was my harrowing D-Day landing experience. The Lord blessed and was with me all the way until the Germans surrendered. I only had a small shrapnel wound on my hand (plus a hurt knee) that I got somewhere along the way. Today I am 80 years old: February 14, 2000, Valentine's Day.

Bernard Pelura (Deceased)
Company G, 2nd Battalion, 8th Infantry Regiment

Pep Talk

We boarded a large ship in southern England and headed across the English Channel for France. All you could see were big ships and lots of smaller boats with men and supplies. Then when it started to get a little dark, a door opened up and out came Major General Raymond O. Barton, 4th Infantry Division Commander, and Brigadier General Theodore Roosevelt Jr., Assistant Division Commander. I was about ten feet from them. General Barton gave us a little talk and said that for the last two years, we pounded discipline up our rear ends. Then he said, "If you fellows ever want to get home, you have to be the meanest, dirtiest son-of-a-bitches the world has ever seen, or you'll never make it home."

General Roosevelt said, "And, don't you ever think for one minute that they won't shoot to kill you." Then, about 2200 hours that night, the sky seemed to light up. A big arms and ammunition ship exploded, and it looked like a gigantic Fourth of July fireworks display.

Around 0230 hours, they threw a big net over the side of the ship and we climbed over the side and down into small boats. There was one first lieutenant and thirty of us. I don't remember his name. We circled around, and at about 0620 hours, we headed for shore. It was hell trying to get to shore, and when we were about seventy-five or a hundred yards from it, the navy man started to lower the end gate. The lieutenant cursed the heck out of him and said, "Put that gate up and get us to shore." But it was down too far, he couldn't get it back up and the boat sank. We were lucky; the water only came up to our chests and we could walk to shore. There was a buddy of mine three or four feet from me. His last name was Walters and he was from Baltimore, Maryland. I said, "Walt, don't you get too far away from me. If I step in a hole, you pull me up." He didn't answer me, and I looked over and half his head was blown off.

When we made shore and headed up from Utah Beach, there was an old man and his wife leaning on a gate at the first farmhouse we came to. The lieutenant asked them if there were any Germans in the house and they shook their heads, "no." Out of the bushes across the street came two paratroopers and they said, "We think they're lying. You fellows watch them while we search the house." It didn't take too long until we heard two shots, and then, out came the two paratroopers.

They said two Germans were hiding under the bed and they had shot them. Then they shot the old man and his wife for lying to them. The lieutenant asked the paratroopers where the 2nd Battalion, 8th Infantry Regiment was. They said, "Straight ahead, in the little village," and that they were pinned down by 88s and mortar fire. They said to watch out for snipers as they were shooting at us fellows from the right and left.

I saw several paratroopers whose parachutes were stuck in the trees four or five feet above the ground. They were shot and bayoneted. All over the small fields, the Germans had posts dug into the ground. About five feet above the ground, they had nailed heavy wire to the top of the posts to cause the gliders to crash when they landed. The gliders were made of plywood and broke up when they hit the wire and posts.

It didn't take us too long to catch up with the rest of the fellows from G Company. They were pinned down by 88s, mortars, and small arms fire. They were lying on the ground all bunched up and close together. Some were from the 70th Tank Battalion. Their tanks were hit and they came along with us for a while. It was hell. I didn't sleep for three nights and days and wasn't ever sleepy.

Philip Fein, Philadelphia, PA
Company F, 2nd Battalion, 8th Infantry Regiment

All For One

Before we shipped out of the channel port, I saw British General Montgomery talking to the troops while he was standing on the hood of a jeep. At the end of his talk, he said, "All for one and one for all!"

John Pfister, Erie, PA
Company E, 2nd Battalion, 8th Infantry Regiment

Going To Live Through This?

John Pfister's arrival in Europe began with circles in the sea, but his journey across France, Belgium, and Germany followed the straight line of duty. From June 6, 1944, to May 8, 1945, John Pfister went where duty took him—from Utah Beach to the Cherbourg Peninsula, from St. Lô to Paris, from the depths of the Hürtgen Forest to the "quiet" posts in the Ardennes Forest, and on to the heart of Germany. But even today, fifty-five years later, he finds himself going around and around, putting himself right back in time to a moment in a foxhole in Normandy—to the day he was wounded—to the tense times in the hedgerows, and to the cold of the Battle of the Bulge. He can flip back to these moments and actually be there.

These first five hours off Europe were spent going in real circles. Company E of the 8th Infantry Regiment, 4th Infantry Division, was sent over the side into landing craft at 0100 hours June 6, 1944. We were in the second line of boats to hit the beach, backing up the rifle companies that would land first. The landing craft was among hundreds assembling in the black of night, getting organized so they could hit the beach at H-Hour—0630 hours.

For hours, the boat plowed and tossed through the rough waters of the English Channel. Equipped with a bazooka and five bazooka rockets, a box of .30-caliber machine gun ammunition and his own rifle (not to mention rations, gas mask, and other items), Pfister, like the other men, got a good dose of seasickness. "We got sicker than dogs. We were throwing up on each other—with all this paraphernalia on," he said.

Even so, we didn't care how sick we were. We knew we had to go no matter what happened. I knew we were going to hit the beach and I was thinking to myself, John, are you going to live through this? It was not only am I going to live, but after the beach, how long would I last?

As landing craft finally neared the beach, the GIs were ordered to line up. American bombers from the Army Air Corps were dropping load after load on the beach and beyond, pulverizing German defenses. Battleships offshore were unleashing their salvoes. Still, the German artillery was firing back. Pfister saw some boats from his wave take direct hits. He also saw amphibious craft that had not taken part in the exercises off Slapton Sands, England, nor off the water of the United States. He saw DUKWs, the tracked vehicle that can go through water and drive on land as well as tanks specially fitted to motor through the water.

When the landing craft's ramp went down, Company E was about seventy-five to a hundred yards from the beach. They inflated their "Mae

Wests'" and jumped out. They didn't know how deep the water was. It was chest high. Even jumping into that, Pfister initially sunk under the heavy load he was carrying but was able to push off the bottom and work his way toward shore. The combination of relatively light opposition (compared to that faced at Omaha Beach), the efficient bombardment and the work of the first companies ashore made the landing itself relatively uneventful. The Germans were putting some machine gun fire down, but it hadn't stopped the capture of the first pillboxes by Companies F and G. Prisoners were running in circles on the beach, their hands in the air. They didn't know what to do. The 8th Regiment pressed inland. Its first-day objective was St. Mére Eglise, a small village about eight miles inland taken by units of the 82nd Airborne Division after fierce fighting. They held it until the 8th arrived. As they worked their way inland, they came under fire from a sniper in a small two-story house in a village. "That's when I fired my first rocket (from a bazooka)," Pfister said. The rocket went right in the window and exploded. Whether it hit the sniper or not, he never found out. However, the sniper fire stopped. Further along, they heard a noise in a barn. Taking no chances, Pfister fired another rocket. This one went right into the structure, too. But this time a horse came running out.

The 8th joined up with the paratroopers at St. Mére Eglise before dark and were ordered to prepare for a German counterattack. During the night, they saw and heard gliders being towed with glider troops of the 82nd Airborne. The Germans fired at them, but it was the landing in the dark, smashing into the hedgerows, that caused heavy losses among the glider troops. "We could hear them crashing and hear the men screaming. The screaming was awful," Pfister said.

Joseph Kraynak, Lansdale, PA
HQ Battery, 29th Field Artillery Battalion

Too Excited to Sleep

Nightfall set in. I dozed off in some dark corner, lonely, and feeling like a hound dog. I clearly remember thinking; this is it, D-Day, Operation Overlord. It was the beginning of the assault on the Normandy Coast and the five major campaigns until the end of the war in Europe. It scared me and no doubt everyone else. I was too excited to sleep, but I do remember the gradual shapes as they came into focus when dawn approached. Up to this time, I had no idea of the number of ships taking part in this invasion. My vision of this event was that the coast of France would be loaded with enemy artillery, rifles, mines, etc., —just waiting for them to have a field day—firing at us like sitting ducks. My thought was, we will probably be history in a few hours…at the light of dawn.

As daylight approached, a vast amount of our ships, and planes of all sizes, came into view. It was at this moment that the sight of these ships, as far as one could see, gave me a sense of such confidence in our strength. I was, for the first time, thrilled to be a part of this historic occasion. Also, I was certain it would be a complete and swift landing with very few casualties on our part.

The 4th Infantry Division was assigned to what was called Utah Beach. There were of course, other beaches being invaded by our Allies along the Normandy coastline. At this time, we drove the truck with a dismantled plane from the LST onto a flatbed for the short trip to an area shallow enough for us to get the truck on the beach. It seemed like the opposition was light, but before going ashore, there were landing craft returning with the casualties of the earlier wave of assault troops. My confidence in a swift and easy assault was slightly altered.

After a few hours, we encountered heavy fire from the Germans about a quarter of a mile inland. The day was warm and the smell of death cannot be described. It was then that it dawned on me why I was disengaged from my unit. Only a small element of my 29th Field Artillery unit was to go ashore immediately and get set up for artillery fire. My job was to assemble this plane in a small clearing the size of a football field and get it ready to direct the artillery fire. At this stage of the invasion, the area was under some small arms fire and artillery shells. The Front, as we knew it, was indefinable.

There were cows and other farm animals killed before we arrived. By noon, the sun was hot and it caused the dead animals to bloat at least twice their normal size. This sight was not easy to forget and I am surprised that it is never mentioned in all the material I have read to date on D-Day. It was under these conditions that I had to enlist the help of some GI to hold the wing, which I bolted to the fuselage. In about one and a half hours, the plane was ready for action.

Shortly afterward, I met some of my old buddies from other units and it was like a reunion to see them. I went in about 0930 hours and it was now about 1300 hours. I am not proud of this, but in our excitement, we saw two planes coming in on us. We immediately opened fire. Fortunately, the two pilots were not injured and managed to land their damaged planes. It was then that we realized we brought down two British Spitfires. The pilots were typically calm British, and made light of our stupidity in our first effort of this war.

By nightfall, we managed to join about ten of our buddies with whom we trained in England. We had no idea where we were and no clear plans or orders. One of the men managed to get a fifth of cognac, which we consumed in about one hour; and all of a sudden, the war looked like a pretty neat place. The sound of planes coming at us, and the great judgment we received from the cognac, gave us the idea we should be firing our rifles. At the time, I remember it seemed real great to be in a war. All we did was bring down some enemy branches from the trees, which was our hotel for the night.

St. Mére Eglise was our immediate goal. Our unit was to meet the paratroopers there and take the town, which was sort of under control by the units before us, but we got in on the celebration with the townspeople of St. Mére Eglise.

Don Fleck, Redford, MI
Service Company, 22nd Infantry Regiment

Bring the Blankets

We were in a blackout on a destroyer for two days, and I was ready when word came to move out. I was on duty topside as we approached France; the roar was deafening. Later, we found out it was Utah Beach. The arc of the tracers lit the sky in their paths towards land. What a sight to behold, this pre-invasion blanket of fire.

At 1030 hours, the beachmaster flagged us to come in. We were told to bring all the blankets we had. Naturally, the enlisted men did not understand. With rough water, high waves, and combat gear—down the rope ladder we went, into the landing craft. This was it! The landing craft stopped, the ramp went down, and out we went. As I stepped off the ramp with my rifle in one hand, the blanket in the other, I was soon chest high in oozing cold water. As I approached the beach I saw six bodies, face up, as if sleeping. I still remember to this day how young they looked. I now understood the request for blankets.

As our platoon reached the midpoint of the beach, an 88 shell hit the beach about fifty yards to our left. Someone yelled, "Hit the ground!" I was already in a puddle of wet sand. Then, up and off the beach, on to many wartime experiences I will never forget.

Stanley McKaig, Princeton, NJ
Company C, 4th Engineer Battalion

Fought as Infantry

I was on a LST that arrived some ten miles or so off the Normandy Beach in the very early hours of June 6, 1944, after being on it for several days. There were only enough bunks on a LST to support about half the persons on board. This meant you were only able to sleep on a cot every other night. On the off night, one would find a back of a truck or some obscure corner to get any amount of sleep possible.

There were all kind of ships including battleships as far as the eye could see. Long before I unloaded from the LST onto a LSVP, the battleships began to fire their sixteen-inch guns onto areas on land beyond the beaches. You could actually see these shells going through the air. The sea was very rough and vehicles were driven onto the LSVP via the front "down-ramps" of both the LST and the LCVP. Because of the roughness of the sea, most soldiers off-loaded from the LST onto the LCVP by nets. They went over the side of the LST, after U.S. Coast Guard boat operators brought the LCVP around to the side. This is the route by which I boarded the LCVP, just a few minutes after daybreak.

The LCVP that I went in on had four vehicles and about a squad of men. We were the second wave of soldiers hitting the beach. The boat operator had trouble finding the new Utah Beach as the location had been changed. When we arrived near the beach, the LCVP operator kept calling out to any other boats within ear range, "Do you know how to get to Uncle Red Beach?"

As our boat neared the beach, we hit a sandbar; the ramp was put down, and the first truck went down the ramp and out of sight. The truck operators energized the air capsules that inflated their life belts. We were not fired upon as we unloaded, and we continued inland on a very narrow road that ran through a German minefield on both sides of the road. A German fighter plane came strafing down this road from the landside. We couldn't get off the road, so we just lay crosswise across the road because a bullet from a strafing fighter plane hit the ground at about six foot intervals. Bullets were off the road a large part of the time so not many people were hit.

Not long on shore, we took a large amount of explosives and placed it on the backside of a pillbox that was firing its guns at incoming troops and ships unloading on the beach. We placed about a thousand pounds of C-2 explosives at the rear of the pillbox and blew it up, knocking it out of action.

The remainder of the day we fought as Infantry, advancing to the little French town of St. Mére Eglise by early afternoon. Later that afternoon, we dug foxholes in a church cemetery on the north side of St. Mére Eglise and set up defensive positions for the night. After digging the foxholes, we made a reconnaissance in a jeep to the area in front of us for several miles. After we turned around, we returned on the same road that we came out on. There was a knocked-out Sherman tank on the road where a German 88 shell had gone through it. To this day, I don't know why we weren't fired upon unless they were lying in wait for a bigger prize than a jeep with a couple of people in it.

We stayed that night in our two-man foxhole, one man at a time staying awake. We were not fired on overnight. The 4th Infantry Division troops handed all their German prisoners over to the paratroopers who had done their mission for the day and were heading back to the beach. From there on, we generally turned toward Cherbourg, and a few days later sealed off the Peninsula. Then, the real assault was on Cherbourg. As I remember, I didn't get to wash or shave for thirteen days as we continued through the hedgerows of Normandy. The first real hot meal we had was in Paris, on August 25, 1944, when the company cooks fried chicken—nothing else but chicken, but it sure tasted good.

Morris Austein, Boca Raton, FL
Company I, 3rd Battalion, 22nd Infantry Regiment

A Sky Full of Planes

The following appeared in the March 28, 1994 Boca Raton, FL newspaper.

The infantrymen in Sergeant Morris Austein's unit were accustomed to training operations, but this was "the real thing" as Supreme Allied Commander General Dwight D. Eisenhower told them. As advance troops, their mission was to open the field at Normandy for the troops behind them, Eisenhower said. "If the advance troops fail, the whole mission fails."

As a staff sergeant, Austein, who lives in Boca Raton, was responsible for forty-two men in his demolition platoon, Company I. Their mission was to destroy all obstacles hindering the advancement of troops up the beach and into the French countryside.

The order to assault came at 0500 hours on June 6, 1944. Thousands of boats circled the waters around Normandy, Austein remembers.

"It seemed as if you could walk from one boat to another, there were so many of them," Austein said.

"The sky was so full of planes you couldn't see the sky any more. Bombers were hitting the coast. We all had things on our mind like the enemy and what we would run in to. There were thousands of troops alongside each other going on to the beach. On the shoreline itself, there were land mines. Germans put them down and if you stepped on one, you blew up. I lost five men that way. There was utter confusion on the beach and soldiers were crying for help.

"We saw Brigadier General Teddy Roosevelt Jr. He was riding along the beach in a jeep, yelling, 'Move on! Move on!'—meaning get off the beach and keep moving forward. The beach was jamming up with men and equipment. He was afraid they would bomb the hell out of us.

"My unit pushed forward off the beach. As we moved forward, we could smell the stench of dead animals and dead German soldiers. We also found American paratroopers dying. They were hanging on the trees. They got caught in the trees when they came down, and the Germans shot them while they were hanging there.

"One of my men got a shell right in the middle of his back. He was sitting in a hole and a cannon shot from a mile away hit him in the back. He never knew what hit him; he was killed instantly.

"We spent the entire day just moving up the beach. We were moving steadily at a reasonable pace and we got about a mile up the beach. I didn't see a German until dusk. I was moving forward around these hedgerows. I looked at him, he looked at me, and he turned sideways to walk away. He didn't know I was an American and I didn't know he was a German; it was too dark. But as he turned, I recognized the helmet. It was in silhouette. It had a different shape from ours and in the excitement, I raised my rifle. At that moment, he realized I was an American and we both started shooting at each other. I thought I was shot for a second, but he missed me. I don't know if I hit him, because suddenly a heavy bombardment hit us. These were mortar shells and artillery rounds.

"The fact that I shot alerted them that we were Americans. The artillery came in very heavily and everyone scattered trying to protect themselves. There were hedgerows all over and we didn't see anything at that time. I couldn't tell if anyone was being killed. We all ran behind hedgerows to protect ourselves and some ran into craters where bombs made big holes. We stayed there the rest of the night. We couldn't move because it was dark. If we moved, we would be shot. There was no talking even, no smoking, and no noise. To sleep, we covered ourselves and took our chances. That is how D-Day ended for us."

Reflecting upon his experience, Austein said that once people go through a war they feel they can do anything without fear. He discovered that each person reacts differently to combat and no one can predict his reactions until the time comes. Some of his men panicked, some cried and others were strong. Austein adopted a fatalistic approach, which he credits with getting him through the experience. "Whatever happens will happen," he figured, adding, "It was beyond my control."

"But it hurt very badly when you saw someone you know get hit. I lost many good friends and it hurt." Austein has no regrets about the war and calls it, "a fantastic experience."

After 21 days of straight combat, Austein was wounded on the outskirts of Cherbourg, France, on June 27, 1944. He spent one year at Walter Reed Hospital in Washington, DC and received an honorable discharge for medical disability. His right leg is still partially paralyzed, but he experiences no pain today.

Darel Parker, Leipsic, OH
Company C, 1st Battalion, 12th Infantry Regiment

Trouble Came Later

I landed on D-Day around 1000 hours, after making my way down the rope netting on the side of a larger boat into the small landing craft. The water was very rough. Coming off the small landing craft into water up to my chest, carrying my M-1 rifle with plenty of ammunition, bazooka and ammo, gas mask, and life jacket was no easy task. Everyone had the same thought and that was to get out of the water. If we could get out, maybe we had a better chance. In the water, we were like sitting ducks.

We landed down the beach from where we should have been so we didn't have as much resistance. Some of the officers got together and got us headed in. After we were in a ways, we came across the flooded areas that the Germans had made to make travel more difficult. Most of the water was about knee deep, but every few yards there were ditches that were six or seven feet deep. For a fellow five feet five inches tall, that was no easy task.

We traveled on without much trouble until well after dark—trouble came later. There was artillery flying all directions all night. I finally lay down in an open field (didn't even dig in) and tried to get some sleep, but it wasn't much. This about ended the first day.

Leo Jereb, Cleveland Heights, OH
Company L, 3rd Battalion, 8th Infantry Regiment

Reality Sets In

After years of preliminary training and anticipation, we knew the time had almost arrived. We had been in our barbed wire marshaling area and gone through dry-run practices. We would load up with all the equipment we could carry with us and then form as we would when it actually happened, only to come back and do it again another day. We all had a number of personal items which we liked to have with us. Whether it was by design or not, each time we had one of these exercises, we'd discard a little something and soon most of us were reduced to a combat-ready load.

Then one day reality set in. Officers and noncommissioned officers were summoned to a small building located in an open field in the marshaling area. There before us, on a table, was a sand diorama of our landing area. Colonel James Van Fleet, commanding officer of the 8th Infantry Regiment, presided at the meeting.

In a voice barely above a whisper, he told us of the impending invasion of Normandy. As he spoke, I looked out through the lone small window and could see the building was ringed in barbed wire; guards walked in circles around it as far as I could see. The 8th Infantry Regiment was to be the assault regiment at Utah Beach and my company was to hit the beach at H-Hour, plus 45 minutes.

On June 1, 1944, we geared up for the last time and headed for the port of Plymouth in early morning. We passed small groups of people huddled together talking in hushed tones. They seemed to sense that this was it. We loaded on a large craft that was to take us to sea and once there, to await the order to load into our assigned landing craft.

Once aboard ship the chaplains were conducting services and, as you can guess, they were doing a land office business. After making peace with God, there was time to while away. Some men were in quiet anticipation and meditation, but it was surprising that some of them gambled in card and dice games. They were using some of the newly printed invasion francs that were issued to each of us.

After a weather postponement, General Eisenhower gave the order early Monday morning, June 5, 1944, to launch Operation Overlord. All units once again went into the attack mode. In the darkness of early Tuesday morning, June 6, 1944, we received the order to go over the top and down the cargo nets. This is where Donald Roddenberry had to part with his guitar. I don't know how he was able to keep it in his possession that long.

Descending the cargo net was no easy job. After you reached the last rung, you had to jump into the LCVP because this "cigar box" type of landing craft pitched badly in the choppy channel. If you didn't jump, you might break a leg, or worse than that, fall between the net and the LCVP into the cold channel. After we were loaded, we went around in circles until the other craft were loaded. When they were, we headed for the assembly area. Once there for a while, we heard the motors rev up, and then we knew the next stop was the beach.

We all stood up for the trip in because there was no room to sit down. I looked out a few times and saw huge sprays of water around us. They were firing at us and missing. I thought there must have been a lot of noise, but I wasn't aware of it until our landing craft stopped. The ramp went down and as I looked ahead into the water, I asked myself, what am I doing here?

Of course, I knew, so I jumped into the water holding my rifle over my head and waded into shore as fast as I could, looking straight ahead. When I reached the shore, I ran as fast as I could to the top of the dunes and took cover. We lay there in the sand wondering what was next as bullets snapped around us. I never looked back. I wish I had, because I would have seen the largest naval armada ever assembled and would have felt more secure.

There was only one exit road across the flooded area where we landed and movement was slow. Later, waves of troops had to wade through the water because things were ganging up as more troops landed. That was a tough job since the Germans had bulldozed furrows into the area before it was flooded. As troops moved through the area, they would suddenly drop into a deep hole and disappear into water over their heads.

I received the order to move out and gave my men the arm signal to do so. As we started forward, the man next to me did not move. My first thought was that he had dozed off while we waited because we did have a few sleepless nights during preparation. I put my hand on his shoulder to arouse him and that is when I saw he had taken a bullet through his head. That was really the start of the war for me. That is when I fully realized that there was a war on and I was in it.

About halfway across the flooded area, we came to a damaged DD tank that had preceded us and was pushed off to the side of the narrow road. It was quiet and no fire seemed to be directed at us. My curiosity got the best of me and I climbed up the tank and looked down through the open hatch. What I saw was a huge pool of blood—another quick, gory reminder of this deadly war I was in. I quickly jumped down because I realized that I made quite a good target up there. After reaching the other side, we spread out and moved into the hedgerow lined farming areas.

Behind the hedgerows, Germans waited for us in well-established defensive positions. They also knew we hid behind the hedgerows and they would direct 88mm fire in a flat trajectory at the hedgerows until they literally blew holes in them. The pounding and the noise of the exploding shells were deafening. And, of course, we were losing men. We knew we would have to be very lucky to survive a war like this one.

As we advanced through the farming areas, women emerged from barns with buckets of milk, which they offered us, but we declined because we didn't know who could be trusted and there was the need to keep moving. The fields were covered with dead cattle, meaning they were mined or the cows were caught in an artillery barrage.

Late in the afternoon, we were moving across one of these hedgerow-lined farms and suddenly found ourselves surrounded by huge balls of fire accompanied by a lot of explosions. After a while, we found that these were gliders being hit by enemy fire as they were trying to land. Others were crashing into the tall hedgerows. It was difficult for them to find room to glide in, and some were probably released too early in order to avoid heavy antiaircraft fire. My buddy, Leo Brislin, ran to one of the paper-thin gliders that crashed near us and tried to pull open the jammed door. After kicking at it for some time, he was able to open it and look inside. In it, he saw a fellow he had gone to school with in Wilkes-Barre, Pennsylvania. His classmate survived the landing and the war. Leo often saw him walking around the streets at home. Leo survived the war too, but he walked around Wilkes-Barre with one leg. He lost the other one later in the Hürtgen Forest when he went into a minefield to drag out a buddy who had stepped on a mine. In so doing, he detonated another mine, which was his undoing. We decided to get out of there in a hurry, lest we get hit by enemy fire or even a glider attempting to land.

After that, it was hedgerows, hedgerows, and more hedgerows. We were fighting Germans at very close range of about one hundred fifty to two hundred yards. We also had to worry about friendly shells or bombs hitting us by mistake, or landing short of their intended targets.

After a couple weeks of fighting, the men became very weary and began to inquire about unit relief. Little did we know they would get only some replacements—to fill slots caused by casualties—but no relief. The 4th Infantry Division would later be cited for exceptional service and be relieved only after 199 days in contact with the enemy.

My war would end on June 23, 1944, when I was wounded by machine gun fire at close range. After being operated on in the beach area for chest and arm wounds, I was flown out from a temporary landing strip. The plane was forced down by bad weather at Thorney Island in the Isle of Wight. I was taken to a hospital in England, then to a hospital ship, and then back home again.

Between Utah Beach and the end of hostilities, there would be many "longest days." Many of our men would lie in military cemeteries in Europe or in the United States if their next-of-kin chose to bring them home. If they could speak, they would say they were happy this D-Day Museum affair was arranged and that they were being remembered. They would thank you for remembering them and ask us not to forget the price that was paid. Their legacy cries out, "Freedom Is Not Free!"

Note: The National D-Day Museum was dedicated in New Orleans, Louisiana, on June 6, 2000. This author hosted 105 4ID D-Day veterans at that event—the largest contingent of any unit to attend.

Fred Stromberg, Concord, CA
Company G, 2nd Battalion, 22nd Infantry Regiment

Get Your Packs On

While in Scotland recovering from a wound received in Africa with the 47th Infantry Regiment, 9th Infantry Division, I elected not to return to that outfit, but to stay in the United Kingdom. I was sent to a replacement camp, "Old Gold," near Exeter, in southern England. It was here we were told we would be the first replacements for the 4th Infantry Division after the invasion.

A few weeks later, midday on June 5, I was ordered to report to the CO with full field pack as I was shipping out. I joined twenty-two others as we loaded into an army 6x6 truck and were driven to the city of Plymouth. We were driven into a large brick warehouse on the waterfront and disembarked. A colonel addressed us: "Men, you are now part of the 4th

Infantry Division that will assault the beaches of the Cherbourg Peninsula in France. General Eisenhower wanted all units over strength and that is the reason for the mad rush of additional troops."

That evening the huge iron doors of the warehouse opened and I could see the transport loaded with troops. The four days of heavy rain had stopped when we were herded up the gangplank and placed on the foredeck. There was hardly room to stretch out your legs. I removed my backpack and placed it under my head as a pillow. The rumble of the engines indicated we were on our way. As night closed in, it became very cold. A six-hour trip in open air left me half-frozen. The transport stopped and I could hear the anchor drop, then the lowering of the landing crafts.

A lieutenant came over and shouted, "Get your packs on. Let's go!"

I then decided to put my pack in front as I felt it wouldn't stop any bullets if I had it on my back. I was constantly reminded I had my pack on backwards.

We were some 7,000 yards from the beach and it would take 45 minutes for the landing craft to reach the shore. The square-nosed craft sped toward the beach, butting against the heavy seas. Suddenly, a huge explosion flipped the landing craft ahead of us end over end as it hit a mine. Yells and screams were heard from the men being tossed all over. We could not stop to help. Heads bobbed up like corks along the way. Most drowned before they reached the beach. Our landing craft was to drop the nose gate on the beach, but it was dropped some distance from shore. The cold water from the Atlantic rushed in and swept me off my feet. Since I was only five feet, three inches tall, the water was up to my shoulders. The force of the water kept me from making any headway as I stumbled. A soldier twice my size next to me grabbed my cartridge belt and lifted me up. "Shorty," he said, "If you don't get your hind end higher out of the water, you will drown."

"Oh," I said, "I'll be all right. I'll make it." With that, he fell forward, blood gushing from his face. I felt so sick. I didn't get to thank him. I didn't even know his name.

I made my way up to the tank obstacles, then to the roadway. One irritating problem was the soaking up the sand of the beach as you crawled, chafing your body all day. However, the pack in front lifted me off the sand enough not to be saturated with it. The hundreds of soldiers being landed almost at once caused mass confusion. A six feet-two-inch first sergeant came crouching over, calling for Company G men. He took one look at me with my pack dangling almost to my knees.

"Soldier, what the hell are you trying to do?" he hollered. "I'm just trying to find which way to go," I answered. "What company are you with?"

"I don't know."

"What Regiment are you with?" "I don't know," I kept replying.

"Well, I'm the First Sergeant of Company G. What is your name?" he asked as he shook me. A lot of the utensils fell from my pack. "You are the sorriest soldier I have ever seen," he said. "How did you get into the Army? You must be the original Sad Sack." I never had the chance to explain my predicament or why I didn't know the units comprising the 4th Infantry Division.

I don't believe anyone had a more auspicious entry into the War.

John Plonski Sr., East Northport, NY
Company E, 2nd Battalion, 8th Infantry Regiment

Many Soldiers Died

Upon leaving the Navy ship on D-Day June 6, 1944, we had to go down the rope ladder to get into our LCI boats. We had to go around in circles before we made our landing on Utah Beach. When we came to the Normandy landing, we were off course and hit the French shore in the first wave, at exactly 0642 hours. I carried a BAR (Browning Automatic Rifle).

Many boats of ours were hit by German fire and many soldiers died, suddenly drowning in the water, as we were pretty loaded carrying extra ammunition. Overhead was the Navy, firing their guns at the Germans, and American planes flying overhead to give us more support. When we got off the Higgins boat, we were lucky to be alive on the French shores, advancing to our goal of St. Mére Eglise.

As we got on land, we came across dead and alive 82nd paratroopers that had landed four hours before us. The first thing they asked us was, "Can I have a cigarette?" We gave them a full pack to help them have company. I never smoked any cigarettes at all. We couldn't help them. We told them the medics were coming and that they would take over.

Our primary job was to go to St. Mére Eglise. By the time we arrived, we sure were tired and hungry.

Bill Garvin, Nottingham, NH
Company K, 3rd Battalion, 12th Infantry Regiment

A Wild Experience

We, the two hundred strong of Company K, 12th Infantry Regiment of the 4th Infantry Division, U.S. Army, went into Normandy, France, at Utah Beach on June 6, 1944, and fought through five campaigns before the European War ended. Unfortunately, most of my company comrades didn't make it through. Others were seriously maimed for life, and some, like me, were temporarily hospitalized with lesser injuries one or more times. To my knowledge, the only unscathed survivors in my company were the kitchen crew that served us hot food whenever we were pulled back from the front for a brief rest. Most of us had rigorously trained together for about two years. We had long marches with full field packs on the hot and dusty back roads of Georgia, weary overnight bivouacs, and maneuvers in the scrublands of New Jersey, and even amphibious training alongside the playful dolphins in the Gulf of Mexico.

We had docked at Liverpool, England, in January of 1944, and established camp in the quiet and tiny community of Exmouth in Devon County. Training activities resumed in a routine manner as German buzz bombs sailed overhead destined for Cardiff, Wales. Invasion preparations intensified in the spring, and in early June, we packed up, boarded trucks, and headed for Bournemouth Harbor where our channel crossing transport awaited. For two days, we nervously waited for the gale force winds to subside. These winds savagely tore away our barrage balloon—our protection from enemy strafing—and hindered subsequent beachhead activities for days.

Crossing the English Channel on the night of June 5, was a wild and memorable experience. All troops aboard were required to remain below decks except for the two company radio operators, Corporal Delevan, and myself. Our duty was to have our radio on for receipt of any messages, but not to transmit. The strong winds and pounding surf engulfed us with sheets of salty spray. Seasickness ran rampant amongst the troops below. It was a long and sleepless night. Well before daylight, the heavy drone of hundreds of aircraft carrying thousands of paratroopers and glider troops passed overhead, bound for Normandy landing zones. Our immediate destination was Utah Beach, and our mission, after the beachhead was secure, was to push inland about two miles through flooded farmlands and relieve the paratroops at St. Mére Eglise. This, we accomplished without serious losses, unlike the unfortunates who had landed on Omaha Beach and the paratroops who preceded us to our objective.

During the days that followed, we became hardened to the realities of war. The enemy had brought in reinforcements and stubbornly held their ground. They had the advantage of concealment, position selection, and withdrawal routes. We, the aggressors, had no choice but to advance into their gun sights if we were to take ground. We began losing men heavily from snipers, constant artillery, and high concussion Neblewerfers or Screaming Meemies (small rockets), fired in salvos with a grinding and wailing sound. The concussion from the close explosion of these rockets was so great that with helmet chinstraps fastened, one's neck could easily break.

On one occasion, it was found that a spare radio battery that I carried under my arm (across a field under enemy fire) had been pierced by a bullet, rendering it useless. Another occasion, equally scary, was being pinned down in a shallow depression by a sniper with an itchy trigger finger. He wasn't far off target with each shot.

Our new mission was to take the high ground that the Germans were using as their last observation point on the beachhead. Onto this beach, they could lob artillery shells and watch the results. While advancing with tank support, enemy action in the form of shelling and automatic gunfire increased. The five tanks with us were all knocked out; the bodies inside charred beyond recognition.

The regular company radio operator, Corporal Delevan, became a casualty from a tree-burst shell and I took over his duties. Men that had become like brothers to each other were being cut down. The Germans were practically looking down our throats; we couldn't move without drawing fire. Company aid men themselves had been wounded. In spite of severe losses, we eventually took "Bloody Hill," as we referred to it afterward, earning a much-deserved breather.

We held this well-exposed hilltop position, less than a hundred yards from the enemy, for several days, reinforcing our foxholes, taking pot shots at the enemy darting across hedgerow openings and trying to dodge incoming rockets and artillery. Whenever the action ceased, it was an indication that patrols had been sent out or a counterattack was imminent.

On one such an occasion, I nervously peeked over the nearby hedgerow and discovered, shockingly, that a German patrol of six men was not more than thirty feet away creeping towards us. With no time to waste, I signaled to my buddies the danger we were in and then jumped up, John Wayne style, onto the hedgerow top. I leveled my carbine on the leader and yelled, "Achtung!" meaning, Attention! It was the only German word I knew that indicated to them that I meant business. The leader got the message and gave a command to his men to lay down their firearms and raise their hands. Motioning them to come forward, we took them prisoners.

A few days later, units of the 90th Infantry Division passed through our ranks heading south, to cut across the Cherbourg Peninsula and seal off the German escape route with the eventual fall of Cherbourg. Capturing Cherbourg resulted in a bonanza of prisoners and a very important port that was not heavily damaged. The city was well fortified by dozens of huge concrete pillboxes and gun emplacements designed to repulse any allied attempt from a frontal assault from across the channel. Our attacking from the east, the opposite direction, fooled them completely.

Ferdinand Glista, Chicopee, MA
Battery B, 20th Field Artillery Battalion

Waves were Rough

I was a corporal in Battery B, 20th Field Artillery Battalion, 4th Infantry Division. Our battalion was made up of 155mm howitzers. We were scheduled to land at HHour plus three at Utah Beach to support our infantry, which landed at H-Hour, about 0630 hours.

We were on a Landing Ship, Tank, at about 0800 hours when the LST lowered its ramp to allow a landing craft, mechanized, to hook its ramp to the LST for unloading. The LCM could only take one howitzer and tractor at a time. Besides the tractors to pull the guns, there was ammunition, supply trucks, jeeps, kitchen trucks, and other equipment vehicles. The sea was very, very choppy and when they hooked up the first LCM, the waves were so rough that the ramp on the LST broke down and the operation was aborted so they could make repairs. The Navy personnel frantically did what they could so the landing could commence; however, several hours went by before we were to make another attempt.

While the repairs were being made, we were allowed to go up on deck. We were still four or five miles from the French coast, but we could see U.S. planes bombing and strafing German positions.

About eight that evening we made another attempt to get off the LST, but again the ramp broke down and the landing was aborted. We stayed in the hold of the ship until it was getting dark. They didn't want us to try landing in the nighttime, so the mission was again aborted and we were allowed to go up on deck again.

It was dark, and we could hear planes overhead. They must have been German planes because the sky became lit up with fireworks. Every ship was firing up in the sky. It was like the Fourth of July fireworks at home—only a thousand times more. It was actually beautiful, but scary as hell. I don't remember sleeping that night.

Jay Pearlstein, Augusta, GA
Cannon Company, 12th Infantry Regiment

H-Hour

On May 16, 1944, the 12th Infantry Regiment departed from Exeter and Exmouth, England, for its marshaling area in Plymouth. We were stationed in former British army barracks, sealed in by security guards. There would be no further communications or contact with the outside world. Top Secret Field Order No. 1, issued on May 20, 1944, outlined the mission of CT-12 (12th Regimental Combat Team) as per landing on Utah Beach in France, and to advance inland to capture Cherbourg.

On June 4, 1944, the 12th Infantry embarked in Plymouth harbor on LCIs, LSTs, and LCTs. I was a platoon leader aboard an LCT that was commanded by a British skipper and crew who had beach-landing experience during the North African invasion. The word then came down:

"D-Day is June 6, H-Hour, 0630 hours." At first light the morning of June 6, there were blustery winds and gusts of cold rain that had been going on for the past twenty-four hours. We were all desperately seasick. Spread out all around us, as far as the eye could see, there was an invasion armada of over four thousand ships of all types (combat, cargo, tankers, supply, hospital, landing craft, etc.) Overhead the sky was filled with friendly aircraft. The landing on Utah Beach was supported by para-troopers of the 82nd and 101st Airborne Divisions.

It was about 1030 hours—H-Hour plus 4—when our unit rendez-voused to hit the Beach. Due to the inclement weather of the past twen-ty-four hours, the entire operation had drifted, and we hit the beach ap-proximately two miles south of the planned landing area. Prior bombing by the Air Corp and shelling from warships had pretty much obliterated our landmarks. This all resulted in mass confusion on the beach, which was covered with burning craft, trucks, and equipment, and was receiv-ing deadly incoming artillery fire from the German coastal batteries. I had mentioned that my platoon crossed the channel on a British LCT. I was in command of the platoon, but the British skipper was in overall command of all personnel on his craft.

When I was initially assigned to the British LCT, I coordinated with the Skipper, the loading and unloading of personnel and equipment by using "to scale" cutouts of the vehicles and cannons. I felt fortunate to be with someone who had experienced a previous invasion landing; howev-er, it later turned out to be a bad choice.

When our wave went in to hit the beach, there were American LCTs on either side of our craft. The American skippers, with no prior invasion experience, went all the way in and dropped their ramps on the beach. However, our British skipper, from past experience, was fearful of be-ing grounded on the beach and accordingly, initially dropped his ramp a good distance from the beach. The first and second jeeps to exit the ramp were not able to make traction and both capsized with resulting loss of radios, maps, etc. My jeep was next in line to exit, but I refused to move despite the screaming order from the skipper to "get off my boat!" During all of this time, we were receiving incoming German artillery and machine gun fire. The skipper finally pulled up the ramp and moved further in to allow the jeeps to gain traction and move onto the beach.

My orders were to move rapidly inland and rendezvous with our company in a pre-designated area. During our stay in the secured marshaling area, we had been briefed on sand tables that were an exact replica of Utah Beach, showing various landmarks to guide us to the rendezvous area. However, all these landmarks had been obliterated by the bombing and shelling. There were painted German signs reading, "Achtung! Minen!" everywhere. Some of these posted areas were actually mined and some were not, however, our engineers were slowly, but surely, opening these areas. We instinctively moved ahead and managed to join up with the rest of our company around dusk. Our orders for that first night were to stand fast—absolutely no movement within our perimeter area. (Even a slight noise would bring fire from trigger-happy soldiers.) Even though it was June, the night air was extremely cold. We wrapped ourselves in the silk parachutes that had been abandoned by the paratroopers.

We captured our first prisoner the next morning. A German soldier was actually sleeping in our perimeter area. When he awoke, he was so surprised he simply threw his hands up and surrendered. For nineteen bloody days after that, the 12th Infantry Regiment and 4th Infantry Division fought through the hedgerows for every foot of ground. On June 25th, Cherbourg was taken.

Bob Kay, Charleston, SC
Company I, 3rd Battalion, 12th Infantry Regiment

"After You, Lieutenant!"

Although my memory has somewhat dimmed after fifty years, as I recall, the time was about 1030 hours, June 6, 1944, when our LCM landing craft ground to a final, scraping halt on a sandbar thirty yards short of the beaches of Normandy, France. With that wallowing stop, the Coast Guardsman at the bow hit the chocks, dropping the boat's metal ramp into the sea, and said, "This is it."

There was no turning back—none of this "dry-run" stuff, none of this "by-thenumbers crap"—this was the real thing. Years of military training and combat preparation were about to be tested. But as the ramp splashed down, I hesitated for just a moment when a tantalizing voice behind me said, "After you, Lieutenant!" It wasn't until forty years later that a surviving Sergeant Milton Shenton admitted in a letter that it was he who piped those words. Subtle humor such as this in the face of possible death can only be found in the free-spirited attitude of American troops that made them so unique. I shall forever treasure this jibing remark.

With a simple command, I said, "Let's go," and 189 wonderfully brave men of Company I, 12th Infantry Regiment of the 4th Infantry Division unhesitatingly followed me down the ramp into chest deep water and waded ashore to a more solid footing on Utah Beach, Green. We were right on the mark, for there on the beach stood a green vertical panel already erected by our Combat Shore Engineers.

The gods of good fortune smiled on us briefly that day for we reached our beach objective without a single casualty. This could have only been achieved as a result of those gallant 4th Infantry Division men from the 8th and 22nd sister regiments who had preceded us onto the beach, according to our assigned invasion plans. Who would have dreamed that by D-Day's end, we would find ourselves six miles inland, hunkered down along a sunken trail, protected by a dense hedgerow?

The destructive spoils of war were immediately evident to the left of our beach landing position. Abandoned personal equipment lay scattered on the sand along with a destroyed two-and-a half-ton truck as well as a 35 ton Sherman tank, dead awash in the surf. Even with its very secret flotation capability, the tank never made it.

As I peered over the ten-foot high sand dune behind a four-foot high concrete seawall, I could see in the distance a group of buildings and a church spire. I "guesstimated" this landmark to be the small French village of St. Martin de Varreville—the first primary objective of the war for the 12th Infantry. My compass heading showed 280 degrees and that's the direction I headed at a trot, with the troops dispersed behind me at extended intervals.

I'm sure the earliest and most impressionable sounds of war were the distant thump and rumble of artillery and the not to be forgotten "rrrrip" of a German machine pistol. It didn't take long for every man to seek cover at the deadly sound of German artillery passing over, ending in an explosive roar ahead or in an air burst puff of gray-white smoke. And, who among us can ever forget the screeching "crank-up" of those electrically fired screaming meemie rockets?Upon discovering the thousandyard-wide flooded zone beyond the beach, we saw that the ridges that we could wade in often ended up as eight foot and ten foot deep water troughs, necessitating the use of our toggle ropes and inflatable life belts to swim our troops across. It was a slow, physically exhausting requirement that eventually took almost three hours to negotiate. Considering those men with heavy weapons, ammunition, and fortification assault gear, one wonders how we ever made it that day.

However, upon reaching terra firma at a point called "Pitcher's Box," a code name for the Regimental CP, we thankfully were able to dispose of our flamethrowers, bangalores, and pole and satchel charges. But even before drying out, Company I received orders to move under cover to a position three-quarters of a mile west, to serve as left flank protection for the regiment and its attacking battalions.

Would you believe that up to that point in time (late afternoon) since landing, our rifle company had not lost a single man to enemy fire? Lady luck had indeed been on our side, but our good fortune as a unit was soon to change.

As our company attempted to establish and secure our flanking position, I was ordered to lead a patrol and check out an area to our front, along a paved highway, to a distance of 200 yards. As we cautiously moved along drainage ditches paralleling both sides of the roadway, our advance was suddenly interrupted with the twilight arrival of maybe a dozen DC-3 towed airborne gliders immediately over our position. They were so low that one of their dropped nylon towlines fell across the very position in which I lay.

With that, all hell broke loose, as the concealed and as yet unseen German forces reacted like a swarm of hornets lighting up the sky with tracer and small arms fire. Suddenly, in the darkness, an attacking German force jumped my sixman point unit located in the ditch on the opposite side of the road from my position. Four men were lost in that brief, "close-in," and intense encounter. A wild but short firefight ensued, ending only after close-in, 60mm mortar support, allowing my patrol to extricate themselves from a seemingly untenable position. Finally, we withdrew to a covered trail and secured our company's position for the night. What a way to end my first day in combat. For sure, the 1st squad of the 2nd platoon of Company I took a big hit that fateful night.

Though vivid combat memories have faded over all these years, the awesome, panoramic view of the sea and the vast armada of ships dimly visible in the dawn's early light as we approached the Normandy coastline was a sight not to be forgotten. Smoke and fires ashore also gave evidence that other troops were already in the fight on the beaches and the cliffs. Our turn was yet to come, and come it did.

Yes, I remember, but fifty years later, I much prefer to only seriously recall the names and faces of those gallant men with whom I had the privilege to know, to train, and to lead into combat as an infantry platoon leader. To them, and to all combatants that day, I commemorate the following paraphrase and transposition of scripture (Phil. 2, verses 5-11), which reads in part: "To them belong all Glory, Laud, and Honor, since they gave up their equality with God, and became obedient to the point of death—even death on a battlefield."

Sigmund Nalewjka, (Deceased) Schenectady, NY
12th Infantry Regiment

Semaphore Light

In our practice runs for the invasion on Slapton Sands, we tried to learn how to send messages with the Navy's semaphore light. It was a little bulky with the rest of the equipment that we carried. On one landing, the lieutenant made a remark that he would shoot the operator of the semaphore in the butt, and that remark got around the platoon. On landing on D-Day, with all the confusion and shooting, everyone was looking out for themselves and who got hit or killed. The second day, the lieutenant asked the platoon leader where the semaphore light was and he was told it was left on the landing craft, still in the English Channel.

George Goodrich, South Plainfield, NJ
HQ, 44th Field Artillery Battalion

Bodies Stacked like Cordwood

(From a news story written by Evelyn Hall for a newspaper called The
Reporter)

Elation sang through George Goodrich's veins as the landing craft
plowed through the water toward the shore. Finally, after long
months of training, he was about to join the battle that would culminate
all his practice and preparation.

A scant two hundred yards off the beach, a German shell struck the
landing craft a glancing blow, causing minor damage and no casualties.
Lieutenant Goodrich's elation immediately died. Fear replaced it, accompanied by the knowledge he and all his companions could die in the
coming battle, perhaps even before they ever set foot ashore. The twenty-
six-year-old lieutenant had two very special reasons to want to stay alive:
the South Plainfield farm girl waiting for him back home, and his infant
son.

At 0700 hours, June 6, 1944, George Goodrich was in the third wave
of Allied forces that landed on Utah Beach. When he reached the low
seawall at the end of the beach, Lieutenant Goodrich saw the bodies of
soldiers from the first two waves were stacked there like cordwood.

He looked over the bodies and saw beyond, a field with the warnings
posted, "Achtung Minen." Beyond that minefield, a German machine
gunner sitting in a tower kept the Allied soldiers pinned to the beach. "I
looked over the wall and no one was past it."

The craft that bore the lieutenant and his companions to the beach
also carried the first artillery piece into the battle that day. When the
tanks landed, they immediately took out the machine gun tower. But
the soldiers' advance was still stalled. The Germans had flooded the land
behind the seawall, leaving only three passable corridors across the flooded area. "Allied troops were supposed to land about two thousand yards
southwest of where they actually did, at a different pass," Mr. Goodrich
said. It was a mistake that worked in the Americans' favor. The other two
passages were heavily fortified.

"Our landing was fairly smooth," he said. But once the troops were
off the beach, "it was Normandy hedgerow fighting" as they moved inland on the second day of the invasion. "Sometimes we would take a
hedgerow and then lose it in the night. I saw my closest friends killed,"
Goodrich said.

Emlin Henry Stelling, Atkins, IA
Medic, 22nd Infantry Regiment

No Turning Back

A round midnight, we anchored several thousand yards off the French
Coast waiting for the minesweepers to clear the beach of mines and
barbed wire. At 0630 hours, June 6, 1944, we climbed down the rope
ladder to LCVP boats that held about thirty men. At this time, the naval
battleships and destroyers were pounding inland to give us protection
along with the Air Corps overhead. We headed for Utah Beach, and I
had about one hundred fifty pounds. of equipment— medical supplies,
plasma, etc.—to sustain us until the beachhead would be established.
When the ramp on the LCVP went down, that was it—no turning back.

Some boats had to stop several hundred yards from the beach due to
shell holes. So many soldiers with their heavy equipment on stepped out
in deep water and drowned before ever reaching the beach. Fortunately,
we stepped out in about one foot of water and headed for the beach wall.
The Germans now knew we were there and were pounding the beach
with artillery causing a lot of wounded.

After reaching the top of the beach wall on D-Day, I saw an officer
scanning the French countryside with his binoculars. To my surprise, it
was Brigadier General Theodore Roosevelt Jr., who came in on the first
wave. I asked him, "How do things look, sir?"

He responded, "I think the Krauts know we are here and all hell is
going to break loose in the next fifteen minutes."

He was right. We left the beach to be with the 22nd Infantry Regiment, pushing inland rapidly to avoid enemy shells raining down on the
beach.

The Germans flooded the few causeways and roads that led inland,
but it didn't hamper us. Our objective was to contact the 82nd and the
101st Airborne, which had dropped east of the beach around St. Mére
Eglise and had helped us to secure a beachhead.

We had accomplished our mission by driving the Germans back five
miles from the beach on the first day. I stayed with the 4th Infantry Division through the entire war. I was in the Bavarian Alps when the war
ended and was very fortunate to be able to come home.

Tom Primm, Wilson, NC
4th Signal Company

A Horrible Sight

After bouncing around in the English Channel for several days, I landed on Utah Beach early in the day with three wire teams, a small truck, and an amphibian vehicle loaded with ammo for the artillery. My mission was to connect the initial infantry and airborne units with wire and telephone communications. The amphibian vehicle was destined to get us across the inundated area just beyond the beach in case the roads and bridges were out. A German artillery shell hit the amphibian vehicle before it cleared the beach, setting it on fire. The shells began exploding and had everyone ducking most of the day.

The beach was littered with clothing left by everyone. Each of us had on three sets of clothing mainly for our protection in the waters of the channel. The initial shock of seeing bodies on the beach and in the water was a horrible sight…difficult to imagine.

One of my men was shell-shocked very early and I placed him in a bomb crater and had him operate the switchboard from that location. General Roosevelt was a real inspiration to all of us on the beach, especially those of us with no combat experience. When shells were coming in, all we had to do was watch him and know when to duck or run for a hole.

Before that day was over, and it seemed to be an eternity, I watched General Roosevelt in his little wool knit cap and carrying a riding crop, lead the troops off the beach and inland.

Irving Smolens, Melrose, MA
Battery B, 29th Field Artillery Battalion

Entire Gun Crew Lost

The 29th Field Artillery Battalion, along with the 8th Infantry Regiment, made up the 8th Combat Team of the 4th Infantry Division, whose mission was to make the H-Hour landing on Utah Beach. Batteries A, B, and C had been equipped with M-7 armored 105mm howitzers instead of conventional truck-drawn artillery pieces, which were standard issue for infantry divisions. Each gun battery was equipped with four guns.

They were lined up on the deck of an LCT, two in front and two in back. Their mission was to fire high trajectory shells onto the invaded beaches in close support of our infantry.

We could do this because the tank treads on the M-7's could cushion the recoil, whereas the conventional artillery pieces could not do this. The trails could not be dug into a steel deck. The LCT carrying Battery B hit a mine in the water. My entire gun crew was lost. Only two members of the battery who had been on board ever returned to active duty.

The reason I am still here to tell this story is that, in anticipation of casualties, the gun crews were stripped down to six men and the remaining six men were kept in reserve on a larger ship. Subsequently, we had to clamber down rope ladders into an LCT with all our equipment for transport to the beach in the late afternoon. Our three-quarter-ton truck (weapons carrier) flooded immediately as it drove down the ramp of the LCT. The skipper had dropped his ramp too far from the shore. It was getting dark and the tide was coming in and weighed us down. As it were, we might have drowned had not a DUKW (amphibious truck, affectionately dubbed by the GIs as a DUCK) driver seen our plight and drove into the surf, came alongside and rescued us.

When we learned of the fate of our battery mates we were dismayed, to say the least. Until the battery was reformed about two weeks later, I was assigned to ride shotgun for a battalion messenger. We sometimes lost our way and became great sniper targets. One other time, we suffered through a head-on collision because of driving in almost total blackout conditions.

Bill Buell, Clearwater, FL
Service Company, 12th Infantry Regiment

We Were Lucky

In mid May, we got notice that we were to leave Higher Barracks and Exeter after breakfast the next morning. After a good night's sleep, we fired up the barracks stove with broken-up wood boxes, courtesy of the ration detail, then off to breakfast. While eating, we heard the fire engines. On returning, we found our barracks on fire. Packing-box wood really made a hot fire compared with the fueldeficient English coke we were supposed to use.

Off we went to a fenced-in camp in Plymouth. We were closely guarded—not allowed out. Another Division did all the work, such as cooking, KP, and maintenance. We were not allowed to fraternize or even to speak to them. After a few days, we were shown maps of where the landings would take place. These maps covered only a space of two to three miles or less. We could tell it was in France, but had no clue as to where in France. We had no reference books or atlas among our meager belongings. What made it particularly difficult to tell where we would be is that we were to land from the east and thence attack north, toward the right flank.

One of the highlights of this long confinement happened one Sunday afternoon. This camp was on a hillside overlooking a valley and the ascending hill on the other side. About fifty soldiers lined up on our side of the hill armed with telescopes and binoculars. They were aimed at the opposite hill where an English sailor and his young lady friend were spending their afternoon in seeming solitude. They were far enough away so they did not hear our cheers and applause.

During this period I was notified that I no longer was to handle rations, only ammunition. In the Regimental Supply Officer (RSO) organization, the group consisted of a captain, a warrant officer, and a buck sergeant. The captain who came to England with us was replaced by Captain Victor Vrabel of McKeesport, PA, who after the war, married a girl he met on the day we liberated Paris. The warrant officer was Max Rodella of Cleveland, OH. All of us, in the future, were given extra duties in addition to ammunition.

Finally, we left Plymouth but not as a group. The S4, Major Kenneth Lay, Captain Vrabel and I left in a jeep driven by Private Licht. Our supply convoy headed for Dartmouth where we boarded a small English boat that held about fifteen small vehicles and about fifty to sixty officers and men. Among them was the Regimental Assistant Commander, Lieutenant Colonel Jim Luckett. This boat was an English vehicle landing craft with a crew of five. There was no underdeck, no kitchen, and no shelter other than inside or under the vehicles, and one latrine that was clogged up within two hours. We survived on 10-in-1 rations. This was our home for the next five nights running around in circles in the English Channel. As you know, we received word the landing had been delayed one day. Vrabel brought along a fishing line with hooks and bait but was never able to use it. We kept busy reading, shooting craps, playing black jack and cooking our rations. One unique item we had—courtesy of our English friends—which I had not seen before or since, was cans of soup that had a wick through the center of the can. You lit the wick and after it stopped sizzling, you had quite delicious hot soup.

Finally, the big day arrived, with the most spectacular air show ever seen. The bombers, the planes with paratroopers, and the planes towing gliders loaded with glider troops, made the sky black with aircraft. Our little English boat hit the beach shortly after 0900 hours, June 6, 1944. They brought the boat right up on the beach. We never got the soles of our feet or the vehicle tires wet. We were lucky. I never looked back to see if the boat ever got off the beach.

We landed with our "lifesavers" (life vests) in case we had to swim across the inundated area behind the beach. We were on the beach quite a few minutes before being bombarded with artillery. Our war had now started. On making my way off the beach, I saw my first casualty, a French woman split down the middle.

That afternoon I dug several foxholes, about fifty percent of all I dug for the entire war. At about five or six o'clock, the major, the captain, Private Licht, and I took off in the jeep to try to find the 12th Infantry Regiment CP. We were a solitary vehicle on a Normandy country road. We came to a crossroad with about a dozen French natives yelling and frantically waving at us. Were they warning or greeting us? Who knew?

Major Lay was one of our most able officers, but his reputation on map reading and natural instinct on directions was shaky at best. He decided to proceed straight through, against the advice we were being offered. The rest of us were sure we were heading into an ambush, but lo and behold, we reached our destination.

The first day, the 12th Infantry established their headquarters in the very same house that had been pointed out to us on the map back in Plymouth. During the night, I finally managed to get some sleep by lying on the cobblestones in the farmhouse creamery. At least that was what the smell was like. When I woke up and was still lying there, I noticed there were flies everywhere, especially crawling on the floor. We had been given bottles of insect repellent made by the Union Carbide Company (something none of us had ever heard of before). I used it on my hands and arms and watched the flies as they abruptly stopped within an inch or so of my hands and arms. Remarkable!

Shortly, a member of the I&R platoon reported they had found a barn loaded with enemy ammunition about a mile away. I was ordered to go with him and take inventory. Off the two of us went, down the unpaved road to a driveway in a heavily wooded area and up the driveway about one hundred yards to the barn, totally surrounded by woods. At this point, my guide left me. Into the barn I went. The big swinging door was lined with small shelves that contained a few hundred frangible grenades (all glass). All of a sudden, small arms fire started coming in from the woods. How they managed to miss me and not set off the grenades and blow the barn up, I will never know. I didn't wait around long to find out.

The first few nights it was cold. We carried no blankets. All we owned was on our backs and lightening our load was our aim. We abandoned our gas masks a day or so later; then of course, we had a gas scare. One night, I had an abandoned parachute to sleep under. Its nylon material made a fine blanket. One morning, I spotted a can of evaporated milk. Was it a booby trap? I took a chance and it tasted great. A nice treat. One afternoon, I found myself being fired upon by a sniper with wooden bullets. The Germans did not trust some of the Polish soldiers they enlisted into the Army with better ammo.

I will close with a few words about the 12th Infantry Regiment's commanding officer, Colonel Russell "Red" Reeder. He was a true-born leader, not averse to spending time at the front line with the rifle companies. He carried an M-1 rifle just like the rest of us and was not afraid to use it. Returning from the front, he rode into the command post almost like a cheerleader, always a positive thinker. In later years, he authored about twenty books. They are enjoyable and I advise you to read some, especially Born at Reveille, an autobiography. Red Reeder was an athlete, an intellectual, and above all else, a soldier. In 1949, when the 4th Infantry Division monument was dedicated on Utah Beach, there were speeches by Sargeant Shriver, then the current ambassador to France; General Omar Bradley, our General Jim Van Fleet, and "Red" Reeder. Reeder brought the house down by giving his stirring speech, first in French and then in English. By the end of the first week in Normandy, Colonel Reeder was wounded and lost one foot. But for that, he would have soon been a general. Red Reeder died in his nineties at the Old Soldier's Home in Virginia, and, per his wishes, was buried on the hill at West Point.

Arthur S. Teague (Deceased)
CO, 3rd Battalion, 22nd Infantry Regiment

Ram the Beach Hard

Bill Boice, Chaplain of the 22nd Infantry Regiment, included the following report by Lieutenant Colonel Arthur Teague in his book, History of the 22nd Infantry Regiment in World War II. –Bob Babcock

The 3rd Battalion, 22nd Infantry Regiment, commanded by Lieutenant Colonel Arthur S. Teague, made the initial assault on Utah Beach, attached initially to the 8th Infantry Regiment. The following narration is a verbatim report by Lieutenant Colonel Teague on the assault landing of the 3rd Battalion, 22nd Infantry Regiment.

From landing craft, we came ashore in LCMs (Landing Craft Mechanized) three of them—operated by Navy enlisted men. An enlisted man on our LCM remarked that this was the third landing in which he had participated and that he didn't mind the initial landing so much as he did the ones afterwards—because he would have to keep bringing in supplies.

Just as we were coming in to the shore, I saw a shell that was fired from up the beach and I knew some of us were going to be hit. I could see the spurts of water coming up. I saw one small landing craft hit, and thinking the same might happen to us, I told the Navy man to ram the beach as hard as possible. He said he would, and after holding it wide open for about two hundred yards, we hit the beach and stepped off on dry soil. A couple of boats behind us—about seventy-five yards back in the water—were hit, and then I saw a number of casualties. Many were killed and quite a few wounded.

I started up by the seawall on the sand dunes and stopped for a moment; it was then that I heard someone call me. It was General Roosevelt. He called me over and told me we had landed way to the left of where we were supposed to have landed and that he wanted us to get this part of the beach cleared as soon as possible. He wanted action from my men immediately after landing and asked me to get them down the beach as soon as I could. This was about 0930 hours.

At this time, we were getting quite a bit of artillery fire from the in-land side of the beach. It was not very heavy, but sporadic. I went on over and called a couple of officers on the staff, got behind the seawall and suggested that we figure out what we had to do. We talked it over and thought about what could happen, then decided the best thing to do was to find Captain Samuels, the Company Commander, and see what troops were already on the beach so that we could take stock of them.

A couple of tanks were on the beach and I yelled to one and crawled up on it. I asked the enlisted men about firing on the beach on the troops we could see. He stated that he had strict orders to just sit there and protect the troops coming ashore, and that was all. I told him for God's sake to start firing so we could reduce the enemy troops waiting for us. He said he had orders to defend until the American troops went through.

We started up the beach and I hollered back to everybody and got them dissembled because I saw two men who were lost on mines. I stayed on the sand dunes to see if I could identify my location on the map. Standing with my back to the water (looking inland), a little bit to my right front was the little round windmill or silo that I had previously observed on aerial photographs and panoramic views of the beach. This gave me the immediate location of where we were. I tried to get higher on the sand dunes, but someone yelled at me that snipers were firing and for me to come down.

I started on up the beach wall and ran into more troops. They said Lieutenant Tolles had been shot. On my way there, I passed a number of "baby" tanks that had electrical wiring and were loaded with TNT. Some troops wanted to fire into one. I told them to stop that action and I posted guards on it. I went on around this little firing trench marked by barbed wire and sandy beach grass. Near this firing trench I went behind a sand dune into an open place and found Lieutenant Tolles lying on his side near another wounded man. I asked him what happened. He said he saw a white flag, and he tried to get them to surrender, but someone had fired on him. I immediately sent someone back to notify a doctor to move him out of the place. I went farther up and ran into members of his platoon who had stopped and were having quite a little rifle fire back and forth. I saw what was happening as they moved along. My German interpreter was with me. We ran and hollered to them and he yelled to the enemy in German. I ran on top of the sand dune. There I picked up an M-1 rifle and called to our men to get going. We went forward and suddenly encountered direct fire. I saw two Germans wounded. About seventeen of them rose up from different places and started running across the beach. Private Meis yelled at them in German. I questioned them and asked them where their mines were and about the number of Germans. They said they didn't know—that they had come only the night before. I told them they did know, and that they would go with us.

I then started a skirmish line up the beach. They went about fifty yards up the beach and yelled, "Mine!" They started showing paths we could take to get out of there. I had seen Lieutenant Burton and Sergeant Mc-Gee wounded by mines along the beach. We moved on down the beach and picked up about forty more Germans. Where they came from, I do not know. Evidently, our troops ran them out. They came with their hands up and ran down the beach. We got on up a little farther and ran into a steel gate that I thought was a T-7 entrance, and now believe it to have been an entrance to U-5 causeway. I got hold of Lieutenant Ramano, Engineer Platoon Leader, told him to open the gate and while he was doing it, to have his engineers go up ahead and to lift out any mines.

I had gone up the beach a little farther and heard that my tanks were ashore so I sent someone down there to get a hold of the tanks and to tell them to come on down the beach. A platoon, under command of a lieutenant from Alabama—I've forgotten his name—came up the beach about this time and we ran across from the little fortification on the beach wall. The Germans were firing down the beach a little and I could see these shots hitting in the water. Some skimmed the tops of our heads and some hit small boats. One of our tanks came up and got fired on and hit by small caliber guns. It was then that we noticed a small steel turret mounted on top of a pillbox. Our tank was about twenty-five yards away, but it immediately elevated its guns and opened fire, knocking the turret completely off the little fortification. Here we got quite a few more prisoners.

In the meantime, our men were having a pretty good fight inland near an old French fort where they had taken about one hundred prisoners.

As we pushed on up the beach, our tanks were firing the whole time. We found another steel gate of the Belgian type on the beach. It had been used quite a bit by vehicles before we landed. I positively identified it myself as being near T-7. I told Lieutenant Manor to get out of the way—I had a tank. I pointed the gates out and he opened that entrance. I waited until he finished the job.

I continued up the beach right in behind several units of our company and ran into Captain Samuels. Captain Samuels talked about one of the little tanks, which had pushed around the entrance to T-7, stopped and was fired upon about three times. The shots ricocheted off the tank and the lieutenant fired the first shot, which went through the pillbox. It was the fortification we were supposed to have landed in front of. About twenty-five Germans ran across the beach with their hands up. The companies pushed on to the fortification and there I was with Captain Samuels, Captain Walker, and almost all the battalion staff. Major Goforth also joined us. Company I was told to hold up this point and L Company was to attack normal buildings and the entrance to Causeway S-9. The attack was supplementary. At the time, we were getting mortar fire, so we three officers, plus Private Buchavellis, decided we would dig into the sand dunes on Tare Green Beach.

We dug about two feet in the sand and finally I remarked that that wasn't going to do any good because we weren't getting any of the other fortifications.

We kept noticing the gunfire that was coming down the beach. I took the platoon leader and he crawled down the beach to see if we could observe where they were firing from. While we were lying there, the Germans saw us and fired two shots. One went over our heads and hit the water. The next one ricocheted off the tank, which was close to us. We called for another tank. Firing continued from the S-9 fortification causing quite a few casualties. Our tank fired a few rounds at it and finally destroyed it.

The mortar fire had let up a little by this time, which had been coming down from the beach. I had just learned that one of our men with a flamethrower ran about twenty-five Germans out of a pillbox. He had taken two American paratroopers from the same pillbox.

I started out from this fortification straight across the minefield. I saw a house on fire. Behind me were Captain Walker and Captain Williams and quite a string of men. As we walked across this area (which had been dry at the time the mines had been placed in the ground), we could see where rocks had been pried up. I took out some white "engineer tape" that we all carried, and we marked them as we went. I told them to step in the same tracks that I had made. As we walked, I heard one explode behind me. Captain Williams hit it, and he got it through the cheeks of the buttocks.

We went on across the minefield and found L Company. Here we met Captain Blazzard, who had machine guns set up and had been firing. I ordered them to assault the house and the S-9 nest simultaneously. This was a matter of about thirty minutes. I yelled for Captain Ernest to hold L Company because I wanted to send K Company into attack.

All this time there was a gun still firing up the beach. It later developed that we could see where two or three shots hit the embrasures, but the Germans had destroyed it themselves.

About this time, I told Captain Ernest we could make an attack. We went out on the S-9 fortification about two hundred yards. The roads seemed to be in excellent shape showing they had been used. We found a French civilian in one of the houses, so we asked him where the mines were. He pointed out that the road from S-9 up the beach was mined. In fact, he showed me about eight or ten mines. You could see where the mines had been put under the rocks. He said that the road hadn't been used for about four months. He said the other road was being used, and to the best of his knowledge, was not mined.

We pushed around for a short time and K Company jumped off and made a flank attack. I went with the battalion staff behind K Company. I started wading in water up to my waist, and in some places, up to my armpits. A long column of men was wading through the water. A sniper got a man just ahead of me. He lay for most of the whole night because he couldn't be evacuated.

I followed K Company on up and encountered Lieutenant Pruzinski. He talked to Captain Ernest and told him that there was supposed to be a flamethrower behind the house, so I sent the lieutenant out.

Then we went on up the beach and hit the causeway. We were getting quite a bit of fire and also quite a bit of mortar. Finally, K Company was able to make the approach to the causeway. Lieutenant Pruzinski had two tanks and he captured that point.

K Company cleared out the causeway and a few buildings at the end of it, and, as it got late at night, I told Captain Ernest that we couldn't make much more distance so we made preparations for the night.

There was a house there that we were afraid might be a booby trap. The men began digging into the place, but it was flooded with water. We were getting machine gun fire from the fortification ahead of us, so I told Captain Ernest that since we couldn't dig in, we would sleep along the road and I would stay with the group. We lay down sometime around 0030 at night, although it was hardly dark. We stayed there for the night. Captain Ernest, Captain Walker, and Major Goforth were with me. (Note: Captain Glenn Walker later became Major General Glenn Walker and commanded the 4th Infantry Division in Vietnam. He retired as a Lieutenant Colonel.) I told Ernest to tell the men we could sleep there, and that we weren't going to give up an inch of ground.

We put two machine guns on the causeway and there was water all around us. It was about 0100 hours before all was quiet. Then we began to make plans for an attack at 0430 hours We worked out the plans on the map. We continued the K Company attack the next day.

Clifford "Swede" Henley (Deceased), Summerville, SC
Cannon Company, 22nd Infantry Regiment

"Jerries" Were Playing for Keeps

Even though it was against regulations, Clifford "Swede" Henley kept a diary during his service with the 4th Infantry Division in World War II. Tommy Harrison, who served with Swede wrote: "The entries were made by Swede so he could relate these memories to Lila, his wife, and other members of his family back in Sommerville, South Carolina. I can remember the times when I was with Swede and he would pull out his little book and recall the happenings of the day. This would usually occur late at night or early in the morning after the outposts were set up and all companies had reported they were secure for the night. Between a couple of slugs of cognac, Swede would make his entries. The following are key entries written not from memory, but on the spot during May and June 1944."

1-15 May 1944. During this period we were getting all our equipment, guns, and vehicles ready to go someplace. Destination unknown. Sergeant Horowitz (Supply Sergeant) began receiving equipment to be used only for D-Day operations. Sergeant Haire (Motor Sergeant) was given orders to waterproof all vehicles. The 105mm (M3) howitzers were waterproofed. All articles of clothing that were unnecessary were turned in. We knew we were going someplace soon, but when and where, God only knew.

15 May 1944. We received orders to move to Y-9 sausage in the marshaling area and await orders. On the afternoon of the 15th under the command of Captain C.M. Henley, 0348106, the company left South Brent Post, South Brent, Devon, by motor for Y-9 camp. We knew that we were seeing South Brent Post for the last time. All of the cooks and unessential company headquarters personnel were sent to Denbury, Camp Newton Abbot, to join us later.

15-31 May 1944. Lived in the marshaling area and took life easy and sweating out what was to come; when and where D-Day, H-Hour would find us. The CO was briefed on May 22, but was not allowed to brief the company officers until the 26th and the company on the 29th. Many hours were spent studying maps of the terrain we were to land on. Plans were made so that everything would work, regardless of what happened. Every man knew what he was to do in case the leaders were knocked off. Orders came for the company to load at Dartmouth on Hard "A" on 2nd of June, on LCT 2045, an American built LCT with a British crew.

1-3 June 1944. Moved out of Y-9 camp at 2025 hours for Hard "A," Dartmouth. Arrived at "Hards" on 0135 hours on the 2nd. The loading was orderly and fast even though it was dark. Lieutenant Colonel Ruggles was assigned to my boat. Colonel Ruggles is Executive Officer of the 22nd Infantry Regiment. After loading, we moved to Brixham about fifteen miles up the coast and awaited orders. D-Day was still unknown. The skipper told us that it would be at least 36 hours after we moved out.

4 June 1944. Received orders to move at 1530 hours and join convoy outside of Torquey.

5-6 June. We were well on the way to France. D-Day and H-Hour was June 5, 0600 hours. A storm hit us and the invasion was delayed 24 hours, making June 6, 0630 hours, D-Day and H-Hour.

7 June, D-Day (Written on June 7, describing the previous day). As far as you could see in all directions, there was nothing but landing craft, destroyers, cruisers, and battlewagons.

All hell broke loose about 4 o'clock as the Navy began shelling the coastal strong points and the sea wall. The Air Corps were doing a good job of divebombing and keeping the Jerries off us. It looked just like another problem to us. We anchored about twelve thousand yards offshore waiting for our wave to hit the beach. Our wave was to beach at H+280 minutes on Tare Green Beach. Nothing unusual was happening as yet. Just like another problem. When we were about three thousand yards off shore we could see the beach, but could not recognize any prominent terrain features of Tare Green beach. Later on, we found out that the Navy landed us two thousand yards south of where we were supposed to land. A usual Navy stunt which made all of our previous planning knocked out.

As we came nearer the shore, we soon found out that it was the real thing and the Jerries were playing for keeps. Artillery was falling every place and when our LCT beached and the ramp was lowered, we unloaded our vehicles and men in about two feet of water. Our first aim was to get off the beach. Long range 88s had made direct hits on several trucks in our vicinity and wounded "Yanks" were being worked on by the aid men. As soon as we cleared the beach, we put our guns in action and then Captain Henley set out to find out what the score was. It was tied up, six to two, in their favor.

As we came nearer the shore, we soon found out that the Jerries were playing for keeps.

Our foot troops were only thirty minutes ahead of us and everything was in a state of confusion. As usual, our boys got everything in line in a very short time and began to push down the beach. By night, we had reached St. Martin de Varrieville.

8 June D+1. Started the push to Raveonville. Rescued a group of paratroopers at Raveonville and continue to make slow progress up the coast. The 3rd Battalion (Lieutenant Colonel Art Teague) was on the right, 2nd Battalion (Major Lum Edwards) was on the left, and 1st Battalion (Lieutenant Colonel Brumby) was in the middle. There was no reserve. Everything was in the fight. The 1st and 2nd Battalions were making progress as the 3rd were hitting one strong point after another until the 1st captured St. Marcour and started out for the strong point at Crisbecq.

Crisbecq was one hell of a strong point but they took it about 1800 hours, and then the enemy counterattacked and drove them back south to St. Marcour. The 2nd Battalion, trying to take Azeville, was being pushed back. Cannon Company was called on for fire in front of the 2nd Battalion to stop the counterattack. We fired eight hundred rounds in about ninety minutes. Our ammunition nearly ran out, but the attack was halted and the Battalions reorganized for the night. Cannon Company had defensive barrages in front of the 1st and 2nd Battalions.

Ernest Christian, Philadelphia, PA
HQ, 1st Battalion, 12th Infantry Regiment

Thank God

We left Plymouth, England, June 5, about 1700 hours Crossing the English Channel was a rough ride. The waves were like mountains; I was so seasick. We crossed the channel, then had a rendezvous, and when we were about a quarter mile from shore, they told us this is for real (as if we needed to hear that). The noise from the shells was so unreal. We finally got close to shore and had to wade water about the last three hundred feet. I had water up to my neck but made it. Then we had gullies to go through in the flooded area past the beach but we made that OK, too. I must say, I was so lucky, I thanked God many times.

Ralph Dragoo, Henderson, KY
Company I, 3rd Battalion, 22nd Infantry Regiment

First Day on the Beach

We were the first company to land on our portion of the beach. We could see the flashing from the guns all night. (We were on the ship waiting for daylight.) I didn't think anything could live through it. Our planes were bombing the Germans all night. I didn't see how anything would be alive, but there were live Germans when we reached the beach. I was a "flamethrower man" and I had to put the flamethrower down. We had eleven of them in the company. I started to step off the ship to get on the landing craft and caught my foot between the boat and the ship. That made me sick.

One of my buddies asked if I was scared. I said, "No, but I didn't know why." When I first got on land, I heard the Germans' machine guns and it didn't take me but a second to get in a bomb hole.

This was my first day on the beach and things would only get worse. I was wounded the first time on June 12, 1944. I was wounded a second time on September 15, 1944. I saw two of my best friends killed on each side of me at the same time.

We never got any rest. I walked in my sleep when we did stop. Most of the time we had to lay in the mud and water. We were so tired that we could hardly walk straight. I remember a good friend of mine; we were drafted together. He told me that he didn't think that he was going to make it home and he would just like to say good-bye. He never made it back home.

Don Lee, St. Louis Park, MN
Company B, 1st Battalion, 22nd Infantry Regiment

First Purple Heart

I remember how I felt the first day in Normandy when I was crawling up a ditch to flame a machine gun and the paratrooper behind me was killed. My nephew could see it still bothered me and pointed out that it was not my fault and it could have been me. I can still hear the paratrooper's last gasp as I crawled past him. The next day I got my first Purple Heart, but just had the medics dig the fragments out of my shoulder and arm. Also, I got a new helmet liner as the next mortar shell punched a hole in my helmet. I kept the helmet, but lost it the next time I got wounded.

Ralph Meynard, Metarie, LA
Medic, Company L, 3rd Battalion, 22nd Infantry Regiment

After the Ramp Dropped

W e departed England on a troop ship where space was super tight. With the bad weather, it appeared doubtful if the landing would take place. Then, on the evening of June 4, word came that the invasion date was canceled. The next day we were advised that we would go in the following day, June 6, 1944.

The morning came, and we prepared to load on the landing craft. This in itself was a harrowing experience. Being the last man to board it took several attempts, as I waited until the landing craft was about to crest before I jumped. Fortunately, the timing was just right. It was a rough ride going into the beach, but we had an excellent coxswain. As we approached the beach, there was an enemy concrete pillbox dead ahead, and to our left was a small clump of scrub trees. The coxswain steered the craft so that we came on the beach behind the trees. The ramp dropped and the men filed out, running across the beach to take up positions behind the sand dune.

The radio man, his cover man, and I were the last to disembark. Unfortunately, the radio man stepped on a mine and the blast killed him outright. The cover man was hit very seriously and I, being protected by the cover man's body, escaped without a scratch. The cover man died before I could do anything for him. I then proceeded to catch up with the platoon. As I was running across the beach, my helmet began to bounce on my head. I brought my head down and reached up to hold it steady. Just then, there was a loud "pop" by my left ear. I dropped to the ground as I felt that a sniper had taken a shot at me.

The platoon leader started to come for me, and I yelled out to him that I was OK. A few minutes later, I ran to catch up as the men were trying to neutralize the bunker. Our BAR man had been hit, and I patched up his arm, making a splint from his legging. The humerus bone in his left arm was broken. Fortunately, there was no arterial bleeding.

Another man had been hit in front of the bunker, and as there was a minefield, we located an engineer with a minesweeper. With him leading the way, we checked on the rifleman. He had been killed outright, probably by a sniper. Another rifleman had been hit in his left shoulder and I patched him up and sent him to the beach to locate stretcher-bearers to take care of the BAR man. The platoon then began to reorganize itself and we proceeded with the advance, reaching our objective that evening.

That night as we were digging in, the glider troops began coming in and they were greeted by heavy antiaircraft fire. Many of them were shot down; later on, we noted that many of them had crashed upon landing.

George L. Mabry Jr. (Deceased)
HQ, 2nd Battalion, 8th Infantry Regiment

On The Beach

In November 1944, as a Lieutenant Colonel and CO of 2nd Battalion, 8th Infantry Regiment, George Mabry earned the Medal of Honor for his actions in the Hürtgen Forest.

The early morning hours of June 6, 1944, found me on a troop ship carrier in the English Channel headed for the beaches of Normandy, France. I was a captain with the 2nd Battalion, 8th Infantry Regiment, 4th Infantry Division. In a few hours we would be going ashore in an effort to begin the liberation of Europe from German occupation.

I had grown up on a farm in Statesburg, South Carolina. After high school I attended Presbyterian College in Clinton, South Carolina, on a baseball scholarship. After graduation in 1941, I received a reserve commission in the United States Army and was immediately assigned to the 4th Infantry Division. After years of training in the United States and several months of waiting in the staging areas in England, I was anxious to experience combat for the first time.

Just before 0200 hours I climbed on deck of the troop ship APA Barnett to watch for the airborne troops who were scheduled to begin dropping on the Cherbourg Peninsula. Only seconds after I reached topside, the German antiaircraft batteries opened up. The sky became alive with thousands of tracer rounds flashing upward in brilliant patterns.

As I watched the awesome display before me, a German plane began dropping chandelier flares to the starboard side of our assault transport ship, flooding it with light. I felt certain that we had been spotted and all hell was about to come down upon us. Everything remained quiet however, except for the AA fire and the sound of our ship slashing through the heavy seas on its trek to the rendezvous spot. When the antiaircraft fire began to subside, I glanced down at my watch. It was 0300 hours. H-Hour was three and a half hours away.

Almost immediately after we arrived at the rendezvous site, Landing Craft, Vehicle and Personnel (LCVPs) began arriving to ferry the battalion ashore. Although our ship had some landing craft aboard, which would be rail-loaded and then lowered into the English Channel, these were not nearly enough to transport the entire assault force of the 2nd Battalion, 8th Infantry Regiment, 4th Infantry Division. Most of the troops would climb down rope nets, lowered over the side of the ship, to board the LCVPs that now cruised alongside.

The task of crawling down the slippery, water-soaked net as that APA heaved in the choppy water to the tiny LCVPs lurching about below, was a dangerous one. The channel was so rough that morning that the landing craft would rise up on waves that reached halfway to the rail of the ship. Then instantly the boat would slip down into a trough so deep that it was impossible to see the craft in the "blackout" condition under which we were working. At one point, a soldier climbing down the cold, water soaked net lost his grip and was whipped upside down with one foot caught in the net. His head was pointing straight down toward the lurching LCVP. Three men who had already climbed into the landing craft protected the soldier's head and shoulders several times as the craft surged up and then fell away. After a minute, a soldier topside climbed down and loosened the soldier's foot. He made his way into the LCVP.

As the loading proceeded, I realized that Brigadier General Teddy Roosevelt Jr.'s boat team number would soon be called. General Roosevelt was the son of former President Theodore "Teddy" Roosevelt and nephew of then President Franklin Delano Roosevelt. Unlike most of us in the 4th Infantry Division, he had seen combat before in North Africa. He had made a personal request of the Supreme Allied Commander, General Dwight Eisenhower, to be allowed to land with the first wave of the invasion of Europe. The request was granted, and General Roosevelt had selected the 2nd Battalion, 8th Infantry Regiment with which to land. I ran down to his compartment where I found the general with his aide, Steve. I told Roosevelt the status of his landing craft and stated that his boat would load shortly. Before I had a chance to withdraw, Roosevelt called out, "Stevie, where in the hell is my life belt?"

"General, I don't know. I've already given you three," the aide said with a slight hint of reproach.

"Damn it, I don't care how many you've given me, I don't have one now."

So, Stevie and I rounded up a life belt and gave it to the general. He received it wearing a little smile on his face.

As we walked together down a narrow alleyway, I asked Roosevelt if he had all of his armaments. He stopped. "Yes, George," he said, patting his shoulder holster. "I've got my pistol, one clip of ammunition and my walking cane. That's all I expect to need."

Even though Roosevelt's boat was to be rail-loaded, it still required a jump of four or five feet down to the deck of the LCVP. The general climbed up onto the edge of the landing craft and prepared to jump when a soldier reached up from inside the boat and said, "Here, General, let me help you."

Roosevelt took his walking stick and lightly tapped the young man on the arm. He said in a friendly growl, "Get the hell out of my way. I can jump in there by myself. You know I can take it as well as any of you." In spite of the tension now at a fevered pitch, the general's remarks brought smiles and a few chuckles from the men in the LCVP. The men loved General Roosevelt. Everyone aboard knew that he had made a written request to General Eisenhower to be allowed to land with the first wave on Normandy.

Finally, after the entire battalion had been loaded, Lieutenant Colonel MacNeely, the battalion commander and I, along with several members of Headquarters Company, rail-loaded into an LCVP. Assigned to what was termed a "free-boat," we could land at any stage of the invasion the battalion commander saw fit. Colonel MacNeely had decided to land just behind the third wave. This position would give us the perspective necessary to gauge the landing's progress and to determine if any on-the-spot changes in the landing should be made.

Once all the landing craft were in the water, we proceeded to organize into waves under the direction of Navy control boats. As we circled, the channel had not calmed at all, and, if anything, the waves had gotten rougher.

The sickening oil fumes emanating from the clusters of LCVPs permeated the air. During the Slapton Sands maneuvers, which were also conducted on heavy seas, hundreds of troops, myself included, had become acutely seasick. But on the morning of June 6, I do not recall that a single man in my boat got sick. Perhaps we were simply too nervous to vomit. Just before daybreak, the final run to the beach began. The early morning sky was stark and gray. A vague outline soon appeared on the horizon, and I strained my eyes in an attempt to spot landmarks in the dim light. Strangely, the landmarks I had studied in my preparation for the landing were not visible. I began to suspect that something had gone wrong in our approach to the beach.

Early in our run to the beach, I spotted a naval control boat that had been designated to mark our lanes to the beach. The ship had hit a mine and was completely turned over in the water. A sailor was lying on the keel of the boat holding onto another man who appeared to be dead. The sailor waved for help, but, of course, we could not stop. This ship was to have been instrumental in directing the landing craft to shore. Its loss, and the loss of another control boat, proved to have a serious impact on the progress of the invasion.

By now, waves of Allied bombers began to come in and obliterate the beaches with bombs. As I watched a formation of bombers, one was hit by antiaircraft fire and exploded in midair. As the bombers finished their runs, the battleships and rocket ships began to discharge their weapons onto the beaches.

Suddenly, a German ME-109 fighter plane dropped out of the clouds and dived directly at our landing craft. Instantly, a British Spitfire locked in behind the German and fired three bursts of its machine gun. The fighter disintegrated in a ball of flame. The plane's propeller, still spinning, crashed down only yards in front of our landing craft.

During the noise and excitement, I had not failed to notice that our boat had fallen well behind the third wave. Colonel MacNeely called back to the coxswain to speed it up. The pilot gunned the throttle for a moment, but soon the boat slowed. Again, we fell farther behind the third wave.

Less than one thousand yards from the beach we passed through the floating DD tanks, which were to land with us on the beaches. They were having a terrible time in the rough seas that morning. The tanks were foundering in the channel and made very slow headway toward the beach. As a tank would begin to founder, the crew would inflate a rubber raft and attempt to abandon the vehicle just before it went under. As we passed a company commander's tank, it too, began to sink. The commander, a man I knew, was climbing out of the turret and then inexplicably stopped. The tank sank and dragged the captain down with it. I looked back but failed to see the man break the surface, and I assumed he had drowned. Later, I was shocked when he rejoined the battalion in France. He told me that his foot had become caught inside the tank and it was not until it settled on the bottom of the channel that he was able to free himself and swim to the surface.

Meanwhile, Colonel MacNeely once again told our coxswain to speed up. Again, the sailor gunned the engine slightly but after a moment, quickly slowed it back down. MacNeely was enraged. He charged back toward the rear of the landing craft. Standing next to the pilot, the colonel drew his .45-caliber pistol and pressed the barrel against the coxswain's temple. "Look, you son-of-a-bitch, I told you to speed up. I'm not going to tell you again. Move it now!"

That cold barrel was all the prodding needed. The coxswain jammed the throttle and we accelerated, leaving a wake akin to a speedboat. Quickly, we caught and then passed through the third wave. We actually caught the tail end of the second wave just as the men from the first wave jumped from their landing craft and began the long struggle to shore. In these final moments, I was still trying to spot familiar objects on shore. I found none. The mouth of the Murrdy Ray River was much too close to us, and there were not nearly as many obstacles in the water as we had been told to expect. Something was indeed very wrong.

The instant the front bottom of our landing craft grazed sand, but while we were still in relatively deep water, our coxswain dropped the ramp. Quickly, the men in front of me began to jump off the ramp as we had been trained to do. Just ahead of me, a soldier named Smokey David jumped off the right corner of the ramp and disappeared. I decided not to follow him and leaped to the front of the ramp. I went under, hit the bottom, and came back up. The water edged around my neck. I looked back just in time to see Smokey David's bald head appear out behind the LCVP. He had apparently jumped into a shell hole, gone down under the landing craft, and back out into the channel. While under water, Smokey had shed most of his equipment, including his combat helmet. He began to swim toward the beach.

While we struggled desperately in the deep water toward shore, artillery fire from our left began to sweep the beach. When I heard a shell come in, I would duck my head down under the water. After what seemed like a long time, I reached water that was only waist deep and tried to run. The water was so cold that after only a few steps my legs cramped, and I collapsed into the surf. I was up again in moments, but every few paces I was forced to hit the water. I noticed that most everyone around me was approaching the beach in the same slow fashion.

When I reached the water's edge, I saw Corporal Speck, one of my baseball pitchers from the team I had coached at Fort Benning, Georgia, lying on the beach. He had been hit in both legs. I ran to Speck and began to drag him forward. He stopped me and said, "Captain, your place is inland. Leave me alone and get moving."

I hesitated for a second and ran on, leaving him there on the beach. Close in front of me, I saw a soldier from F Company carrying a cloverleaf of 81mm mortar ammunition over one shoulder. As we ran forward, a German round dropped and hit the man right on the top of his helmet. The enemy round detonated the shells the soldier carried. He disappeared and something small hit me in the leg. It was a thumb—all that was left of him.

Though I moved forward, my advance was agonizingly slow because my legs still were not working properly. Just to my left, a human stomach was lying on the beach. No one dead or alive was near it. It was a starkly grotesque sight.

Before I reached the seawall, I was convinced that we had landed in the wrong place. The best I could determine, we were eight hundred to a thousand yards too far to the left. The original plans devised by Colonel MacNeely had called for Companies E and F to proceed directly inland. One half mile behind the beach was a vast flooded area with three causeways running across it. Companies E and F were to seize causeways two and three located directly behind the planned invasion area. Company G, landing behind E and F Companies, was to follow them inland several hundred yards, then turn left toward causeway number one and take out any enemy resistance they encountered.

The airborne troops were to land behind the flooded areas and proceed to the three causeways and hold them. At these critical points, airborne and sea borne troops would link. Seizure of the causeways was absolutely crucial. Should the Germans blow the causeways, we would be trapped on the beachhead, and a strong enemy counter attack would push us back into the sea. If my initial calculations were correct, the battalion had landed far left of Causeways 2 and 3, directly in front of Causeway No. 1. If this causeway closest to us could not be seized quickly, we could face disaster. With the other causeways farther than expected, it was likely that they would be destroyed before we could reach them.

As I neared the seawall, a squad of seven men from Company G went over the seawall and began to clear a path through a barbed wire fence. Since my job was to follow Company G, I began to run toward them. The squad leader, a redheaded sergeant, had started through the fence when he stepped on a mine that set off a series of deafening explosions. All seven men fell to the sand, dead or wounded. Some of the men were screaming. Without hesitation, I ran through them into the dunes beyond.

Rifle fire began to crack and bullets pounded into the sand around me. I fell to the ground and scanned the area, looking for a glimpse of smoke from the German rifles. Unable to spot anything, I jumped up and scrambled on a few yards farther. After one more short rush, I looked at the sand around me and realized that I was in the middle of a minefield. The wind had blown the sand covering them and mines lay exposed all around me. I considered going back to the beach, but decided that my mission was inland. If I was going to hit a mine, I might as well be heading in the right direction. I made another short dash forward and dived to the ground. On my next rush, enemy rounds were smacking into the sand so close to me that I lunged toward a large shell hole. In midair, my foot caught a trip-wire, which set off a large mine. The force of the explosion slammed me against the side of the shell hole for which I had been aiming. My right foot was completely numb. I was afraid that it had been blown off. Very slowly, I looked down and was relieved to discover that I had not even been touched.

As I lay there trying to regain my senses, I glanced behind me and saw a lieutenant from E Company moving forward. I called to stop him, but my warning came too late. A mine exploded and the lieutenant crumpled to the ground.

While crouched in the shell hole, I decided that the Germans must think that I was dead because their rifle fire had tapered off. Again, I jumped up and ran straight for the spot where I thought the Germans were positioned. As I reached the tip of the dune line, I spotted a group of foxholes. The nearest was empty but was surrounded by hand grenades and ammunition. I dived into it and quickly realized my mistake. Surely, the enemy had seen me land in the hole. I scrambled out at once and looked to my right. Within thirty feet of me, a German in a foxhole was about to toss a grenade at me. I wheeled around and shot him in the throat. At that point, Germans began standing up all around me with their hands up in the air. I counted seven: two NCOs and five privates. I segregated the NCOs from the enlisted men as we had been trained to do. This was the first and only occasion that I took the trouble to separate prisoners in such a fashion. In combat, one really did not have the time.

After corralling the Germans into two groups, I glanced over my shoulder toward the beach. Through a gap in the dunes, a vast panorama lay before me. An incredible mass of ships in all sizes choked the channel for as far as I could see. I understood why the Germans had surrendered so easily.

I was now confronted with the problem of what to do with my prisoners. Fortunately, I spotted a lone soldier one hundred yards on my right heading toward the beach with a bloody cloth wrapped around one hand. I signaled him to join me. The soldier turned out to be Sergeant West of Company G. He said that his company had been halted by a minefield and was located two hundred yards to our right rear. Until that moment, I had been convinced that Company G was well in front of me. I instructed West to escort the prisoners back to the beach and warned him to avoid the minefield I had already negotiated.

Shortly after the sergeant had left, three other men from G Company arrived. I decided that instead of returning to find G Company, we should push on toward Causeway No. 1 and try to reach it as rapidly as possible. After an advance of almost one hundred yards, we came upon a huge German pillbox. As we approached the bunker, machine gun fire opened on us, and we dived into a deep ditch nearby. We crawled down it until we were within one hundred twenty-five yards of the German position. I told one of the men, Ballard, whom I knew to be a crack shot, to spray the gun slits of the bunker with his BAR. He gave a few wellplaced bursts and ducked back down into the ditch. Instantly, two machine guns began to chatter, sending a stream of bullets over our heads. I did not believe that the four of us could damage the pillbox, so I sent one man back to the beach in search of a tank.

The soldier soon met tanks driving inland. In only thirty minutes, two DD tanks arrived and began to blast the pillbox. The Germans returned fire until one of the tanks maneuvered forward and stuck its gun muzzle directly into one of the bunker's firing embrasures. At that point, a white flag appeared, and Germans began to file out with their hands raised. Ballard and I, who were quite close by then, counted 36 of the enemy leave the pillbox.

I directed Ballard to march the prisoners to the beach. Then I selected another soldier from G Company to accompany me forward. We crawled down the same ditch. According to my map, it led in the direction of Causeway 1. I wanted to reach the objective quickly, regardless of when the rest of the battalion might arrive. After one hundred-fifty yards the ditch ended. I dashed across a road to a shallow ditch. No one shot at me, so I waved my companion across. From our position, I could see a hedgerow that appeared to run straight toward where I thought that causeway was located. To reach it, we would have to cross a field surrounded by a barbed wire fence, an indication of a minefield. I recalled a piece of intelligence I had been given while in England, which stated that if a length of straight wire extended skyward from the corner posts, the mine field was a dummy. On the other hand, if the wire was curled like a corkscrew, it was a live mine field. I saw that a straight line extended from the corner post closest to us. I told the soldier about the wire and said I would test the veracity of our intelligence. If I hit a mine, the soldier was to head back and contact Company G.

I crawled through the wire fence and into the field. I moved as gingerly as possible and saw no disturbances of the earth, either fresh or old; the minefield was indeed a fake. I motioned the soldier to follow. We quickly reached the hedgerow, and, keeping low, began to creep down it. After we had crawled some distance, I peered over the top of the hedgerow. There, only a hundred and fifty yards away, I saw our objective—Causeway No. 1. At this time, we began to hear rifle fire coming from across the flooded area opposite the causeway bridge.

When we reached a point only forty-five yards from the causeway, we were forced to stop. To get closer we would have to go over the hedgerow to a ditch on the other side. Although there were only two of us at the causeway, it had to be held at all costs. I decided to make a dash for it and told the soldier to cover me. If I did not get pinned down, I would wave him across.

I made it to the ditch. It was filled with nearly two feet of water. I had received no fire, so the soldier promptly followed me. I noticed then that the rifle fire had begun to pick up on the far side of the causeway bridge.

We had moved up to a position just ten yards from the causeway when three German soldiers began running down the road from the direction of Pouppeville. I told my companion not to shoot until they got to the bridge. When they reached its edge, we opened up. All three men fell. Immediately a squad of seven or eight Germans appeared and moved off the road to their right. They approached the bridge in skirmish formation. They were clearly trying to outflank us, and we began to fire on them.

The gunfire on the far side of the bridge was quite close now. In fact, I felt that some of the shots were directed at the same Germans we had engaged. American paratroopers must be closing in from the other side of the bridge. I pulled out my square of orange cloth, which identified us as Allies, and hoisted it on a stick well over my head. I spotted a reply. An orange flag waved back and forth from a spot on the other side of the bridge. It had to be the paratroopers.

Several minutes passed since I had spotted the friendly flag. The German rifle fire tapered off and then ended. I decided to run across the bridge to contact the airborne forces. The soldier covered me as I dashed across the bridge. As I ran, I spotted a huge aerial bomb wired for detonation lashed onto the bridge. The three Germans we had shot had probably been on their way to blow the bridge.

When I reached the far side, I saw the three Germans sprawled on the road. They were dead. Several yards away, I noticed other German soldiers all around. Some were lying on the side of the road and others were in a shallow ditch a few yards away. One of the Germans appeared to be shaking, so I gave him a hard kick to the leg with my boot. He quickly jumped up and surrendered. Suddenly, all the Germans around me began standing up. I gathered them into a group. I had a total of eight prisoners.

Before I could consider what to do with them, I heard a noise in front of me and looked up. An airborne soldier jumped over a hedgerow with his rifle at the ready. The soldier was a member of the 101st Airborne Division. We shook hands, and he told me that General Maxwell Taylor, Commanding General of the 101st Division, was just across the hedgerow and would surely be glad to see me. Seconds later, General Taylor, preceded by two men, crawled over the hedgerow into the road. I saluted, and we shook hands. Only minutes later, Brigadier General Gavin, the Assistant Division Commander of the 82nd Airborne Division, came over the hedgerow along with Lieutenant Colonel Julian Yule, a battalion commander, and ten airborne soldiers. It was obvious that the paratroopers had been badly scattered in the nighttime drop. As a result, the division commander and a battalion commander were in direct command of no more than a dozen troops.

Later, General Taylor would say, "Never have so few been commanded by so many."

I glanced down at my watch. It was 1040 hours. The first link between the airborne troops and sea-borne troops had been made.

Joel F. "Tommy" Thomason, (Deceased) Fort Belvoir, VA
CO, 29th Field Artillery Battalion

The Fog of War

At about 0400 hours on June 6, 1944, I awakened, cold and damp from the English weather. My sleeping bag was in the midst of a large stack of cases of rations on the upper, open deck of an LCT off the coast of Normandy, France. The invasion was about to be launched. I had burrowed into the middle of the pile, stacking ration cases up on the sides as a windbreak. My poncho served to ward off rain. That morning I lit the fuse of the heating element for a can of cream of asparagus soup for breakfast. During the week that I had been on board the LCT I had been reading A Tree Grows in Brooklyn. I never finished the book and left it on board.

I was the commander of the 29th Field Artillery Battalion, the main fire support unit of the 8th Infantry Regiment, which my unit was attached to. I had taken command of the battalion during the summer of 1942 when I was 24 years old. With concentrated training, the batteries of the battalion were ready for combat— the officers and men were eager to go. There were five batteries in the battalion: Headquarters Battery, Service Battery, and three firing batteries: A, B, and C. The battalion, with a fifteen percent over-strength to cover initial casualties, consisted of about seven hundred men, including forty-five officers. The unit was equipped with self-propelled 105mm howitzers, M-7s.

Our units were in the 4th Infantry Division, which was reactivated at Fort Benning, Georgia, in 1940. The division had about 18,000 men, and with several years training prior to deployment to Europe was, without question, the best-trained division in the United States Army. The 8th Infantry Regiment was commanded by Colonel James A. Van Fleet. I was on the command vessel with Colonel Van Fleet and our units were the initial assault units of the 4th Infantry division making the amphibious landing on Utah Beach. Colonel Van Fleet was a West Point classmate of Generals Eisenhower and Bradley—class of 1915. General Van Fleet saved Greece from communism after WW II, and later he commanded the United Nations forces in Korea. He died in September 1992, at the age of 100.

We had loaded our units on various landing craft on the Dart River in Dartmouth, England, in late May. We sailed on June 4 with the intention of making the landing on June 5. However, the weather was bad and the seas were high, so we pulled in behind the Isle of Wight when higher headquarters delayed the assault twenty-four hours. As the darkness gave way to early morning light, I could see a vast armada of boats and ships of all types. It was an awe-inspiring sight. They were so numerous that it appeared one could walk from England to France on them. The atmosphere was electric with excitement, and that was my feeling— one of great excitement. This was the day for which we had trained and awaited so long.

By 0600 hours the battleships, cruisers, and destroyers were delivering their fire on the beach. The big guns of the battleships roared and the five-inch guns of the destroyers cracked. It was an impressive sight, and we hoped their fire would destroy the enemy strong points and make our landing easier. Airplanes of the Army Air Corps, with their new invasion markings, were overhead throughout the entire day. Of greatest importance, they had complete air superiority and quickly destroyed or drove away the German aircraft that tried to intervene and get into the action. At about 0700 hours Colonel Van Fleet and my small command party transferred to smaller naval craft for the run into the beach. The initial waves of assault troops had landed some thirty minutes earlier. As we approached the shore, I studied the terrain; nothing looked familiar. We had all memorized the photos that submarines had taken earlier in the spring. That morning we could find nothing that looked like the photos. I had a sinking feeling in my stomach—something was wrong.

The small landing craft ground to a halt on a sandbar at what appeared to be a half-mile from the shore. Had we entered the water at that point, we would have encountered depths well over our heads before we reached the shore. We managed to get the naval officer to pull in closer and we jumped into water about halfway up to our hips. Our individual equipment seemed to weigh a ton. Much of it we discarded shortly thereafter.

Enemy fire was falling on the beach as we reached the shore's edge. My first action was to sit down on the beach, light a cigarette, and pull out all my maps and photos. It was critical that we find out where we were. The other members of my party and I examined the terrain inland, compared it with our maps and photos, and finally determined our exact position. The Navy had landed us more than a mile south of our designated beaches. Therefore, we had to adjust our plans to conform to our actual location. It was a case of Clauswitz's "Fog of War."

There was a strip of dunes and firm ground with some vegetation that extended inland for several hundred yards from the water's edge. Behind this was an inundated area that could be crossed in places on foot, but vehicles would have to use the causeways. Initially we would have to find positions for the five assault elements of the batteries among the dunes, and move inland on the causeway, when permitted by the shore party that controlled the beach. Of course we wanted to be off the beach as soon as possible. We would not be able to fire our howitzers from our initial positions on the beach because we did not know the location of the airborne units that had parachuted inland during the darkness of the early morning hours.

My party was able to find fair, although crowded, positions for the assault elements of the five batteries. They landed about 0800 hours It was then that I learned that the LCT that was carrying Battery B had been destroyed by a naval mine about a mile off shore. That was a great tragedy. Of the 59 men on board, 39 were killed at the time. The remaining 20 were severely wounded to the extent that only three or four were able to rejoin us many months later. The battalion had lost one-third of its firepower before we even entered combat.

Our next task was to get the battalion off the beach where enemy fire was adding to the toll of our already-heavy casualties. I set out on foot with another officer to find firing battery positions inland. By midmorning, we had established contact with the airborne troops, and knowing the position of our own infantry, we were able to fire from our initial position inland. During the afternoon we moved the battalion to a position southeast of St. Mére Eglise, some seven or eight miles from the beach. There we fired some missions throughout the afternoon and night in support of the three battalions of the 8th Infantry Regiment. When darkness came at about 2230 hours, we set up the harassing and interdiction fires on suspected enemy locations and key road junctions. In our final position, a German sniper fired sporadic rounds into our command post, but he never hit anyone. A couple of paratroopers took care of the sniper.

At about midnight, I lay down to try to get some sleep. I was very tired, but my thoughts were of the many casualties we had suffered during the day. Of the 28,000 men landed on Utah Beach on D-Day, the total casualties were remarkably light—just under two hundred. Unfortunately, about one-third of that number came from one small artillery battalion— the 29th Field Artillery Battalion.

John C. Ausland (Deceased), La Crosse, WI
Headquarters Battery, 29th Field Artillery Battalion

A Soldier Remembers Utah Beach

This article by John Ausland appeared in the International Herald Tribune *on June 6, 1984.*

As the time for the attack on Hitler's Europe approached, General Omar Bradley gathered in Exeter in southern England with the officers of the U.S. divisions that were to make the assault landings in Normandy. Bradley's purpose, no doubt, was to let us meet the man who would command the American ground forces. In the course of his talk, he sought to rouse us to the occasion by pointing out that we would have a front-row seat for the greatest military operation in history. For a few seconds there was silence, and then a roar of laughter swept across the room. Bradley looked about, clearly puzzled. A professional soldier, he was approaching the greatest moment in his career. Most of us, however, were civilians in uniform. We were well aware that we were about to participate in a historic event. We were all conscious, however, that a number of us would not witness the end of the first act of the drama that was to unfold, let alone the final curtain.

When the 4th Infantry Division, which I had joined two years earlier, went ashore at Utah Beach on June 6, 1944, I doubt that it ever occurred to me that we could fail. After several years of intensive training in the United States, the division went to England in early 1944. There we made a number of practice landings on the South coast at a place called Slapton Sands. This area was chosen because of its similarity to Utah Beach and its hinterland. As the level of training intensified, so did the level of tension. Finally, the 29th Field Artillery Battalion, in which I was a 24-year-old assistant intelligence officer, moved to its assembly area near Dartmouth. Those of us who had already been informed of the plans for the landing briefed the rest of the battalion.

At last the day arrived when we went to our embarkation point in the River Dart. By this time our battalion commander, Lieutenant Colonel Joel F. Thomason, decided that several of us would go on the same landing craft as Colonel James Van Fleet. He commanded the 8th Infantry Regiment, which made the initial assault on Utah Beach. Van Fleet's headquarters for the crossing of the English Channel was an LCT, a flat-bottomed boat just large enough to hold four tanks. In addition to the boat's crew, the only person who got a cabin was Van Fleet. The rest of us made out as best we could on the upper deck.

As we sailed from Dartmouth on June 4, we all assumed that the next morning would find us in France. We had not counted on the weather, which, when we were at sea, turned foul. As a result of General Eisenhower's decision to delay the landing a day to allow the weather to improve, we found ourselves bobbing around in the wind and rain for an entire night. Slowly but surely, seasickness took its toll. Even though I was one of the happy few who did not succumb, I was as relieved as the others to see the French coast in the gray morning light of June 6. All around us were thousands of ships and landing craft that had made their way across the channel undetected. The reason for that, we later learned, was that the Germans had not sent out their patrol boats in the belief that no one would attempt a landing in such terrible weather.

Although we were too far out to make out what was happening on shore, the sound of loud explosions from aircraft bombs and naval shells left no doubt that the beach was an inferno. As soon as Colonel Van Fleet got word by radio that the first waves had secured the beach and were driving inland, he announced that he was going ashore.

The run into the beach in a smaller landing craft, to which some of us transferred, was a bizarre experience. Most of us were happy to cower behind the little protection provided by the metal sides of the landing craft. One officer from regimental headquarters, however, insisted on sitting in a chair above us, where he was exposed to enemy fire.

Arms folded, he announced that he did not want to miss a moment of this spectacular show. (A few weeks later, under similar circumstances, he collapsed with a bullet through his head.)

When the landing craft hit the beach and the front ramp went down, I waded through some shallow water and ran to the shelter of the seawall that ran along the beach—barely glancing at several soldiers who were lying on the sand as though asleep. I could hear rifle and machine gun fire beyond the dunes, and some mortar shells fell not far away.

My task, once I was ashore, was to guide our three artillery batteries to firing positions that we had selected in England from a detailed foam rubber relief map of the beach. After crossing the sand dunes that lay just beyond the seawall, I was unable to figure out where I was. When I asked an infantry officer to help me, he laughed and said that the Navy had landed the first wave several thousand yards south of where we were supposed to land.

Fortunately, Brigadier General Theodore Roosevelt Jr., who had joined the 4th Infantry Division shortly before the landing, had volunteered to go in with the first wave. He later told some of us that he had gone forward to reconnoiter the beach. Finding that Major General Maxwell Taylor's 101st Airborne Division, which had dropped during the night, had captured the causeways over the inundated area behind the beach, Roosevelt decided that to try to move the landing northward would only cause confusion.

As it turned out, the Navy's error was fortunate. The beach on which we landed was much more lightly defended than where we were supposed to have landed, and the German resistance was overcome relatively easily.

When I went back to the beach, I told Colonel Thomason that I could find only two firing positions, not three, in the limited area between the sand dunes and the inundated area. As calmly as if we were on a practice landing, he said, "It's all right. We'll only need two. Battery B hit a mine on the way in and the landing craft sank."

Before I could think very long about the sixty men on the boat, Thomason told me to get moving and guide the other batteries to their firing positions.

After the batteries were in position, Thomason suggested we go inland to find the infantry. After crossing a causeway over the inundated area, we found ourselves in the middle of a field. We froze when we heard a soldier on the other side of the field shout, "Don't you fools know that you are in the middle of a minefield?" After discussing our predicament, we agreed to separate so that if one of us stepped on a mine, we would not both be blown up. It was a long way to the other side of that field. Discussing this incident not long ago, Thomason and I agreed that the soldier was right. We were fools. We should have had someone clear a path out to us with a minesweeper.

Late in the afternoon, after our batteries had moved inland to support the infantry, the clear blue sky was filled with colored parachutes. From these were suspended boxes of supplies for the paratroopers. The colorful sight turned to horror, however, when the gliders, loaded with soldiers and equipment, started to circle and land. Unnerved perhaps by the German antiaircraft fire, some of the pilots crashed their gliders into the hedgerows that surround the small fields of Normandy.

Whenever I recall that scene, I can still hear the screams of pain that filled the air around me. My last memory of that day is watching multicolored tracer bullets arch through the sky over St. Mére Eglise, which had been captured by our paratroopers but was still surrounded by German forces.

I fell asleep well after midnight in a ditch by the road—a road that would lead us first north to Cherbourg, and then to St. Lô. After that, we participated in the liberation of Paris, the nightmare of the Hürtgen Forest, and the crushing of the German midwinter offensive. After crossing the Rhine, we fought sporadic engagements until we found ourselves south of Munich. There we stopped simply because there were no more German units left to fight.

Bob Pryor, Herkimer, NY
Company H, 2nd Battalion, 8th Infantry Regiment

What to Expect

The success of the Utah Beach invasion rested with the U.S. 4th Infantry Division. This unit had never been in combat and was the only division scheduled to land at Utah Beach on D-Day. "This was all so new," said Corporal Joseph Kenefick. "This division had never landed under enemy fire, and no one really knew what to expect from the Germans."

Most men remember the English Channel crossing as tense, sleepless, and crowded. Some soldiers had been living on the ships for four days prior to the invasion. Private First Class Robert Pryor of Herkimer was below deck and said that when the hatch covers were dropped, "it sounded as if we were being bombed. Nobody could sleep." And there were more card games than usual as invasion francs had been issued to the men.

Joe Kenefick's career got off to a curious start. "I wasn't even an American citizen when I got drafted," said the Irish-born Kenefick. But he was sworn in anyway, and a short while later he was made a citizen. Now, he was in the middle of the English Channel, putting together his 90-pound field pack. He couldn't remember how many times he did this, trying to lighten the pack. "Most men carried about three days' worth of rations," explained Kenefick. The cooks weren't expected to land in France right away. He couldn't sleep and managed to get up on deck in the early morning hours of June 6. Navy battleships began shelling the beach area, and Kenefick recalled that the Navy guns "lit up the sky like the Fourth of July. It was quite a sight."

By 0700 hours the 4th Infantry Division was loaded into a small armada of LCVP carriers. The American and British Navies shared the responsibilities of ferrying the men to France.

Corporal Everett Rickard of Cold Brook recalls that a New Zealander drove the LCVP he was in. In the back of the craft was a small coal-burning stove with a full teapot. Rickard was a little shocked at how young the British sailors appeared. He estimated that a few were not even 18 years old. "They didn't even know where they were going," recalled Rickard. "They thought it was a maneuver."

Sergeant Martin Halpin of Herkimer was in a LCVP with three half-tracks. He could clearly see the first troops land and walk ashore. He thought, "Maybe this isn't going to be so bad."

"Just as the ramp dropped," recalled Bob Pryor, "a machine gun bullet ripped the wood off," a section of his LCVP.

Most men jumped into water that was chest high. They moved inland as quickly as possible and did not stay on the beach. "You've got to understand one thing," Rickard said with pride. "We were a moving division." Pryor remembers getting ashore and being told, "Get off the beach, or you're a dead man." Joe Kenefick also remembers being told to get off the beach. By the time Halpin had arrived, engineers were preparing to put up barrage balloons to prevent enemy aircraft from strafing the area.

Of the Utah landings, Marty Halpin said, "It was the only time during the war our division ever did anything on time—and we hit the wrong section of the beach." And, in a Medal of Honor performance, Brigadier General Theodore Roosevelt Jr., elected to hold the position and move ahead. Roosevelt had landed at the beach with the first wave of 4th Infantry Division troops. According to Ricard, Roosevelt was, "tough on the officers and fair with the men." Pryor called him, "fearless," and Halpin thought he was "a terrific man."

Not long after moving inland, the 4th Infantry Division linked up with members of 82nd and 101st Airborne Divisions. Pryor estimated that he had been in France only a half-hour before meeting the para-troopers.

Rickard was worried about the Germans and the French. "I didn't trust the French in that area." Rickard explained that a lot of the French had traded and done business with the Germans. He wasn't sure how the French would accept the Americans. The Normandy coast hadn't seen an invasion and, "an army can really beat up a countryside."

And the Germans? "They knew the country, and the Americans never did. We had to travel by map. They knew the road junctions and the places they were going to defend," added Rickard.

Truer words were never spoken. That same day Halpin ordered his men off a half-track. "We jumped off and the forward tank had its turret blown off." The Germans did know where to defend.

Pryor said his company was instructed to watch out for Waffen SS Troops. "They conducted themselves a lot differently than the regular (German) troops."

Some men remember where they were at the end of the day. Joe Kenefick says he was still helping to establish battalion headquarters. Bob Pryor remembers sleeping in a hedgerow close to St. Mére Eglise. He still remembers a paratrooper hanging from the church steeple in the town square. Only after he read Cornelius Ryan's book, The Longest Day, did he discover that the paratrooper hadn't been killed but was just playing dead.

Marty Halpin had his first drink of French wine interrupted by Gen-eral Roosevelt. Somebody offered the General a drink and he accepted. "I don't want any of you guys getting brave," Roosevelt said, cautioning the men about getting drunk, "or you'll be up there fighting the Germans all by yourself."

No one deserved a drink more than Roosevelt at the close of the day. The beachhead was secured, and the division was taking offensive actions inland. Roosevelt had taken a potentially disastrous situation and turned it to his advantage. Total casualties for the 4th Infantry Division were fewer than 200.

All of the men interviewed said that the Utah invasion was tough but not their most difficult task during the war. They all agreed that the Hürtgen Forest was about the worst battle they went through. "We didn't have it as tough as those poor guys at Omaha," said Joe Kenefick.

Samuel Arthur Ricker, Greeneville, TN
Company B, 4th Engineer Battalion

Never Saw Him Again

Through my mind's eye I remember seeing Utah Beach for the first time. There was a gray haze along the beach. In the distance paratroopers had dropped behind Utah Beach. Our engineers were unloading from LSTs at 0630 hours Along the beach we saw German artillery shells exploding on shore. When we came ashore one of our men jumped in a bomb crater. Artillery shells hit where he was, knocked him out of the crater, and I never saw him again. The night of June 6 I dug a foxhole, and German snipers fired all night long. As we went inland, we could see paratroopers hanging from trees, shot by Germans. The 4th Infantry Division fought gallantly to free Montebourg as they started eleven months of combat.

Vincent Sammartino, Oceanside, CA
Company C, 1st Battalion, 12th Infantry Regiment

A Beach Strewn with Bodies

Landing on Utah Beach, I lost my colonel, Colonel Montelbano. I was running about twenty-five or thirty feet behind him, and he caught a direct hit from an 88 that pulverized him. In turn, I was bleeding from every orifice from the concussion. I fell on the beach and passed out. I regained consciousness about an hour later. I struggled to get up. I looked back, and the beach was strewn with the bodies of our GIs. I don't know how I did it, but I managed to find my outfit and rejoin them. So many lives were lost that day, including my colonel's, who was such a wonderful man. Ironically, after the war, I discovered that Colonel Montelbano's family owned an Italian bakery in my Brooklyn neighborhood where I used to buy bread every Sunday.

Armand Torre, Rutherford, NJ
Company H, 2nd Battalion, 12th Infantry Regiment

The "Resistance"

While crossing the channel en route to our D-Day landing on June 6, we were briefed about coming in contact with various French Resistance Fighters, especially a certain Frenchman on a bicycle. We were given passwords to determine their identities. Around midday on June 6, we met three men. By exchanging passwords, we knew they were indeed the "Resistance."

Through one of our men who spoke some French, they gave us the location of some German pillboxes and machine gun emplacements. One of the Frenchmen was on a bicycle. He was probably the one they briefed us about. His name was Guillaume Mercader. When I was in Normandy, in July 1999, I looked up his name and found the address, where he welcomed us into his beautiful home. My daughter took French in school, so we were able to communicate somewhat. We stayed about an hour and a half, and he showed us all his artifacts and photos he had about the war. He also had a mock-up of the D-Day invasion.

John K. Lester, Stone Ridge, NY
Battery B, 29th Field Artillery Battalion

Battery B Struck a Mine

On D-Day, June 6, 1944, Battery B lost its entire firing battery, which consisted of four self-propelled 105mm howitzers. The landing craft struck a floating naval mine about a mile off Utah Beach. It is my understanding that it sank almost immediately with the loss of all sixty men and equipment. When I reached the beach on another landing craft and learned of the loss, I was devastated. How quickly I lost so many good friends and buddies! What a way to enter into conflict!

The rest of that day draws a blank. I cannot recall much of anything. I do remember being with Private First Class Richard E. Showalter and Tech/4 George Doolittle that first night. We didn't know what was happening. On June 7 I was reassigned. I went back to being a jeep driver for a forward observer.

Gerald Darr, Toledo, OH
Company F, 2nd Battalion, 8th Infantry Regiment

No Parachutes Opened

I got on the Navy ship after being transported there by a launch or something like it from the harbor at England on June 2, 1944. We clambered up a rope ladder to board this vessel, which was to be our quarters for the next four days.

We got in the invasion craft on the morning of June 6, 1944, and were lowered to the channel. Our pilot maneuvered the craft, and finally, we were lined up with the respective boat teams. Heading into the land, I saw one of our bombers take a direct hit and pieces came tumbling down. I did not see any parachutes open up.

I was a runner for an officer, and we waded to shore in waist deep water. We wore life preservers. The Germans were plopping shells on the beach and in the water. Sometime later, I heard that the First Sergeant of Company E, 8th Infantry Regiment, jumped off and stepped into an 88 hole and drowned as he was laden with a lot of equipment like everyone else.

While I was pinned down on the beach, the concussion of a shell blew my helmet off. A canteen landed near me, and I had to feel to see if it was my own, but it was not. My officer said, "Let's get out of here. This is too hot." Along the cement seawall were the wounded where I spoke with a member of my company. I heard he died the next day in England. Before we got to St. Marie du Mont, I saw Colonel Van Fleet talking with General Maxwell Taylor and General Gavin. They had jumped with their men of the 101st and 82nd Airborne Divisions.

The night of June 6 and the next morning, I observed a sight I will always remember. It was the Glider Army coming in from England. The Germans had planted poles in the open field to thwart their landings. A number of gliders were smashed. I guess they were constructed of plywood. That was scary for the troops aboard as the pilot had quite a task to maneuver the craft to a landing in avoiding the obstacles. I do remember the minefields with the signs, "Achtung Minen" on both sides of the road on the way to St. Marie du Mont and St. Mére Eglise.

Malcolm Williams, (Deceased) Greenville, NC
HQ, 2nd Battalion, 12th Infantry Regiment
Ready To Do It

About two weeks or more before D-Day, we left our barracks at Exmouth and transferred to near Plymouth. No one could go out, call out, or write. We were sure then that D-Day was next for us. I guess we had really known for six months or more. (My brother-in-law in Northern England got a three-day pass and came down to Devonshire to see me, but I was nowhere to be found, so he knew then that D-Day was near at hand.)

We had final instructions and were briefed on what to expect when we landed. Not only were we shown the map of the beach, but we also studied it until we knew it by heart. I think all of us were ready to go.

We boarded boats or ships on June 4. I am not sure how many men were on our boat, but I would say three hundred to five hundred. I think the boat was called an LCS. There were about ten or twelve of us who asked if we could stay on deck as air guards. The sea got so rough it was coming over the bow. To stay dry we stayed in the head. Water was about one foot deep there, so we put ten-in-one ration cases on end to sit on. At least that way we kept our bodies dry. We got no sleep at all that night. We were transferred to a small boat or craft some distance from the beach. This was very risky since we had to go down a rope ladder, and both boats were rocking like hell. There was the usual seasickness, everyone was scared s—tless, but we knew what our job was and we were ready to do it.

The craft hit the bottom, and the ramp went down. All of us were out in water about waist deep. We all made it to the beach and across it. (General Roosevelt was on the beach.) That is when the trouble started. Only one causeway was open. Heavy equipment was on the causeway and was drawing enemy fire. We decided to cross the flooded area. We had been told it was about three to five feet deep and if we stepped in over our head, to swim for about six feet, and we would be back in water we could walk in. That is what we did until we reached the other side. We could hear machine gun fire in the distance, but felt better about that than being on the causeway when enemy fire was falling.

About that time we had our first person wounded. It was Major Gray—he was "walking wounded," so he was not hurt too bad. My section was able to stay together. Sergeant Noe and I always paired off as buddies. We were the best when it came to digging a hole. Noe had a bullet hit the stock of his rifle, clipping a piece of wood off the stock that hit his face. Boy, that got all of our attention.

The first night the glider troops came in. That was a pitiful, bloody thing to see and hear. We spent most of the night helping them back to the aid station. I landed with a carbine rifle but exchanged it with one of the glider troops for his M-1, which I carried with me for the rest of the war. We got no sleep that night either. We all were really lucky to get ashore as safely as we did. Now we felt we had a chance to live a little longer.

Finally, I should tell you that there were 886 men in my battalion when we landed on D-Day. Of that 886, only twenty-one of us came home together at the end of the war.

Glenn Warren, Hardin, KY
Battery C, 29th Field Artillery Battalion

My Time Had Come

Excerpts from Glenn Warren's letter to Bill Cole in 1997

Our getting in touch has brought back so many memories, pleasant and sad. Each year I invade Normandy and also experience the events of December 29, at about 1300 hours when I was wounded. If I could put on video all my memories from June 6, at approximately 0600 hours to December 29, at 1300 hours, there would be several full-length movies. I will relate some of them.

On D-Day morning, before good daylight, we (Company K, 8th Infantry Regiment), Lieutenant Winters and I, got into the landing craft and headed for Utah Beach. After reaching the beach we assembled and proceeded through this minefield. The engineers had cleared a path for us and had laid a tape for us to walk on, but one of the infantry boys stepped off it onto a mine that exploded and he was seriously wounded. We made contact with the paratroopers that afternoon. The next morning we were along the side ditches of this country road when two Germans came in from the rear and killed two infantry boys. In a firefight one German was killed, the other captured. The one captured kept saying "Me Polish, me Polish," as he was being taken to the rear. That same morning the infantry colonel was killed by a sniper.

We were the first "on-foot" troops to enter St. Mére Eglise. I remember seeing a trooper hanging from the church steeple, still in harness. I thought he was dead, but a newspaper article in Hockert's hometown gave some statements about the fiftieth anniversary from five different branches. It stated that a trooper who jumped into St. Mére Eglise and was hanging from the steeple was pretending to be dead. He had been wounded in the upper leg.

The description of our OP was perfect. I had the same feeling as you when we walked across the clearing. Thinking about that day I was wounded—everything had been quiet until then. When I heard those three mortars fire, I knew that my time had come.

I was in the hospital near Bath, England, until April 4, I believe it was. Anyway, I was carried by stretcher onto the Queen Elizabeth on the 6th of April, landed in New York April 12, stayed in the hospital there for a few days and was sent to a hospital (nearest my home in Hardin, Kentucky) in Palo Alto, California. How about that?

I came home on a thirty-day leave and married (as any husband would say) the most wonderful person, on May 23, 1945. Her name is Dorothy.

Jim Flannigan, Allen Park, MI
29th Field Artillery Battalion

To Liberate France

I was cold, wet, seasick, and most of all scared, but that part you don't let anyone know about. I was nineteen and 140 pounds of American fighting man. It was 0615 hours June 6, 1944—H-Hour.

The men in the landing craft with me were all infantry, and they knew we were artillery. We were never very close to each other in the army way—you do your job and everything will be OK. Some of the guys were sick and throwing up; some were scared, some praying, some just thinking. I guess I was doing all of these at once.

We saw the beach being hit by Navy fire, and then we saw the water erupt from the German shells landing around us. I saw two landing craft sink, one of them on fire. I saw people in the water, cold and wet…then noise, smoke, shells, more noise, false smiles, cussing, praying. The whole invasion was here on our craft. This was the whole thing—thirty-five men. We were going to liberate France.

I'd read the letter from General Eisenhower. I knew I wasn't alone, but right then I was.

The ramp went down and we started forward. I was in water, three feet deep holding the 610 radio over my head. Keep it dry, I thought.

At 0622 hours, H-Hour, I was scared and yelling, cussing and praying, and mad at the world. I saw my first dead GI who was half in the water, half on the beach. The water pushed him up and then pulled him back. I was sick…sand, rock, noise…GIs everywhere…shells, small arms, men (bless them), and more noise.

The lieutenant said to find B Company, "Now!" We moved about fifty yards up the beach and the lieutenant was gone—they said it was an 88. We found B Company later and fired our first fire mission about 0645 hours Then we just seemed to walk inland. We started to meet the airborne. I guess it was planned, but to me the whole world was chaos.

Later, in Germany, Jim Flannigan earned the Distinguished Service Cross, for gallantry in action while volunteering to go through enemy lines to deliver a message to headquarters. —Bob Babcock

----

Harper Coleman, Tucson, AZ
Company H, 2nd Battalion, 8th Infantry Regiment

First Wave

The 2nd Battalion, 8th Infantry Regiment was the first unit to go ashore on what is known as Utah Beach, Uncle and Victor sections. The book, Utah Beach to Cherbourg, shows the beach to be named Tare

Green and Uncle Red. I don't know which is correct, but I went in on Uncle Red or Victor section.

I was with Company H of the 2nd Battalion and went in with the first wave of assault troops. Shortly after the larger ships came to a stop, we were to go into the small LCVP. Being with the first waves had its advantages. We were not required to go over the sides of the ship. We were put on the LCVP while it was still on the larger ship and were let down into the water with the craft. As the small crafts entered the water, they began to gather and form groups, which took some time and required going in circles, and, in very rough water. Our circle was around one of the large battleships—the Texas, I believe. It was firing the large guns as fast as could be done, I guess. Each time they fired, it seemed as though it would take your head off right along with it. You could actually see the large projectile going through the air.

As we started to move toward the beach in lines, we passed rocket launcher ships, and as we were going past, they were releasing many salvos of rockets onto the beach. It must have been about 0530 hours to 0600 hours. It was daylight, and we were all standing up in the craft watching the show on the beach, still some distance ahead. It seemed the beach was almost hidden from view by smoke and shell bursts plus the fact that there were also aircraft over the area.

Shortly, we had to get down in the craft in rows as we would be going off. I did see the craft in front of ours being blown up with some sort of direct hit, which left ours first in line. Before we reached the shore, something came through the side of our craft and tore quite a hole in one side and out the other. It tore a goodsized piece out of my backpack, too. I don't recall how I replaced it, but it must have been soon thereafter. Also, while on the way in, I recall seeing some sort of a Navy ship lying on its side with many people on it. We did not stop to assist.

The history books say we landed a greater distance to the left than we were supposed to and that this was one of the easier landings. I don't know if this was good or bad. It did not seem good at the time. We went into the water somewhat more than waist deep and a good distance from dry land. When we came on shore, we had a "greeter." How he got there, I don't know, other than that he was in one of the first landing craft. Brigadier General Theodore Roosevelt Jr. was standing there waving his cane and giving out instructions as only he could do. If we were afraid of the enemy, we were more afraid of him and could not have stopped on the beach had we wanted to. Our squad of six was down to four very early; we lost one person on the beach and one when we came to the higher ridge just over the sandy area. We made a left turn as we came over the top of the beach on what seemed to be a path. Moving as fast as we could we came to a road that came down to the beach. This took us through the swamps that were behind the beach and had been flooded by the Germans. We came up on the small town of Pouppeville. This is where we begin to see the results of our work—our first dead enemy. Shortly beyond the town we began to meet some of the airborne troops. As I recall, they were rather glad to see us and joined in with us where they were needed.

Roger Cole, Rhinebeck, NY
Medic, 22nd Infantry Regiment

See the Explosions

Sailing out of New York harbor, the 4th Infantry Division went to England at the end of January 1944. In late May 1944, we were sent to a marshaling area to prepare for the invasion. There we were told, at last, what we were going to do— invade the coast of France. Fortunately, amphibious landings at Camp Gordon Johnston, Florida, were part of my three years of army training.

We were loaded on an LST with all the machines and other equipment to get ready to cross the English Channel. Of course, it was very windy and rough. Almost everyone got seasick. The night before the invasion I couldn't sleep and stayed on deck watching waves and waves of bombers flying in advance of the great invasion of Europe. If the ship went down, I sure didn't want to be caught below. I wanted to be on deck where at least I could get off.

Off the French coast that we called "Utah Beach," we transferred from the LST to an LCT along with trucks, jeeps, and guns. Although I couldn't yet see the shore from where I was, I could see the explosions where the shells were hitting.

I was able to get up on a two-and-one-half ton truck and got to shore without getting my feet wet. There were many casualties in the beach area—though our first order was to get clear of the beach. The Germans had flooded an area that we had to go through and there was sniper fire all around. There were a few German dead, too, but most of the defenders were farther inland, and we didn't really start to see large numbers of dead Germans until later.

Our first objective was to get to St. Marie du Mont. We bedded down in foxholes that first night and watched the fireworks in the sky provided by the German guns. I spent the next eleven months fighting across Western Europe.

I would be remiss if I didn't mention May Michel de Vallavielle of St. Marie du Mont and Utah Beach. He was a remarkable man and helped the Allied forces in so many ways. He was a French youth forced to work as a cook for the German Army. He gathered vital information about the location of German gun positions. On D-Day, when the Allied Forces attacked the coast of Normandy, a young man dressed in the white uniform of a German army cook raced toward the shore, waving his hands to attract attention. He was seriously wounded when an American infantryman shot him by mistake. After telling the American commander about the guns, he was taken aboard a hospital ship to England and cared for. He later became the mayor of St. Marie du Mont.

John C. Clark, Spring Hope, NC
HQ, 29th Field Artillery Battalion

D-Day Preparations

We all left for Dartmouth on the last of May 1944. There were GIs by the thousands camped that night in the fields about the town. Pup tents were everywhere. Sleep did not come easily with all the excitement and activity. I'll admit that sometimes ideas of danger and death entered our thoughts, but if you were smart, you put those thoughts out of your mind. We could not afford to dwell on such ideas.

The next morning one guy from each section went to the quartermaster area and drew ammunition for everyone. I was chosen to go from my section and drew shells for our new Garand, .30-caliber, M-1 rifles; for the .45-caliber automatics, and the .50-caliber machine gun mounted on our 4x4 truck. I also drew grenades and the 50-pound package of explosives I was to use on the beach as I worked with the engineers. I also drew my four chocolate "D-bar" rations.

There was a lot to do. We spent all day Thursday and Friday gathering and packing our equipment. We knew we'd be in water, so we had to try to waterproof the ignition parts of our motorized equipment. To be sure that the motors could get air and would not flood out in the water, we finished waterproofing our jeep, our three-quarter-ton-truck, and their exhausts. We also waterproofed the gas tanks. If the vehicle were to go under water, the driver had to hold his hand over three copper tubes to keep the water out until the vehicle surfaced.

We all tried to carry in whatever we might need. We wore a suit of khakis, a suit of fatigues, an army field jacket, leggings, and high top shoes. We wore webbed belts from which we could hang equipment. From my belt hung six extra clips of .45-caliber ammo, a holster with the .45 automatic, and a twelve-inch knife with brass knuckles welded on the handle for hand-to-hand fighting. Also on the belt were my first aid kit, a canteen with cup, and a shovel. From the webbed suspenders used to hold up the belts, six grenades were attached to the rings on the front of each strap.

My field glasses were on a strap around my neck, and my gas mask hung from my right shoulder and rested over my left hip. The Garand rifle was slung over my right shoulder. My "Musette" bag was carried against the back of my head and neck and was fastened to the suspenders with snaps. It contained extra socks and underclothes, toilet articles, and a piece of shiny metal to use as a mirror. Any extra space in this bag, or anywhere else, contained ammunition. I estimate I carried at least 50 pounds of ammo. The Musette bag was about a foot square and served as a pillow on occasion. I had wrapped my raincoat around this bag to make it as waterproof as possible.

On my back was a 610 radio pack, strapped to a frame that had saddle straps for each arm. I would use this radio to contact the field artillery to give directions for firing. We radiomen were referred to as "Sparks." All of this equipment and the explosives were so heavy that I found I had to wear two life belts to stay afloat.

On Friday night, our chaplain held services in the field for all of our battalion. It was not required that everyone attend, but I think most of us were there. We all realized that for some of us, this would be the last service, and we hoped God would hear when the chaplain prayed for our safety.

Saturday, June 3, was a typical British cloudy day. When we looked out over the harbor, we could see ships everywhere. The loading of the men and equipment began and went on all day. Each battery of guns, with their supply trucks and cook truck, were to load on a separate LST.

I was told that I would board a different boat. Since I was one of the scouts, or artillery spotters, I was to go in on the first wave along with the scouts from other units. We scouts were told to go to a staging area to await our boat. From there, we watched our friends go aboard their LST. As I watched my section load on to the boat, I thought about the fact that we scouts had been told that our odds for survival were one in six. That was the reason for each of us being loaded on a separate boat. I watched the infantry soldiers being carried on small boats out to the larger ships where they had to crawl up rope ladders to get on board. I just sat there and watched—knowing that I was watching history being made.

It was about midnight before we scouts were loaded onto our LCVP that carried the engineer's jeep, the twenty-eight engineers, one scout, and the three sailors who would operate the boat. I knew that these were the men with whom I'd work to clear the beach so tanks and trucks could get to the beach. We had been shown pictures of the sea wall we had to break down. Then I was to set up radio communication with our 29th Field Artillery Battalion headquarters.

Of course sleep was impossible, although we tried to rest. It was still cloudy, but, thankfully, it was not raining for there was no shelter from the elements. The seas were not very rough as we went around and around in the English Channel. About midmorning on Sunday, June 4, the rain began—showery, sometimes heavy—and we all got soaked. The seas got rough, and that was when we really began to bounce. It wasn't quite so bad after the sailors pulled up to the lee side of one of the LSTs. The bad part was that only about ten at a time were able to sit down.

Monday was more of the same. We all felt that maybe the weather was too rough for an invasion, and we weren't surprised when we headed back toward England. It seemed everything was off, but as soon as it got dark, we changed direction again, heading away from England. We began to see that we must be going in after all—the sailors thought so, too.

D-Day—was this the day we'd anticipated for the past two years? There was certainly nothing glamorous about it. We were all very wet and miserable, and a bit hungry, for we couldn't eat much. We were seasick and ready to get off that flat-bottomed boat. We knew that the code name for where the 4th Infantry Division was to land was Utah Beach, but we didn't know where Utah Beach was.

About an hour before daylight, all the LCVPs and the LCMs left the rest of the convoy and headed toward the beach. The air was heavy and so thick with burnt powder that we could hardly breathe. It seemed as if we could see the shoreline when the sailors predicted about five minutes until we beached.

I was thinking of what I would have to do and was getting my gear arranged as conveniently as I could when I found myself in water so deep that it was over my head. To this day, I still don't know what happened. We were about five hundred yards from shore when our boat went down—without warning. When I came up to the surface of the water, all I could think of was to start to swim toward shore. I swam on my back so I would have the least exposure possible, especially with the fifty pounds of dynamite on my back. As I considered the facts later, I think what happened may have saved my life. By the time I got to shore, I was in the third wave; there were heavier losses in the first wave.

Everything was mass confusion. The sea was alive with ships. As I approached the shore, I began to see many bodies floating in the water. I could not stop to investigate or to help, for I was needed on shore to help break through the sea wall and other obstacles for the incoming M-7 tanks and the 6x6's loaded with ammo and supplies.

One of the men had a Bangalore, or pipe bomb, and we blew a hole in the barbed wire fence wide enough for our tanks to get through. I started for the sea wall to start setting the dynamite to breach the wall when an engineer told me to wait, that a pillbox had the area under fire. He pointed to a buddy with a flamethrower crawling up to the pillbox from the side in order to get close enough to burn them out. In a few minutes, he gave them a good shot of fuel oil, then sent the flames into the narrow slit they were looking out of. That stopped the machine gun fire from that pillbox, and we were able to start setting the charges to blow the sea wall. The "Free French" had given us the right specifications we needed to break it up. The first two charges split the wall, and the third lifted it out of the way. I must confess, I put two extra sticks in each charge to be sure of it.

I was down on my knees behind the wall, working on my radio, taking the waterproofing off it, when I heard someone yell, "Hey, Sparks! Look out!" I just rolled and shot a German captain in the leg with my .45-caliber pistol still in its holster. He was a prisoner from another pillbox and was headed for the back of my neck with a pocketknife, both blades open and the corkscrew between his fingers. The infantrymen apologized, saying they had frisked him but they missed his pocketknife. It was a good lesson for me. From then on I didn't give anyone any chance at all.

I had already set up my guidon flag and had contacted my unit by radio. They were still waiting to come in.

They had not learned that the infantry had secured the causeways that our tanks needed.

There were medics giving all the help they could to the wounded on the beach, but there were many, many dead bodies. We pulled some of them up on the beach to keep the boats, tanks, and tracks from running over them when they came in.

While I was working on my radio behind the wall, someone yelled that a boat had capsized and the regimental officers it carried were in trouble out in the ocean. Some of us swam out and helped these men to shore.

The infantry officers kept yelling for everyone to get off the beaches and make room for the others coming in. They kept telling me to move on, but I told them I was field artillery, not infantry, and that I was trying to get our tanks in to help them. After I heard on my radio that my battalion could see my guidon flag, I went with the infantry and engineers.

We ran into a few machine gun nests on the way to the swamps. We had to watch out for snipers while the engineers built us a pontoon bridge across a part of the causeway. The Germans had blown it as they retreated.

After the initial beach assault, we did not see a great deal of opposition until we reached the hedgerows. The paratroopers who had gone in before we did made our job much easier. The hedgerows were where the real fighting began for us. There were rows and rows of hedgerows around the small fields of Normandy, with Germans dug in behind every one of them. There seemed to be no end to them.

As soon as our tanks got across the swamps, we had them blow a hole in the hedgerow near us. If we could get behind the hedgerow, we could clean it out all the way down the row, for the Germans were exposed. We got across several hedgerows this way before darkness set in and the fighting slowed down.

That night I was sitting down behind one of the hedgerow trees. Every once in a while snipers would cut loose, but we felt pretty safe after a long hard day. My buddy said something to me, and I turned my head to speak to him. Just then, a bullet hit the tree beside my head. Some sniper had zeroed in on my cigarette, and if I hadn't turned my head I would have been killed. I spat out that cigarette, and to this day, I have never smoked another one. One of the infantrymen from Company B, 2nd Battalion, 8th Infantry Regiment that we were with came by and asked if we knew where the sniper was. We pointed in the direction that the bullets came from and he took off in that direction. In a few minutes, we heard two different guns fire, and when he came back by us, he said we didn't need to worry any more.

I had seen many terrible sights—pieces of bodies lying on the beach, guys blown all to hell....I think the thing that bothered me most was seeing a tank with a blade moving up the road and shoving the bodies into the ditch so they wouldn't be run over by the advancing tanks and trucks.

We were so keyed up that nobody even tried to sleep. You'd see people resting but not really sleeping. You just tried not to think too much about what was going on, just what you had to do and how you would do it.

I felt something hit my shoulder during the night, but thought I had brushed a tree limb or something. In the morning, I felt a slight itch on my right shoulder, so looking to see what it was, I found a green wooden bullet. The green paint from the bullet had caused the wound to fester a bit, so the aid man gave me some sulfa and a bandaid. Talk about luck.

A more important discovery that morning was that the Germans had brought in their 88mm guns, which were very versatile and very accurate. This upset our plans for knocking out the hedgerows and caused fierce fighting. We experienced days when our infantry could move no farther than a few hundred yards during a day's fighting. Loss of life was heavy on both sides as we fought our way toward Cherbourg.

Anthony Ferrara, Daytona Beach, FL
Medical Detachment, 22nd Infantry Regiment

Jeeps in the Water

I didn't want to get wet, so I asked Major Kirtley if I could go in on the six-by-six truck with Service Company. He said, "Yes," and I got on. The truck went a little ways and stalled out. Little by little, the tide pushed the truck into deeper water, and the two fellows and I got out and got on the top. Along came a Jerry airplane and strafed us. We jumped into the water and held on to the side of the truck. I came up; the two of them came up crying and yelling, and I had to jump in and pull them out. A personnel carrier got us to the land, and we were hit by artillery. I had their two field packs and rifles and led them by the hand to the first aid station.

Major Kirtley saw me and said, "Ferrara, you've got five jeeps to get out of the water."

I replied, "OK, Major, I'll get them." With the help of each driver we got the jeeps all cleaned up from salt water and got them running. It took time and we were done about 0100 hours, in the dark. In addition to taking care of the vehicles, we took care of the wounded. We covered them, gave them cocoa and cigarettes, and talked to them to keep them calm.

Bill Garvin, Nottingham, NH
Company K, 3rd Battalion, 12th Infantry Regiment

Wildest Night of My Life

Following four months of regular and specialized training in England, we packed up and were trucked to Bournemouth Harbor in early June 1944 for the exhilarating voyage across the channel. We were finally going to get a piece of the action.

We waited for what seemed like days in Bournemouth aboard our troop ships for the ceaseless wind to ease and the channel crossing to begin. The wind was so savage it ripped away nearly all the barrage balloons that protected us from potential enemy strafing. Finally, on the night of June 5, we lifted anchor and turned eastward out into the night and the scary unknown. It was required that all army troops remain below decks for the crossing with the exception of us company radio operators. We were to maintain radio silence, operating the radio for message receiving only.

It was the wildest night of my life. The gale-force winds whipped the turbulent sea into sheets of salty spray that constantly engulfed the entire ship as it pitched and rolled at crazy angles. We had secured the radio from being heaved overboard and tried to do the same for ourselves. A mid-ship stanchion gave us some protection from the spray. We didn't think about getting seasick, but we learned later that those below had a nightmare of seasickness and a limited area in which to vomit.

Well before dawn, the heavy drone of aircraft loaded with paratroopers and gear was heard above the crashing surf. Those were followed later by more planes towing gliders. As dawn broke, an unbelievable armada consisting of thousands of ships appeared as far as the eye could see. Our ship's progress slowed to a crawl as we neared the coastline of France. Big guns from several large ships began lofting shells inland as early waves of infantrymen in Higgins landing craft raced toward the shores. My company was scheduled for the ninth wave, when we climbed down the rope ladder to our bouncing LCI. The wind had eased somewhat, although it was still strong.

We rendezvoused in a circle of about seven boats before striking out for land. The LCI pilot was kind enough to drop us solidly on land, which we soon discovered was nothing more than a sandy spit. A few yards beyond the beach lay two miles of inundated farmland with flooded irrigation ditches about one hundred yards apart. We barreled out of the craft expecting to run into a hail of bullets and exploding shells but were fortunate to find the immediate area undefended.

Our mission was to work inland as quickly as possible to the town of St. Mére Eglise and relieve the paratroopers that had descended on the town hours earlier. We began wading through the hip deep water and floundering across the irrigation ditches. Having retained our life preservers from the channel crossing helped immensely. After about one and a half hours, we reached solid ground where a dead German lay—a realization that we were nearing face-to-face combat. Soon, both dead Germans and dead Americans became visible as we approached the town. Torn parachutes hung in trees. Buildings showed extensive damage and we came across bedraggled troopers herding German captives to a central collecting point.

Our mission accomplished, we continued to expand the occupied land and establish defensive positions. At one point, when my Company K stopped for a short break, I strolled off a short distance to a shallow gravel pit to relieve myself. All went well until I straightened up to dress, at which time a sniper's bullet threw sand in my face. After a few minutes, I shifted positions and tried again, only to be narrowly missed a second time. After the third attempt, I realized I'd be left behind if I didn't join my company quickly. So, though only partially dressed and bent over, I made the fastest waddling withdrawal known in military history. Probably the sniper was laughing so hard he knew his accuracy would not have improved had he fired.

Though we did our job with little effort, we still hadn't decisively engaged the enemy. That would happen soon and continue for many months before it ended with costly losses and much suffering from our many engagements with the enemy.

Roy Wahlstrom, Marquette, MI
Company K, 3rd Battalion, 8th Infantry Regiment

Trunk Full of Purple Hearts

It was early morning on June 6, 1944, and the weather was clear as we began climbing down the rope ladders to the waiting LST. Paper bags were issued to everyone in case of seasickness, as the waves were rough, tossing the boats against each other. We suffered our first casualty of the day when our sergeant fell from the rope ladder on his way down. Ours was one of the first boats to reach shore. 35 men unloaded into waist deep water. Our first good surprise was that the beach was not flooded by the Germans, as we believed it would be.

One of the first things that happened was our machine gun section was hit by 88 fire. We lost our section leader to a hit in the arm, which put me into the job. We began our forward progress with no maps to guide us, just a general order to "go in that direction." There were supposed to be lieutenants out in front of us, but I never saw any. We were showered by "screamin' meemies" (rockets that were sent out in groups), but our ship support fire was excellent; they could have hit you in your back pocket if they wanted to.

They looked at my wounds, reached into a trunk full of Purple Hearts, gave me one and sent me back to the fighting.

I was hit in the hands with shrapnel that day, so my Commander sent me back to the aid station on the beach. They looked at my wounds, reached into a trunk full of Purple Hearts, gave me one and sent me back to the fighting. I carried that Purple Heart around with me for the rest of the war.

I saw a glider landing with troops and equipment at one point. The gliders were made at the Ford plant in Iron Mountain, Michigan, which was close to home. At another point we heard the Germans were going to launch a forward assault at us, so our machine gunners and some extra 4th Infantry Division machine gunners were told to line up on high ground along a road and shoot at will to show our fire power. We used up a lot of ammo there.

I was all alone when I came up to a hedgerow with a road on the other side and heard a vehicle approaching. At first I thought it was one of ours, but then I heard them chattering away in German. I stayed where I was until they passed hoping to be able to throw a grenade into the car, but I didn't get a chance. About suppertime, I ran into a couple of paratroopers sitting by a hedgerow eating supper. I didn't get too close because of the chance of being shot by mistake.

That first night we were separated from our company. All of us were out in this big field thinking about how easy it would be for them to send in artillery at us. There was a beginning to that day, but when I think about it, I can't remember its end.

I spent almost one and a half years in Europe. I'll never forget when we got to Paris. After the fighting was over I was standing alongside the street with my friend when a four-year-old boy came up and wanted us to go with him. My friend and I followed him to his home where his mother had the most wonderful hot meal all ready for us. It was much better than K rations. I saw him and his mother again when I went back to Paris for the 25th Anniversary of D-Day. We met at the hotel and when she walked through the door, I knew who she was right away.

Claude Hockert, St. Paul, MN
Battery C, 29th Field Artillery

Get Off that Beach

From an article that was published by the Minneapolis Star-Tribune *on the 50th Anniversary of D-Day.*

We were eighty some people in our boat, four tanks and a couple of jeeps. I remember going round and round in the harbor, waiting for the go. We could see some of the big warships farther out. It was open in the boat and cold out there— very windy. We had little gas stoves to cook our rations, but a lot of guys couldn't take the sea. They just got sicker and sicker. Man, I was so damn proud of myself. In our whole boat, there were just three of us who didn't get sick.

Bad weather over the English Channel forced a 24-hour delay. Eisenhower's decision to go on the 6th was an agonizingly tough call since the weather hadn't improved much. But that night you could sense it. We could watch the signals going from ship to ship, and then everything began to move out across the channel. Just before daybreak we could see the big battleships in the distance behind us when they opened up, and the shells came whooshing over us. Then we could see the shells exploding on shore. By that time we were so sick of being on that boat we couldn't wait to get on shore ourselves. I don't think there was a man who didn't want to get on land at Utah Beach.

Hockert's artillery battalion was divided into three batteries that were to follow the assault troops and set up covering fire as they moved inland. As the boats approached shore, the LCT carrying Battery B hit a mine and blew up, killing 59 men on board. Hockert's C Battery was nearby. Everybody got really tense after that. It was, "Come on, come on! Let's get off of here! Let's get on land!"

The front end of our craft began to open. When the boat could go no farther, the ramp dropped down and we ran out into water up to our waists. We waded in the rest of the way, our rifles above our heads. There were not too many shells then. What I remember best is bodies floating in the water. They were our own guys. There were maybe half a dozen that I saw. Then the tanks came splashing off the craft and set up firing positions on the beach. As the troops organized, the German shelling intensified. They were gunning now for our tanks. An officer asked for volunteers to make contact with the infantry and I said I'd be happy to go. I wanted to get off that beach. I really felt it would be safer up at the front.

With a radio pack, two other men and I hiked about half a mile inland and caught up with the infantry company. The resistance got kind of weak, and we kept going. We came upon American paratroopers, dropped before our landings. Some were alive, and they joined with the advancing infantry. The ones who hadn't made it…still hanging from their chutes where they had landed in the trees. The infantry was advancing fast, however, at dusk, the advance was halted for the night. Early the next morning, D+1, the advance continued but came to a quick halt. Some of our own shells were falling around us, and there was German rifle fire in front and to the rear of us.

It was at this time the company realized we were pinned down and were beyond the front lines. The company commander was killed. They had taken some German prisoners. One was really scared. He wasn't very old. He started moving off to the side and then he ran. "Halt, Halt," someone yelled, and then they shot him. He was the first one I ever saw shot right before my eyes.

I tried to radio for help but the batteries were dead. My officer in charge told me and the fellow paratrooper (who had a jeep close by) to make a rush through the front lines, make contact with our troops, get them to stop firing on us, get help, and get a new battery. It was a wild ride with some bullets zinging over our heads. I remember deafening, unrelenting noise and the smell of gunpowder mingling with swamp gas. The thought came over me every once in a while, it will be a miracle to get out of this alive. I don't think I had any fear then—we were too busy. But I thought it would be a miracle to survive. I found my unit, briefed the CO, and he sent a replacement with a jeep and new radio to the front.D-Day, June 6, 1944.

John Vitous (KIA), HQ, 2nd Battalion, 8th Infantry Regiment

Somewhere in France

Donald Vitous, North Versailles, PA, brother of John Vitous, wrote: "John Vitous was killed near Aachen on September 17, 1944. He landed on D-Day with the first wave of troops. He was wounded at Cherbourg, sent to England, and patched up. He was sent back to his old outfit and then was killed. I came across a letter he wrote my father dated June 15, 1944. You may use it for your book. John wrote me V-mail letters the day after June 6, but, being in the service myself, I was not able to save them. By the way, June 6, 1944, was John's 25th birthday. John did not come back to tell me of his war days, but this letter tells some of it a week after D-Day." – Donald Vitous

Somewhere in France, June 15, 1944

Dear Dad (Personal to you only), I hope this finds you well and in good health. I'm fine and O.K. I guess you've gotten my V-mail of the 13th by this time. As I told you before, I'm in the combat—your son was among the first to land on the beach. It was a great show and I hope I can tell you about it some day. But, along with the show, you see the worst part of war also. You're a man and know what it's all about so don't tell Mom about it. Sherman was right when he said, 'war is hell,' and I don't care who knows it. One gets used to it though, and you have to harden yourself to it. It's no fun seeing your buddies getting killed or wounded and it scares you a bit....everyone's that way.

We have no use for the Germans and they're as tricky as the papers say they are. They don't like close fighting and give up when they're licked that way. Our riflemen really hate them. I'm on the front line also, but I have a different job. You know what it is and the snipers try to get us for that. Their snipers are "bum" shots, though. I've had some close calls so far, same as everyone has had. I've learned how or when to duck an 88 or mortar shell though. "Mother Earth" is your best friend and the slit trench your best protection.

"Mother Earth" is your best friend and the slit trench your best protection.

The French people are pretty nice and I pity them for their homes and property being wrecked. We get plenty of bitter cider to quench our thirst and some good wine. Some fellows even got some good whisky. We lived on K-rations and chocolate bars at first, but now we've had better rations in a rest area. I've shaved, washed, and feel much better now. So much for the war now.

Dad, don't kick about going to work as you're doing your share there. I'd never kick about working in a steel mill again if I get there again. I hope your car is running O.K. I made PFC today, or, Private First Class. It makes no difference to me about that. Must close now; take good care of yourself and Mom.

Loving Son, Johnny

Fred Stromberg, Concord, CA
Company G, 2nd Battalion, 22nd Infantry Regiment

Yogi, the Pilot

At Mickey Mantle's funeral, Yogi Berra and other Yankee ballplayers were the pallbearers. Subsequently, Yogi was interviewed by a sportscaster. The conversation led to the question, "Were you ever in the service?"

"Yes," Yogi replied, "I was in World War II in the European Campaign." "Were you in the invasion?"

"Yes and no," Yogi replied.

"What do you mean, yes and no? You were either in it or not."

"Well, I piloted landing craft #114, ferrying troops to the beaches during the invasion. I was in and out and didn't stick around to see what happened. I was only nineteen then."

That was the number of the landing craft that I had been on. I swore that if I ever had the opportunity to meet the pilot, I would have a few words with him for landing us so short of the beach. I am still waiting to meet him.

Bill Knowles, Geneva, IL
HQ, 4th Infantry Division

Behave Like a Soldier

O n June 6, 1944, Bill was with the 8th Infantry Regiment and landed on Utah Beach. While resting, Bill said he found himself on the
sand looking up at the war's greatest air show. Frequently, an Allied or
German plane would hit the earth and crash. While looking up, he recognized pockmarks from bullets entering and circling around him in the
sand. He then said, "I had a serious talk with myself: No more curiosity.
Behave like a trained soldier, play it safe, and keep in contact with God."

Jack Fox, Jacksonville, FL
Medic, 1st Battalion, 8th Infantry Regiment

Combat Medic

F or those of us who participated in this momentous event, it will never
be forgotten. I was a combat medic, assigned to the 1st Battalion,
8th Infantry Regiment, 4th Infantry Division. The 4th Infantry Division
arrived in England in January 1944, and training for the inevitable invasion of Europe began immediately. I vividly remember every training
exercise leading up to the invasion, including the disastrous amphibious
landing exercise that was penetrated and attacked by German E boats
off Slapton Sands, England. This was my first exposure to the tenacity,
mettle, and resourcefulness of the enemy, and it would not be my last.

Towards the end of May 1944, we were moved to a marshaling area
near the coast. Although not given a firm invasion date, we all knew our
time in England was drawing short. During this period we were subjected to German air raids; fortunately, our casualties were light. On June 3,
1944, we boarded ships where we received final briefings and given our
specific assignments. We were told we would be part of the greatest invasion in the history of the world and that the fate of our nation and western civilization was riding on our shoulders. Believe me, that was quite
an awesome responsibility for a young man from Brooklyn, New York,
to comprehend. I remember wondering if I would be brave under fire.

Could I do my job with someone from the other side trying to kill me? I really think I was more afraid of being afraid than of being killed. I knew that whatever happened, I would never be the same man after that day. I did not realize that none of us would ever be the same after that day.

We were told that we would be landing on the Normandy coast on a beach code-named "Utah" at dawn, June 5, 1944. We were given invasion currency, which consisted of two 100-hundred franc bank notes. I lost one of the bank notes playing poker. I had some of my buddies sign the other bank note. Later, I managed to get autographs from Ernie Pyle and Ernest Hemingway. I carried that autographed 100-franc bank note throughout the war, and it is still encased in my den at home. I plan on leaving it to my heirs for their safekeeping and in remembrance of my comrades-in-arms who never came home. During June 3, the weather turned bad and we were told that the invasion was on hold. Soon afterward, we were informed that there would be a break in the weather and General Eisenhower ordered a "go" for June 6, 1944.

About 0130 hours on June 6, 1944, we climbed down rope ladders into the invasion landing crafts. The water was very rough and many of the men began to vomit. We passed by many large battleships and cruisers, all firing at the beaches. I remember looking up at the night sky and seeing hundreds of airplanes heading towards the beaches. When the dawn came, I finally got to view the invasion armada. It was the most awesome sight I have ever witnessed. The noise of the shelling was deafening. The smell of sulfur, vomit, and fear was permeating. Our landing craft was under fire from German shore batteries. I don't know why we were not hit and killed at that time. I remember the bullets flying over our craft and also seeing the ricochets hit the water. The landing craft's door fell open and we all ran into the surf. We were in very deep water and I thought I was either going to drown or be shot before getting on land. By the grace of God, I made it ashore and started running through the deep sand towards the seawall.

I had saved my medical equipment and stopped to help a wounded soldier lying on the beach. I turned him over and realized he was dead. I recognized him—he was a friend of mine. I was shocked, scared, and angry at the same time. The sobering sight of seeing my friend killed in action, a buddy lying on that beach, made me realize that war was indeed a noisy, chaotic hell. I got my gear, ran to the seawall, and joined up with members of my unit.

Within a few minutes, our Assistant Division Commander, Brigadier General Teddy Roosevelt Jr., came to our position and started forming up the men. He was a great heroic man—a natural leader who later died of a heart attack in Normandy. He received the Medal of Honor for his valor on D-Day. General Roosevelt told us we had landed on the wrong beach, but we would move inland from there. The battalion was breaching the German fortifications and we all began to go about our day's work. I attended many wounded that day and slept in a ditch off the side of a road that night. I often find it impossible to believe that I survived when men all around me were being killed. I received a battlefield commission and later received a Purple Heart for wounds suffered in the Hürtgen Forest. I received my second Purple Heart years later while seeing action in the Korean War. I remained in the Army and retired as a lieutenant colonel in 1966.

Bob Walk, Atlanta, GA
HQ, 22nd Infantry Regiment

A Rough Place to Be

As for our training, we went on a lot of problems (exercises) practicing for D-Day. We landed on Slapton Sands. It turned out that it was much like the beach—Utah—where we had landed on D-Day.

Being one of the "over strength" guys, I was assigned to different boats on different problems. (Over strength was for the Division to be ten percent over our required division number of personnel. This was to allow for our initial casualties). I remember being on an LCIL.

At first I was in 2nd Battalion Headquarters Company, and then I was assigned to Regimental Headquarters Company. The biggest thing I noticed was that instead of getting stew, one got steak.

I was assigned to doing typing in the HQ office during that time. I happened to see the title of the next exercise on the typewritten sheet next to me. The name was "Bigot Neptune." An officer or someone saw me glance at that typewritten sheet and I was immediately ordered to go into the "Blue" Room." It was a secret room. From then on I was

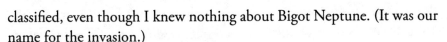

classified, even though I knew nothing about Bigot Neptune. (It was our name for the invasion.)

I remember the last exercise we went on before the invasion. We were all loaded with everything we would need for the invasion, including live ammunition. It was the exercise we learned only a few years ago, at the insistence of an English man who lived nearby, that over 750 Americans were lost. The Germans sent PT Boats out to attack us. A man I grew up with, Elmer Ashway, who had lived a half block down the street from me, was on the deck of an LST that was hit. Elmer was on the top deck when it was hit by a torpedo and was knocked down to the tank deck. Being a captain, he was able to find where I was. I got a pass and visited him in the hospital. He was going to be "OK," they said. I still stay in touch with him.

I was still working in the Regimental HQ office when one day, three weeks before the invasion, I was ordered to go to the motor pool and check out a jeep. I was introduced to my new superior, Lieutenant John Deedy. He was fresh from the States and told me that he had been able to see his new baby daughter before he left.

He was to be a liaison officer and I was to be liaison sergeant. I had no idea at the time as to what that was, except I was told that he would keep a situation map, just as I would. That was if in case something happened to him, I could temporarily take over. At the time, all three battalions of the regiment were put onto the marshaling areas in preparation for the invasion. Lieutenant Deedy and I were assigned to Division HQ as liaisons between Division and our Regiment.

Lieutenant Deedy was not at all pompous or the "I'm an officer" type. I always felt he was too good to be true. In our trips back and forth to the battalions of the regiment, driving on the wrong side of the road (the left side), British style, one incident stands out. It illustrates what I said about Lieutenant Deedy. Coming back from the battalion one day, on one of the main two or four lane roads, he saw a couple of English sailors hitchhiking and ordered me to stop and pick them up. He was just trying to be helpful, not thinking about himself. We had barely pulled out on the road when a command car with some brass in it (colonels probably), pulled alongside and motioned us to pull over.

Lieutenant Deedy went up to their car, saluted and got his ass reamed for picking up these sailors. The reason being, he had been briefed about the invasion, and England was supposedly crawling with German spies. These English sailors could have been spies themselves. We had to follow the command car back to Division HQ. Lieutenant Deedy had to go inside and I assumed that he was reamed out there. He could have been busted for this. Thankfully, he wasn't.

The English Channel is a rough place to be in a storm. I remember one time walking to the back of the boat. It was so low in the water that you could have walked right into the water.

The next big happening was when we got the orders for D-Day. I drove my jeep to where we were to board our assigned landing craft. I remember the hospitality of the British women. On one of our problems at Plymouth, we were lined up along the street to get on the landing craft (I didn't have a jeep then), and the British women came along and gave us cookies. I drove my jeep on to our landing craft, an LCT. It was a beautiful, sunny day. As we got out into the harbor, there were boats and ships as far as the eye could see. More boats and ships than I have ever seen. Our landing craft held three liaison jeeps, three radio jeeps (one for each regiment), and I guess a couple of three-quarter-ton trucks.

My biggest worry (not thinking that we were going into the big one where I could be killed or maimed) was that I didn't know how to put my jeep into low range and four-wheel drive. So I asked some of the other jeep drivers. The liaison sergeants and lieutenants for the other two regiments, the 8th and 12th, had jeep drivers, too. My regiment was cheap, so I was the jeep driver and liaison sergeant. Incidentally, this was Saturday, June 3, 1944. The invasion was to be Monday, June 5.

But God had other plans, and on Sunday, June 4, it rained and stormed. The English Channel is a rough place to be in a storm. I remember one time walking to the back of the boat. It was so low in the water that you could have walked right into the water.

I was amazed to learn that the crew of our landing craft was Coast Guard. Our landing craft also had a Coast Guard crew. There was no place for the enlisted men to go except to stay with their jeeps on the deck. The officers were able to get inside somewhere. What I did was lie across the front seats of my jeep and cover myself with my raincoat. As long as I lay there and didn't move, I didn't feel or get sick.

After a while I would get hungry, get up, and go into the little galley nearby on the deck. Someone always kept the coffeepot full and hot.

There were also some self-heating (British) cans of soup that I heated up and ate with crackers. When I started to feel a little woozy, I'd run back out to my jeep and lie down. Those cans of self-heating soup were heated by, as I remember, a tube down in the can, with a wick that you lit. When the stuff in the tube was used up, the soup was hot.

It seemed to clear up on Monday, June 5, and we got the word that we were pulling out. (We didn't know we had pulled back into the harbor.) The invasion was back on for Tuesday, June 6. Let me interject some information here before I continue: The clothing that we wore was ODs (olive drab uniform). Over the top of them we wore impregnated fatigues (protective clothing against gas attacks). We wore no division insignias, and as I remember, no rank insignia either. These two sets of clothes kept us warm in Normandy.

Tuesday morning, June 6, finally came. We could see the French coast in the distance. That was a thrill to me. Again, I was not thinking about what may lay in wait for us there. I remember seeing Navy ships—they looked like battleships—shelling the coast. I also saw some planes (ours), but not a whole lot.

The line company (infantry units) guys and the general and other officers were on large troopships. The line company guys were lowered into landing craft when they left the ships; however, officers like our commanding general, Major General Raymond O. Barton, came on board our landing craft. With all the liaison jeeps, radio jeeps, etc., it was his command post. When he came aboard, he announced that the hour was changed from 0530 hours to 0630 hours.

It's a source of pride to me that General Barton put his situation map on the hood of my jeep. The first thing we heard on the radio was Colonel Van Fleet (8th Infantry Regiment Commander) calling in to General Barton and saying that he was going in and that everything was going according to plan. His regiment and the 3rd Battalion of the 22nd (my regiment) were the initial assault units on Utah.

A little later, my regimental commander, Colonel Hervey Tribolet, called in and said he was going in and that everything was going according to plan.

After we heard that, General Barton said, "That's good enough for me—let's go!" I thought to myself, "Hey, we're on the General's boat. We shouldn't be going in so soon."

I have to honestly say, my next memory was getting in my jeep and being worried that I wouldn't be able to get my jeep into low range and four-wheel drive in case they didn't pull us in close enough and we got stuck in the sand and water. They did pull us in close enough that the water only came up to the hubcaps. At that moment, I didn't see or hear any shells coming in.

I remember that we were all bunched up on the beach (including General Barton and his staff). There was a long seawall, maybe five feet high, and the division engineers were already there with the steel to build a road through the hole they had blown in the seawall. We didn't go that way though.

I was standing there wondering whether I should take the shovel off my jeep and dig a foxhole, when all of a sudden, I got my baptism of fire. I instinctively dived into a foxhole that one of the engineers had dug. He dived in on top of me.

When the shelling stopped, he said, "It's OK. You can come out." I told him I couldn't move because of the sand, so he got the sand off me, and I got out.

I think one of the shells slightly wounded one of General Barton's aides, a First Lieutenant. We got the order to move up to the right along the beach. It was then that I saw my first dead GI. It struck me like a bolt of lightning. Hey, these guys are trying to kill me. Why? I didn't do anything to them. It may sound silly, but that's the way it hit me.

General Barton set up the first 4th Infantry Division Command Post just up over the seawall on level ground right next to a blasted house that obviously was used as a zero point for the German artillery. "General, how could you?"

All I remember of that spot was that I was digging in the ground with a bayonet style knife with a handle guard, that I had bought in Harrisburg, Pennsylvania, before we left for overseas. Anyhow, when we pulled out from there, I left it. No big deal—I just hated losing it.

The rest of the day is just a blur to me. Lieutenant Deedy had to go on foot and find our regiment (the 22nd), and report back to the general. I just had to keep moving along with the CP. I didn't see Lieutenant Deedy until that evening when we pulled into a little wooded area for our night command post.

I remember lying down on one side of a hedgerow. On the other side were dead, bloated cows, killed by artillery. Some time that night (D-Day night), we had to go down along the beach (I guess to a battalion HQ). While I was waiting for Lieutenant Deedy to come back, I thought I would cover myself with my raincoat and light up a cigarette. A bad idea. As soon as I did, I heard a rifle shot and got that cigarette out in a hurry. I also remember a small plane zooming low over the beach. I don't know if it was theirs or ours.

I just remembered some other things that happened during the day. I remember going through the little village of St. Martin de Varrieville. It was our first objective after landing. Also, I remember seeing paratroopers' chutes caught in the trees and some with the paratrooper's bodies in them. The Krauts had shot them as they came down. I, and many others went over and cut a piece of parachute off—not the chutes with dead paratroopers in them—and used them as scarves, as a badge that I had landed on D-Day. That is, we wore it until the Battle of the Bulge and Patton took over. He ordered that no one was to wear anything that wasn't GI. (However, I still have mine).

We also saw gliders being pulled by C-47 transports. As I remember, this was in the afternoon. The Germans had put poles (about the thickness of telephone poles) in the fields. This caused the gliders to crash on landing. In fact, I didn't see one that wasn't crashed. We also saw the paratroopers being dropped. Speaking of the paratroopers—82nd and 101st—I remember seeing (either on D-Day or the next day), outside a pillbox, one dead paratrooper and about eight to ten Krauts.

My admiration for the paratroopers went up 100 percent.

Peter Triolo, Pueblo, CO
HQ, 1st Battalion, 12th Infantry Regiment

Sat On My Shovel

On or about May 28, 1944, while stationed in England, I was called and told to report to regimental headquarters. Upon arriving there, I noticed the other two battalion S2s (Intelligence officers) were there. We were told that one of us would be assigned to a special duty. After an hour or two, the other two battalion S2s were told to go back to their unit, which meant I was it. I was informed that my equipment was coming up and I was to be reassigned to a special duty. When my equipment arrived, I was loaded into an army truck with two other officers and a guard. We rode around in the enclosed vehicle for two or three hours. We finally arrived at a farmhouse. We were taken into the office and told that we were being assigned the duty as liaison to the 82nd Airborne Division for D-Day. We went up into the big red barn, and on the wall was the D-Day landing plan from D-Day until D+26. On returning to the office, we were assigned a bodyguard. He was assigned a password and instructed that if anyone approached me without the proper password, he was to shoot him. I also had a password with the same instructions.

On June 5, 1944, I was called into the office and informed to take a special message to the 4th Infantry Division located at Plymouth, England. They were already loaded on the ships. I didn't know then, but my message was changing D-Day from June 5 to June 6. I flew down in a D-6 twin-engine cargo plane. On the way back to the 82nd Airborne, we were attacked by three German aircraft. My pilot was calling, "Mayday! Mayday!" and looking for help. I was told to lie down on the floor, but I didn't, I looked out the window. We were flying so close to the ground I could have picked apples off the trees below us. Upon landing, I was informed by the pilots that British aircraft shot down two of the German planes.

D-Day morning: At 12:00 midnight, the 82nd Airborne paratroopers took off for France. They landed anywhere from five miles inland to many miles inland.

Their job was to distract and confuse the Germans so they couldn't tell what was going on, or where. The gliders from the 82nd Airborne took off at approximately 0200 hours, headed for France. I was in the first glider, with the Chief of Staff of the 82nd Airborne. It was an American glider made of aluminum tubing and canvas with plank seats and a walkway. Most of the troops were in British gliders made of plywood.

As we approached France, we continued inland and then turned back to land on the return leg of our flight. Radio teams had been dropped to guide us into our landing zones. The first two signals we approached, the Germans had neutralized or captured. Finally, on the third signal, the colonel said to release and go on in. Riding in the glider was like the Fourth of July upside down. All the lights and flashing were below you instead of above you. I asked the colonel, "What is this pluck, pluck, pluck sound I hear?"

He said, "That is the bullets going through the canvas; aren't you sitting on your shovel?"

I said, "No!"

He said, "You'd better, to protect your family jewels." I looked at all the other fellows and could see the handle of a shovel sticking out between their legs. So I sat on my shovel, too. I have always shared with my kids and grandkids that I rode in on D-Day on a shovel.

When we landed in France, we landed in an orchard about ten miles away from St. Mére Eglise. Upon landing, the American glider I was in collapsed but no one was hurt. However, the British gliders made of plywood splintered on landing. I saw American boys with boards the size of a two-by-four through their bodies because of the damage from British gliders on landing.

We landed about 0430 hours The colonel organized the men that weren't dead or wounded. We went on to St. Mére Eglise. We arrived there at or about 0600 hours, then started fighting to help control and take the city. St. Mére Eglise was important to the success of D-Day because it controlled the two major highways leading to the beachhead. I can remember the early hours of the morning, crawling up and down the ditch of the road to keep away from German artillery fire. An American soldier tapped me on the shoulder and said, "Lieutenant, you are wounded." I looked down at my right leg and the calf of my leg had been hit by artillery fragments. My leg was bleeding, and the cut was four inches long and a quarter inch deep. I asked him where the aid station was, but he didn't know. I didn't know either, so I stayed where it was safe.

Around 0800 hours at the 82nd Airborne Headquarters, a naval officer, an Army Air Corps officer and I were talking to the colonel. The colonel asked the Air Corps officer if he could get a strike order. There were two columns of German troops moving toward St. Mére Eglise. The Air Corps officer was informed that it was too overcast to fly. The Navy officer said, "I think I can get support from the battleship USS Texas, out in the bay about ten miles behind us." The Air Corps officer, the Naval officer, and I went up into the steeple of the famous church in St. Mére Eglise. The naval officer called the battleship USS Texas on the radio, informing them he had a target. He gave a map-reading of the

German locations. The Texas fired one round. The Naval officer gave him a correction. They fired the second round. He then gave them a corrected reading and told them to fire on the target. I didn't know how many rounds they fired, but if you've ever heard a freight train go by blowing a whistle and making all the noise it could make, you understand. That is how the shells sounded going over our heads. They hit their targets and stopped the lead German tanks between the hedgerows, which blocked the vehicle columns and their assigned infantry. Later that day, the Air Corps came over and finished the job.

On D+1, the Chief of Staff called me into his headquarters. I was told that I was to lead a patrol of 82nd Airborne men to contact the 4th Infantry Division. As I was standing there, one of the soldiers asked me if I was going to shoot my .45- caliber Thompson machine gun. I said, "Yes, if I have to."

He said, "You'd better load it then."

I didn't realize until then that while crawling around in St. Mére Eglise, that I had lost my clip. The next thing I did was turn around to the soldier behind me and ask him if he'd be willing to trade my Thompson machine gun for his M-1 carbine rifle. He said, "yes," and we switched. I carried that M-1 for the next five and a half months.

I left the 82nd Airborne on D+3 to rejoin my outfit, HQ Company, 1st Battalion, 12th Infantry Regiment, 4th Infantry Division.

George Comella, Newark, NY
Company B, 4th Engineer Battalion

Hit June 7

I am now a paraplegic. I was hit June 7, 1944, on the beach. It was a bomb concussion.

This short comment from a 4th Infantry Division veteran is included to remind us that so many men have worn the scars and disabilities of their service with the 4th Infantry Division all their adult lives.—Bob Babcock

----

Peter Russo, Brooklyn, NY
Batteries B and C, 29th Field Artillery Battalion

The Great Pinochle Game

D-Day minus three found the crew of this artillery battery crammed aboard a Navy Landing Craft Tank. An LCT resembles, and is about the size of a sand-carrying barge. Carefully squeezed into its hold were four self-propelled 105mm howitzers, one supply truck, and one jeep. Walking between vehicles was next to impossible. Little walking would be done during the sea voyage.

We were barely out of the protection of the English harbor when the greater part of the gun crews succumbed to seasickness. There was a mad scramble for position on this small craft. The men who were neither the fastest nor the strongest were to take up topside resting areas. The winners nestled near two toilets: one on the starboard and the other on the port side of the bow. All but the pinochle players remained wet throughout the trip. If the drizzle did not keep one wet, the sea spray did.

The great "pinochle game" began as soon as we reached open water. Four of us chose partners, ducked under the truck tarp and began the game, which was to last three days. We preferred the outdoors and bright light, but the weather, sea spray, and vomit kept the game under the tarp.

On the evening of June 5, 1944, a meeting was called. The few able to attend gathered around to hear of the postponement of the invasion. Word was passed on to the sick men and eventually a rumor was spread about. Some color appeared to return to the faces of the sick when the word of a return to England reached their ears. In short order, the paleness returned along with the seasickness, regardless of the good news. The pinochle game continued.

One more crummy day passed into night and the sea was as rough as ever. Another meeting was called during the early morning hour. Again, those able to attend gathered around. This time the word was "Go." The invasion was on for this day, June 6, 1944. All at this meeting were briefed as to the enemy strength, our landing spearhead force, and the beachhead assigned. We were directed to pass this information on to others when possible. There would be no return to England. The spearhead infantry was ours, so we would land on their backs on H-Hour. Back to the game for the pinochle players.

Daylight was now approaching, and the volume of planes flying overhead was noticed. Bombs were landing on the beach in hopes of destroying enemy gun emplacements. The Navy guns joined in pelting the same area. We stopped the pinochle game to watch the rocket-carrying craft speed in front of us. A few hundred yards off our port side, the rockets were unleashed. We looked on as the tiny lights of the fired rockets created a Coney Island fireworks scenario.

Our attention was diverted by a large boom to our left flank and no more than fifty yards from our center. The boom was followed by a huge puff of smoke. Battery B was leading the 29th Field Artillery Battalion toward the landing site on Normandy. It struck a mine in the water and was gone. We could see very little debris and a few bodies as we rode by. All on our LCT were up and looking at what was left of Battery B personnel, the landing craft, and the equipment. Seasickness was replaced with horror and fear. We were introduced to our first exposure to combat. We focused on the enemy artillery rippling along our landing zone and thought about the losses to be added to that of Battery B.

Not a sound was to be heard on this craft until we landed. We became seasoned veterans before one round was fired in support of our infantry. The pinochle game was over.

Edward Gallucci, Stamford, CT
Company L, 3rd Battalion, 22nd Infantry Regiment

Where's the Award?

On the D-Day landing, John Wood and I were in the same assault section and on the same LCM. The 3rd Battalion, 22nd Infantry Regiment landed at H-Hour, 0630 hours, June 6, 1944. They made a right turn on the beach heading for Quinéville, our Regimental objective. Companies I and L led the attack on D-Day, capturing two strongpoints. There were mine fields, tank traps, and barbed wire over the whole beach. (Captain Edward J. Gatto, the CO of Company L, was killed by a sniper June 9, 1944 at a crossroad beyond Azeville.) All assault divisions were awarded the French Croix de Guerre except for the 4th

Infantry Division. Why? That's an interesting story that maybe some of you guys can answer for us. I have Major General Ruggles' story about why he thinks you did not get the award, and it has nothing to do with your courage in battle or value to the liberation of France.

Sam Nelson, Ladson, SC
Company H, 2nd Battalion, 22nd Infantry Regiment

I Could Get Killed

After loading into the assault craft and heading toward the beach, we were stopped and dumped in about waist-high surf. I dropped my telephone in the water. Being well trained on the importance of not losing our equipment, I spent a few minutes stopped in the surf trying to find the telephone. I finally thought, What am I trying to do? I could get killed out here. I then moved on to the beach and we headed down a road into Normandy. The artillery came in, but we were not hit.

Victor Bonomi, Pittsburgh, PA
Service Company, 22nd Infantry Regiment

Gas!

I am going to write about an event that happened in Normandy a few days after the landing. We were stopped in an apple orchard and everyone dug slit trenches and prepared to spend the night. The weather was warm. We were just preparing to settle down when we heard from the hedgerow next to our field a loud shout, "Gas!" Then we heard the clanging of the dinner bell alarm and shouts of "Gas!" from other fields nearby.

We whipped open our gas bags, black plastic roll-up types that were strapped to our left thigh. I put mine on, and after a few minutes, I felt a slight burning on my neck. I immediately thought, whatever kind it is, it burns. I remembered seeing the lesions of the mustard gas. It turned out the burning was from the residue of the tear gas we had used when we tested them in England before the invasion. While I was sitting there contemplating the kind of gas the Germans were using, a jeep pulled into the field and the driver and a captain were standing on each side of the vehicle. They had a gas mask between them and were pulling it across the seats shouting, "This mask is mine," and "No, it's mine." Finally, they both jumped into the jeep and drove out of the field and back to the beach. Later, I heard they panicked the boys there with the news.

Now, back to the field. Sitting up in his slit trench was a soldier named Otis. He didn't have his gas mask on. In fact, he didn't have a gas mask and was sure wishing he had one. At this time, we were sure we were having a gas attack. This poor fellow sat there moaning in a pitiful way, "Please get me a mask." I felt sorry for him but thought it was his own fault. Within a few minutes, we heard, "All Clear." There was no gas and, of course, we removed our masks. For some time thereafter we kidded Otis about his breathing problem—which usually resulted in some swear words. Shortly after this, the whole Army piled our masks in a big pile in a field there in Normandy and we never saw them again.

Francis W. Glaze Jr., Clearwater, FL
HQ, 8th Infantry Regiment

Teddy Earned His Keep

We first saw "Teddy" Roosevelt in Honiton, Devon, at a surprise Regimental Assembly. The regiment was formed in a square around the outdoor boxing ring when suddenly the staff cars started pulling in to the area. The brass headed for the ring and the murmur of recognition started through the regiment as they mounted to the ring: Generals Eisenhower, Bradley, Patton, Roosevelt, Montgomery, Barton; Ike's Deputy Air Marshall, Sir Arthur Teddar, plus Winston Churchill himself.

Finally, we all recognized what a position of honor we had been given: an assault division on D-Day. To ourselves, we recognized this moment of honor in its true light; for example, "Oh, Sh-t!"

The second time we saw General Roosevelt was on Utah Beach. I was in the fourth wave; Teddy had come in earlier. We had landed about fifteen hundred yards south of the emplacements that were our first objective. We were deciding to attack and get to our original objective when

Teddy earned his keep. He said, "Gentlemen, the war starts here! Go inland any way you can, we'll worry about those bastards another day!"

So we did, and we took all our D-Day objectives.

Another time—and typical—Teddy escaped from the Division Command Post and was reviewing the situation with Colonel Van Fleet, our Regimental Commander, when a tremendous German barrage started. For once, it wasn't for us. It was landing three or four miles to our rear and obviously aimed at our Division CP. Teddy was enthralled. He got up on a hedgerow, hooting and hollering. "Give it to them—that will make those bastards back at division get off their asses and down in the foxholes," he said. He was cheering the Germans on at a great rate.

The last time I saw Teddy was one morning after we had taken Cherbourg, when we were starting the attack out of the bocage country toward the St. Lô-Periers Road. The attack was the first of nine days attacking on a regimental front against the German 6th Parachute Regiment. The 8th Infantry Regiment started the attack, but each regiment got in its three days worth. The 6th was well dug in and we only made 200-300 yards a day. After nine days we reached our objective south of the St. Lô Road. The German 6th made us pay dearly at a three to one casualty rate, but they no longer existed as a unit.

My driver and I had been up with the assault battalion for the jump off at 0400 hours and then reported back to the Regimental CO. My driver was very proud of his brand new jeep. It replaced the old one that died after three and a half weeks of combat. The new jeep was three days old and did not have a scratch on it. It was about 0700 hours. I was tired, so I crawled into the sack to catch a few winks. About an hour later, my dog-robber wakened me to report to the CP "ASAP!" Colonel Van Fleet and Teddy needed a guide to the battalion HQ, and I was volunteered.

I went looking for my jeep and driver but found only the jeep, so I drove myself back to the CP. The other two jeeps fell in behind, and we took off. The attack battalion CP was on a forward slope, so we stopped about one hundred yards behind the ridgeline and went forward on foot. At the CP the Battalion CO joined us by the side of the road and discussed the situation with Teddy and Van Fleet.

Teddy Roosevelt, Jr. looked down at me and said, "You are probably smarter than we are. Why don't you lead us back and out of here?"

About then some enemy shells came moaning in, just cleared the ridgeline, and exploded yonder. Since I was just a captain, I felt more vulnerable than the high-paid help, so I lay down in the ditch by the side of the road. Their discussion seemed to speed up, and then Teddy looked down at me and said, "You are probably smarter than we are. Why don't you lead us back and out of here? We've been brave and stupid long enough."

We quickly went back to the jeeps, and I noticed the new shell crater about ten feet to the left of my new jeep. The side was a sieve, the muffler was no more. The windshield, cover, and half the steering wheel were gone, and the spare tire was history. It sounded like a tank, but the four wheels were round and the motor "moted." I led my little entourage back to the 8th Infantry Regiment CP and then I went back to my Company CP. There my driver was waiting with folded arms. He fell on me from a great height, berating me for going without him. He had believed me to be dead and buried, and he held me fully accountable for breaking his new jeep. It is difficult to watch a grown man cry, but he insisted that I go along to the Service Company Motor Pool and explain why he needed a new jeep after only four days. He got a new one, so I was back in his good graces again.

Ray Saul, St. Louis, MO
HQ, 22nd Infantry Regiment

Go On!

I was preparing to dig in when Brigadier General Roosevelt walked up to me with his .45-caliber pistol in his hand and said, "Soldier, we are not going to stop here. We are going to go on," and he pointed further inland.

I said, "Yes sir," and further inland we went. Just over a month later he was gone, passed away of a heart attack.

Delbert Bendrick, Canton, IL
HQ, 3rd Battalion, 22nd Infantry Regiment

He Remembered My Name

Lieutenant Colonel Arthur Teague, CO of the 3rd Battalion, 22nd Infantry Regiment had attached me to the 8th Infantry engineers. They were sent in before the invasion to do some demolition work, so I landed with them before dawn. My job was to survey the situation and report to the 3rd Battalion of the 22nd Infantry Regiment when they landed with the 8th Infantry Regiment. When the engineers left to begin their demolition work, I was left alone on the beach. I was sitting against a little wall when a man dressed in fatigues walked up to me. It was General Roosevelt. I asked him why he was there, and he said he'd gotten special permission to land ahead of the troops. He asked my name, and then he walked on.

The invasion began. Our objective was to take Utah Beach. We fought from dawn until about 2100 hours Toward the end of the afternoon, two or three Germans came out of a pillbox waving a white flag. A few of our guys started up to get them, but the Germans shot them, and then retreated back into the pillbox. I had started up the hill with the men, but had stopped to take a radio call. After that, one of our tanks with a big shovel attached started piling sand on the pillbox. They didn't stop until there was twenty to twenty-five feet of sand on top of the pillbox. I guess they're still buried there.

About a week or ten days later, I went to check in with an outpost. General Roosevelt was there. He said, "Sergeant Bendrick, I see you made it." I was honored he remembered my name.

Letterio Bongiorno, Boynton Beach, FL
Service Company, 22nd Infantry Regiment

Like a Traffic Cop

On June 1, 1944, I was on a landing craft with my jeep and seven trucks, with ammunition and supplies for five days on the rough sea. On the morning of June 6, D-Day, about 0600 hours, the sky was

full of planes and the ocean full of battleships. I was first off, heading
for the beach—Utah Red Beach. On the beach, I met Brigadier General
Theodore Roosevelt. He was like a traffic cop. He showed a lot of GIs
where a German helmet with a sharp point was on the fence with a wire
hanging down. He said do not try to get it because it was a mine. He
received the Medal of Honor.

Bill Parfitt, Elmira, NY
Company G, 22nd Infantry Regiment and HQ,
4th Infantry Division

Hogwash!

*Bill Parfitt was an aide and bodyguard for BG Teddy Roosevelt. He accompa-
nied General Roosevelt ashore on D-Day. Bill sent an article from the March
1999 American Legion magazine, which said that General Roosevelt was
unarmed as he moved about on Utah beach. The article stated: "Armed only
with a cane..." Bill clarifies General Roosevelt's armaments in his reply. —Bob
Babcock*

I note the clipping says that General Roosevelt carried nothing but a
cane. That is hogwash. I know because I cleaned and oiled every weapon that was on the jeep every night. I wanted to be sure that they worked.
The general had a Model 1911 .45-caliber pistol, usually in a shoulder
holster. I know. I kicked my butt many times for not keeping the general's .45. I was also informed that when the general's stock of cognac
was below a half case, I was to get more— anything I had to do to get it.
When opportunity would prevail, I would get two cases and hide one in
the jeep trailer.

I did the same thing with cases of canned premium tuna and anchovies that we had liberated in Cherbourg. I remember the day on the
beach that the general was knocked down by some artillery, or he tripped
and fell. This was when the helmet he was wearing, which was unusual in
itself, came down on his nose as he hit the deck, and it busted his nose.
He had a beautiful swollen nose, and I do not know who, but someone
put him in for a Purple Heart for it. You know, he was all over the place
from D-Day on, but I think this happened on the beach. I have the

picture taken on the seawall, at the first CP that he had with General Barton.

I can also remember General Collins chewing his ass but good for failure to wear his helmet. I also remember that as Collins walked away, General Teddy tossed the helmet into the jeep. He hated the helmet and wanted to wear the little knit caps we all were issued. I also remember meeting General Roosevelt's son. He was an officer in the artillery and was some place on the Cherbourg Peninsula at the time of the general's death. I have read accounts that vary like the devil on this. The story that he carried no weapon was one, and that he was buried with no family present is another. Incidentally, General Roosevelt was buried next to an enlisted man.

Joel F. "Tommy" Thomason, (Deceased) Fort Belvoir, VA
CO, 29th Field Artillery Battalion
Submitted by Irving Smolens

Who's the Wise Guy?

It was either D-Day or D plus one. General Roosevelt was coming out of the 8th Infantry Regiment command post in either a farmhouse or a barn. There was a Signal Corps photographer standing by to take his picture as he emerged from the command post. Tommy said that when it came to his uniform, the general was the worst looking soldier he had ever seen. If he had on leggings, one pant leg would be inside and the other hanging on the outside of the legging. Tommy went to the photographer and told him not to take the general's picture as he emerged from the building, but to ask him to stand in front of a compost pile. The photographer did that and took the general's picture there.

The general soon realized what had been done and demanded to know who was the wise guy who thought, "I looked like a pile of horse sh-t." Tommy said that he didn't want anybody else to get in trouble for what he had done, so he had admitted that it was he who was responsible. The general then went over to Tommy and put his arm around him and said, "That's OK, Tommy."

I think the entire story deserves to be in the book that you are preparing because it demonstrates the spirit and camaraderie among the officers of the 4th Infantry Division, which transmitted itself down to the enlisted men and contributed to our success as a fighting unit.

Theodore Roosevelt Jr.
Medal of Honor Citation

For his conspicuous gallantry and leadership on D-Day, Brigadier General Theodore Roosevelt, Jr. earned the Medal of Honor. Following is the citation.
-Bob Babcock

ROOSEVELT, THEODORE, JR.

RANK AND ORGANIZATION: Brigadier General, U.S. Army, 4th Infantry Division.

PLACE AND DATE: Normandy Invasion, 6 June 1944. ENTERED SERVICE AT: Oyster Bay, New York BORN: Oyster Bay, New York

G.O. # 77, 28 September 1944

CITATION: For gallantry and intrepidity at the risk of his life above and beyond the call of duty on 6 June 1944, in France. After two verbal requests to accompany the leading assault elements in the Normandy invasion had been denied, Brigadier General Roosevelt's written request for this mission was approved and he landed with the first wave of the forces assaulting the enemyheld beaches. He repeatedly led groups from the beach, over the sea wall and established them inland. His valor, courage, and presence in the very front of the attack and his complete unconcern at being under heavy fire inspired the troops to heights of enthusiasm and self-sacrifice. Although the enemy had the beach under constant direct fire, Brigadier General Roosevelt moved from one locality to another, rallying men around him, directed and personally led them against the enemy. Under his seasoned, precise, calm, and unfaltering leadership, assault troops reduced beach strong points and rapidly moved inland with minimum casualties. He thus contributed substantially to the successful establishment of the beachhead in France.

George Gosselin, Manchester, NH
Company A, 4th Engineer Battalion

My Country Owes Me Nothing

I have always felt that one of the greatest experiences of my life was to have served with the 4th Infantry Division for 44 of my 47 months in the Army of the United States. It was one of the top outfits of World War II, and at the risk of sounding corny or crazy to some former GIs, it was my home away from home.

One has to have warm ties after spending four Christmases, four Easters, and four birthdays with the same group of men. We served with the greatest, and depending on where you stood, the greatest served with us. We stacked up enough firsts to be reckoned with: first on Utah Beach, first at the liberation of Paris, and one regiment managed to be first into Germany. Another notable hard fact that is hard to argue with is that we suffered 22,454 battle casualties. Generals Barton, Roosevelt, Blakeley, and Colonel Van Fleet were all there with points to make and ground to cover, not lose.

Interesting anecdotes from quiz books on WWII: "Who were the first U.S. troops to link up with elements of the 101st Airborne on D-Day in Normandy?" Answer: Soldiers of the 4th Infantry Division.

"Identify two U.S. generals who actually directed traffic as Utah Beach troops began moving inland?" Answer: Generals Barton and Roosevelt.

Somewhat interesting when your children and grandchildren find, and read you these facts from a book they bought you. Patton was right—we are proud that we didn't shovel sh-t in Louisiana. I was there when Van Fleet's 8th Infantry Regiment earned the Presidential Unit Citation. I was there the afternoon that Captain Maroney, Company A, 4th Engineers, braved the wrath of an armored column for the safety of his men sweeping the area for mines. We were camped near Perriers just before the great breakthrough at St. Lô when the word came that General Roosevelt (over twice the age of his men) had suffered a fatal heart attack on the very day that he had been appointed Commanding General of the

90th Infantry Division. Real heady stuff when you read the chronicles and find that you were a part of all this. There wasn't a better bunch of guys to serve with. Much courage and valor were common because we had trained so long together.

My love and endless admiration goes out to the men we left in the sprawling cemeteries of Europe. We are now full of years, and our numbers dwindle every day. There could have been worse ways to spend four years of my life. I take great pride in being a veteran, not just any veteran, but one who served with the 4th Infantry Division.

My country owes me nothing. It called, and like millions of others, I answered. No war is a good war, but the enemy we faced was obsessed in taking our freedoms. It seemed not only right, but also morally responsible to prove them wrong.

Fighting in the Hedgerows and On to Paris
June, July, August 1944

After the successful landing on Utah Beach on June 6, 1944, the 4th Infantry Division began some of the toughest fighting in their history as they fought through the hedgerows to participate in the liberation of Cherbourg, which took place on June 25, 1944.

From Cherbourg, fighting continued to St. Lô, where the 4th Infantry Division, along with the U.S. 2nd Armored Division spearheaded the "St. Lô Breakout," known as Operation Cobra, on July 25, 1944, and started the drive across France, which culminated in the liberation of Paris on August 25, 1944. These are stories about that tough hedgerow fighting and the liberation of Paris.

Chronology of the 4th Infantry Division, 7 June 1944 through 28 August 1944

Courtesy of Robert S. Rush, Ph.D.

7 June. 4th Div, with 22nd Infantry on right and 12th on left, drives northward toward line Quinéville-Montebourgh until halted by strong opposition from permanent fortifications at Crisbecq and Azeville; 8th Inf columns converge on St. Mére Eglise, where they assist elements of 82nd A/B Div in throwing back major enemy counterattack from N. Tanks of 70th and 746th Tank Bns also give valuable assistance.

8 June. Azeville-Crisbecq: VII Corps begins all out drive on Cherbourg with 4 regts505th Para Inf (82 A/B Div) and 8th Inf (4th Div) on W and 4th Div's 12th and 22nd Regts on E. Enemy again halts assault of 22nd IIInnff aaatt eeeddggee oooff Azeville-Crisbecq fortifications; 12th Inf fights bitterly for Edmondeville. On W, attack reaches general line from Montebourg highway through Magneville to the Mederet.

9 June. Azeville: 4th Div makes significant progress at some points as it continues drive to Cherbourg: on right flank, 22nd Inf forces German garrison of Azeville fortifications to surrender and organizes TF Barber to drive on Quinéville through Azeville gap; 12th Inf thrusts quickly northward from Edmondeville, seducing strong-

point at Joganville; during hard and costly fighting, 8th Inf overruns enemy positions at Magneville and drives to Ecauseville, from
which enemy withdraws after nightfall.

10 June. Azeville: TF Barber, on 4th Div right, makes little headway
through Azeville gap toward enemy's MLR on Quinéville ridge,
since enemy is disposed in strength on the TF flanks; efforts to reduce Ozeville and Château de Fontenay are futile; 12th Inf reaches
positions just below MontebourgQuinéville highway in region E of
Montebourg and is well ahead of rest of 4th Div; 8th Inf gains its
objectives along Le Ham-Montebourg highway.

11 June. 4th Div's TF Barber continues futile efforts to break through
Azeville gap to Quinéville ridge in coastal sector; 12th Inf gaiiinns
its objective W end of Montebourg-Quinéville ridge-but pulls back
behind Montebourg-St. Floxel road since its flanks are exposed;
8th Inf digs in along le Ham-Montebourg road when enemy fire
prevents forward movements to the RR.

12 June. Ozeville: 39th Inf of 9th Div, attached to 4th Div, is given part
of 22nd Inf's sector along coast and takes Crisbecq, from which enemy has withdrawn as well as Dangueville and Fontenay-sur-Mer,
forcing enemy back to his MLR on Quinéville ridge. With strong
fire support, including naval, 22nd Inf makes concerted assault of
Ozeville and captures it; 12th Inf moves forward again to les Fieffes
Dancel, at W end of Quinéville ridge; 8th Inf makes limited attack
on Montebourg, but finds it strongly held and pulls back.

13 June. 4th Div sector, 39th Inf (attached) makes limited progress
against coastal strongpoints S of Quinéville; 22ndInf gets into position for drive down ridge to Quinéville; 12th maintains positions
at W end of Quinéville ridge; 8th contains enemy at Montebourg.

14 June. Quinéville: Enemy's MLR on N crumbles under attacks of
4th Div: 39th Inf (attached) overcomes strong opposition in—
Quinéville and finishes clearing coastal region to S with capture of
Fort St. Marcouf; 22nd Inf clears heights W of Quinéville.

19 June. 4th Div, on VII Corps right encounters firm opposition from
forces deployed for defense of Cherbourg. 8th and 12th Regts attack on either side of Montebourg, which 3d Bn of 22nd Inf finds
clear of enemy, well before dawn, 8th reaching positions just SE of
Valognes and 12th abreast it to right. 24th Cav Squadron, 4th Cav

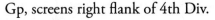

Gp, screens right flank of 4th Div.

21 June. Hill 158: 4th Div closes along the city's main defenses to right—Hill 178—NW edge of Bois du Coudray—Hill 158. 22nd Inf gets bn on Hill 158, cutting lateral road between Cherbourg and St. Pierre-Eglise.

22 June. Digosville: 4th Div attacks with 3 regts; on left, 8th Inf makes limited progress toward La Glacerie; 12th in center, makes main effort toward Tourlaville but is held to small gains; to right, 22nd Inf, with mission of Digosville, becomes surrounded by enemy and is unable to advance.

23 June. In 4th Div zone, 12th Inf, assisted by tanks, advances steadily toward Tourlaville, but units flanking it make little progress.

24 June. 12th Inf continues to make main effort of 4th Div. Reinf by bn of 22nd, the regt overcomes strong resistance in Digosville area and enters Tourlaville u opposed at night. 8th Inf reduces strong positions E of La Glacerie, on div left. 22nd Inf, on div right, contains enemy in Maupertus area.

25 June. Maupertus: In 4th Div zone, 12th Inf gains its objective with drive to coast E of Cherbourg; when orders are changed to permit div to participate in capture of Cherbourg, 12th Inf enters the city and clears assigned portion in E part; 22nd Inf is ordered to take Maupertus airfield.

26 June. Maupertus: 22nd Inf, 4th Div, begins attack on Maupertus airfield.

27 June. Maupertus: 4th Div takes over garrisoning of Cherbourg; its 22nd Inf overruns Maupertus airfield and quickly clear Cap Lévy.

30 June. 101st A/B Divs relieves 4th Div at Cherbourg and latter starts S for coming offensive.

2 July. US First Army commits VII Corps, with 4th, 9th, and 83d Divs under its command, between VIII and XIX Corps.

6 July. VII Corps commits 4th Div to W of 83d as attack toward Périers continues against unabated opposition.

9 July. In VII Corps area, 4th and 83d Divs gain several hundred yards toward Périers in violent fighting.

10 July. VII Corps continues attack with 3 divs—4th, 83d, and 9th, from W to E—and reaches general vicinity of St. Eny, Tribehou, and Le Désert.

11 July. To W, 83rd and 4th Divs continue forward slowly.

15 July. VIII Corps, now holding initial objectives along Ay R except for town of Lessay, maintains current positions while regrouping to include 8th, 79th, 90th, 4th, and 83d Divs.

19 July. 22nd Inf attached to 2nd Armd Div.

20 July. US First Army continues to prepare for Cobra, shifting 4th Div from command of VIII to that of VII Corps.

25 July. St. Lô: VII Corps attacks across Périers-St. Lô road on narrow front at 1100 to force passage through enemy positions in Marigny-St. Gilles region, 9th Div on right, 4th in center, and 30th on left advance steadily and force enemy back about 2 miles to line La Butte-LaChapelle-en-JugerHébécrevon.

26 July. St. Gilles, Canisy: 4th Div speeds S to La Conviniere. 2nd Armd Div attacks through 30th Div on left flank of corps and takes St. Gilles and Canisy.

31 July. le Mesnil Herman: Div and CCB, 3d Armd Div, drive forward beyond Villedieu-lé-Poëles. 2nd Armd Div thrusts spearheads to Notre Dame de Cenilly and Fervaches.

28 July. Villebaudon, Moyen, Percy: CCB of 2nd Armd Div reaches St. Desin-leGast. CCA thrusts S through Villebaudon to vicinity of Moyen.

1 August. Tessy-sur-Vire: 4th Div, reinf with CCB of 3d Armd Div, pushes forward toward St. Pois. Tessy-sur-Vire falls to CCA, 2nd Armd Div.

2 August. 4th Div continues toward St. Pois. 22nd Inf relieved from attachment to 2nd Armd Div.

3 August. 4th Div continues to close in on St. Pois.

4 August. 4th Div, which releases CCB of 3d Armored Div to 1st Div, battles vigorously but indecisively for St. Pois and heights about the town.

5 August. 4th Div overruns St. Pois and advances slightly beyond there. 6 August. 4th Div is pinched out W of St. Pois.

7 August. To help stabilize center of corps line, 4th Div and 2nd Armd Div are committed at once, latter being transferred to XIX Corps. 4th Div is reinf by RCT 39.

9 August. 39th Inf, 9th Div, is detached from 4th Div.

10 August. Le Teilleul: 2222nd Inf, 4th Div, is committed to right of 35th Div in Le Teilleul area.

13 August. 4th and 9th Divs await new mission.

14 August. 4th Div disposed along the Varenne, is out of contact with enemy. 22 August. 4th Div is transferred to V Corps from VII Corps.

23 August. 4th Div, preceded by 102nd Cav Gp (less Tr B) follows Fr armor along southern route and reaches Arpajon, S of Paris.

24 August. PARIS: 102nd Cav Gp units, screening for 4th Div, reach the Seine S of Paris. Ordered by Gen Bradley to push into Paris at once, 4th Div, less one RCT, attacks toward the city from S in conjunction with Fr attacks from SW. One RCT of 4th Div retains mission of securing crossings of the Seine S of Paris.

25 August. PARIS: 4th Div enters from S soon afterward, following Tr A, 38th Cav, which enters at 0730. 22nd Inf, 4th Div, establishes bridgehead across the Seine S of Paris.

26 August. PARIS: 4th Div returns to positions SE of the city and protects Seine bridgehead and airfields in the area.

27 August. PARIS: In V Corps area, against scattered resistance, Fr 2nd Armd Div and 4th Div, former on right, drive NE to outskirts of Paris, French overcoming strong opposition at Le Bourget airfield.

28 August. PARIS: Fr 2nd Armd Div and 4th Div continue attacks NE of Paris.

Morris Austein, Boca Raton, FL
Company I, 3rd Battalion, 22nd Infantry Regiment

Here They Come!

My most memorable years are of the times I served with I Company, 3rd Battalion, 22nd Infantry.

I landed at Normandy at 0600 hours on D-Day. I was in the first wave on Utah Beach. I was a demolition platoon leader. My first night after moving from the beach was spent behind a waist-high stone wall. We were all nervous and exhausted. We were half asleep around midnight when someone shouted, "Here they come!" We all got excited and started firing in the direction of the noise. We fired until everything got quiet. Checking things out in the morning, we found the place full of dead animals.

The second night I patrolled the hedgerows in the dark. I came face to face with another soldier, not knowing if he was German or American. We turned sideways, and I noticed the cut of his helmet. I raised my rifle the same time he did. We both fired in the excitement. I felt something hit me in the mouth. We missed—it was my rifle butt. Another incident: We were in foxholes in a hedgerow area getting air support in the front lines. One of the planes was dropping a bomb that hung up and didn't drop. As the plane was swinging upward over our lines, the bomb came loose. Fortunately, it didn't explode, but it made a huge crater and the sand rained down for what seemed like an eternity, half burying me.

The final incident crossing my memory is when we were dug in overlooking Cherbourg, and we were getting sniper fire. Young and foolish as we were, I put my helmet on my rifle and raised it. The sniper fired at it. I kept doing it and played with him for a while. Shortly, a group of soldiers came forward to us with a white flag and suitcases. One said, "Me Polish, going to America." I turned the prisoners over to Captain Glenn Walker. I returned to my unit and was talking to my men through a window in the antitank ditch. I was lying flat on my face when a mortar shell landed inches from me, blowing me up and back down into the bottom of the ditch. It was June 27, 1944, and the end of my Army days of combat.

All these incidents made me a fatalist. My number didn't come up, and I still am a fatalist.

Donald Ellis, Richmond, ME
Company G, 2nd Battalion, 8th Infantry Regiment

Lived and Learned

The next day, June 7, 1944 the Company was reassembled, and as we advanced we began to get into the hedgerows. These hedgerows were interwoven and as thick as your wrists. The farmers used these as we would use a fence. The enemy, having been there for some time, had zeroed in their guns and mortars to cover the gate. Some of these areas were fifty to a hundred yards in depth. At times we would fight all day to take one field. After penetrating the area, we would use their foxholes. As we got into the holes, the Germans would drop mortar shells on us because they had zeroed in on these holes, too. We wised up and dug our own holes.

Upon securing our positions, we would establish outposts and then begin our patrols. In the beginning the patrol would check with the outposts to alert them with a password and counter password to identify us upon return. When we returned, the Germans would attach a couple of their men on the end of our patrol. After catching a couple in the act, we established a procedure of giving the number in our patrol to the outposts. You lived and learned... You've got to realize the Germans had been at war long before we got there. We learned their tricks and counteracted with some of our own.

Montebourg was the first big town we hit. After digging in for the night, Rip Colbath, some others and I, decided we would go into town to scout around. A common practice of the town folk was to hide in cellars of the bombed out houses. When we came in contact with them, they would tell us whether the Germans had left or were hiding out. In checking out several houses, we entered a partially demolished large apartment building. Entering the cellar, we came upon a large group of French men, women, and children. We spent most of the night there trying to converse with our pidgin French and their poor English. They shared their meager food and wine, and we shared what rations we had with them. Just as it began to get light, we decided to go back to our lines. As we emerged into a large courtyard in a strung out line, a burst of machine gun fire hit and killed one of the two guys ahead of me. My buddy, Rip Colbath, was stitched up. I picked up Rip and took him back to our line. Upon returning to our lines, we were met by a medic and Captain Haley. He radioed HQ that our patrol had discovered the town was very lightly defended. Having learned this information, it precluded a fullscale assault. As a result of this, we earned the Silver Star.

As we captured them, we would immediately separate officers from enlisted men because the privates wouldn't talk with the officers present. Breaking out of the hedgerows, we began to hit open country and thus made better progress. We would ride on the back of tanks and tracks, but when we hit resistance, we'd dismount and fight. Outside of St. Lô, we were told to dig in as there would be a huge bombardment by the Air Corps. After we dug in, we would go about two hundred yards in front of our forward position and put out an orange colored panel to mark our front lines. There was always a forward observer from the artillery with us who was in communication with their outfit, so he could adjust fire by radio. Also, we had an air corps man to do this via radio with the bombers.

Later, when I was hit by machine gun fire and suffered a broken leg, a medic got me back to our line. As I lay on a stretcher, the bombardment started. Wave after wave of bombers came over. The bombs looked like a ladder reaching to heaven. All I could think of was how devastating it would be to be on the receiving end. The first couple of waves raised much dust, and it began to hide our panels out in front of our lines. Each following wave began to bomb too soon, and we began to receive casualties until our air corps observers could contact the bombers. The error was soon corrected. This is called "friendly fire," which also happened with artillery when we advanced too rapidly or had so called "short rounds." I might mention here that the hardest thing to do is to advance when fired upon by mortars or artillery, because the tendency is to lie down and dig in, thus increasing your chances of being hit.

Conrad "Frenchy" Adams, Gulfport, MS
Company E, 2nd Battalion,
8th Infantry Regiment

Captured

Before I start, let me tell you that I am very proud that there were six of the Adams brothers who served in World War II, and, thanks to the good Lord above, we all made it home alive. And second, let me tell you that I believe in miracles. I have highlighted the miracles that happened to me in my story below.

Then came D-Day. There were around ten thousand GIs on board the ship as it pulled out of New York harbor, horns and sirens blowing, whistles…We thought the local population was there to see us leave. We were told two hours later, at sea, that the invasion had started. We crossed to Europe in five days. On reaching England, we boarded another ship, and in the afternoon of D+7, we came off the ship off the Normandy coast. I came off the ship as an eighteen-year-old 120pound young man. With my heavy pack and equipment, going down that rope ladder into the invisible boat, I struggled to stand up. When the sailor opened the front ramp as we neared the shore, I couldn't touch bottom, being only five feet, six inches tall. Thanks, to the tall GI next to me who carried me where I couldn't touch bottom, or else I would have drowned. (That's my first miracle).

I came to Company E, 8th Infantry Regiment, as a rifleman. A sergeant asked me if I knew anything about 60mm mortars. I told him, "yes," so I thought I was a mortar man, but when I woke up the next morning, I had two ammo boxes for a .30 caliber machine gun by my foxhole.

When we made our first push against the Germans, some machine gun opened fire. I didn't know which machine gun it was, so I hit the ground and started to sweat as I was some scared. I almost dug a foxhole with my helmet.

We got up and started on with the regiment fighting the Germans. July 25 came and while we were in the foxholes, we saw around five thousand bombers dropping bombs. This was St. Lô. People wondered why Americans were killed by our own bombers. The reason was when the smoke bombs were dropped, the good Lord above had the wind change, and the bombers didn't know, so they dropped the bombs short. They hit us just outside of our foxholes. Only my buddy Bell, did not survive. He died of a concussion, leaving me and the others to go on fighting the Germans. And boy what a feeling. (And that's another miracle). Then as the joke goes, someone hollered, "Get some Greyhound busses to catch up with the Germans!"

I turned nineteen, and our objective was a railroad depot. That was early in the afternoon. The 4th Infantry Division wasn't satisfied, so we kept on pushing and passed a well-camouflaged German tank. We went into position, not knowing we had passed a tank.

As you know, the riflemen guarded one flank and the BAR man and his assistant, along with the machine gunner and those assistants, guarded the other flank.

The camouflaged German tank came from our rear and started firing at us. Then the riflemen jumped over the hedgerow and we had to cross the field to the other side. The machine gunner ran across and we heard him holler. We figured he had been shot. After one assistant gunner tried to go across, we heard him holler. I told my buddies, the BAR man and his assistant, that we should back up and jump the hedgerow around the back. One jumped, then the other jumped, and then it was my turn. By then, the German tanks had seen us and as I jumped over the hedgerow, my helmet came off and a bullet creased my head. Just a quarter of an inch lower and I would not have been able to write this. (Again, that's another miracle).

As we jumped over the hedgerows, we jumped into the German hands. They had captured the BAR team of Brown, from California; Clarence, of Fort Wayne, Indiana; and me. The first thing the Germans asked us was if we had American cigarettes, but none of us smoked. Then they questioned us about our Army and how many, etc. But they seemed to know more than we did.

I put a bandage on my head. I was weak from the loss of blood. The bandage was white and green. They started taking us to the rear and marching us to a Stalag. Eventually, the American airplanes must have seen my bandage and started spraying us, not knowing that some of us were Americans. We were not hit. (That's a miracle).

On the third or fourth day of captivity (I said I was weak from loss of blood), I dug into the pockets of my jacket and found two hand grenades. I'm glad no one said anything because the Germans could have killed me then. (I say again, another miracle).

We started to march at night and hide in the day. A week passed and we were stopped along a hedgerow. When they heard the walking and heard American soldiers, the German lieutenant pulled out his Luger pistol from his holster, pointed it at my head, and told me if the American soldiers opened fire that I would be the first to die. No one opened fire. (Another miracle). By the way, that lieutenant could speak better English than I could.

When we heard machine gun fire, we would hit the hedgerows, and then some of the Germans would pass me up. I don't know what happened to the lieutenant. I guess it was everyone for themselves so I lay down and let the Germans pass me up. I waited ten minutes or so then started to walk back the way we came from. I would walk at night and hide in the daytime.

One morning, I ran across a field to a barn and must have walked in a circle, because when I went into the barn, I walked right into the same Germans. (Another miracle). This time they, too, were tired and hungry. They had hidden their weapons under the hay.

I heard the American tanks coming. I asked "Luxembourg," who was dressed in a German uniform, if he could understand French, and he said he could. I told him I was going outside and stop the tanks. I stopped the first tank, and all full of blood, not shaved, and dirty, the tank man pointed the .50 caliber machine gun at me, but he decided not to shoot me. (Again, a miracle).

When I got on the tank, I told the captain there were German soldiers in the barn. He asked me if I was an American and I told him I was, but had no tags on me. Then he saw my ODs under my fatigues.

They picked up three truckloads full of German prisoners and made a pile of weapons four feet high and fifteen feet long.

I told him of the Germans in the barn and in the woods. They picked up three truckloads full of German prisoners and made a pile of weapons four feet high and fifteen feet long. That was the 2nd Armored Tank Division that saved me.

They took me to G-2, in the rear and I was questioned a lot. I told them what happened and that the Germans were out of fuel, food, communications, and transportation. I know because they made me carry two 88 shells. The information I gave them helped Patton and Montgomery to close in that pocket much sooner. The captain said I would be awarded the Purple Heart, Silver Star (which I never received), and the Bronze Star.

Then I was brought further on with G-2 to a radio station. I was to make a speech that would be broadcast by a New Orleans radio station, telling on the radio just how I had escaped and so on. After the speech, they said I was like Superman, and then they asked the American people to buy more American war bonds. I refused to make the broadcast. I am sure the Germans would have picked up that radio broadcast, and I figured the next American to be captured would not be as lucky as me. I thanked God for what he had done for me. They told me to go back to America for a 30-day furlough. Then I would be transferred to the Pacific theater. Having the experience of combat, I chose to stay in the European theater and not go home.

As I was going back to Company E, I met up with a good buddy from Ringgold, Louisiana. His name was Sergeant Mavin Pike. He was coming from being hit for the third time. When we got to Company E, they put me in the rifle squad, and the sergeant said to me, "'Key,' tonight, you go on patrol.' Then that night, he called for "Key" and then the next day the sergeant said, "'Key,' I wanted you to go on patrol." I told him that my name was not "Key;" it was "Adams." Then Sergeant Bob Beverly heard me talk and recognized my voice. He told them I belonged with him, back in the machine gun section. Bob Beverly was a great guy.

We then went on to liberate Paris. As far as we knew, we were the first in Paris, and then they took us out of Paris. Myself and six buddies can proudly say we went into Paris. We went to a city park and made a big "round." I would ask the French if there were any Germans. They would say, "Bosch left ten minutes ago." I could understand the French people talking to each other. They wondered if we were American or Canadians. Then I told them in French that we were Americans.

Boy, were they glad when I said we were Americans. They gave us wine to drink. That was my first time drinking wine. On my second glass, things were spinning. I wish I could meet some of the GIs I was with. I would also like to know what part of Paris we were in. I have been back three times with the National 4th Infantry Division Association, and I am very proud of this.

Al Miljevic, Havre de Grace, MD
Company F, 2nd Battalion, 22nd Infantry Regiment

Five Days of Captivity

My platoon was several kilometers from St. Mére Eglise, a member of Company F, 22nd Infantry. On or about June 22, 1944 Sergeant Pollock summoned me to the front of the platoon. He and the platoon leader ordered me to proceed as "point man" (we called them "first scout" in WWII) to be on advance patrol. I asked how far was I to go, and the platoon leader's reply was, "Until you meet someone," meaning the Germans.

I then proceeded to advance on the road with a second point man fifteen yards behind me. The main body of our platoon was approximately thirty to forty yards behind us. Along the roadsides were tall hedgerows. I was more concerned about what would be behind the hedgerows than what was on the road in front of me. I noticed a French woman trying to make contact with me. It appeared she was trying to warn me of something. I halted the column and told the platoon leader about the French woman. He ordered me to continue with the patrol.

The road had a sharp left 70-degree turn. The point man on the right side of the road and behind me could see further up the road ahead then I could. All at once he shouted, "hit the dirt." As I looked in front of me, there appeared approximately five German soldiers with machine pistols firing at me. The bullets were hitting the road, and sparks were flying all around my feet. God was with me that day because not one bullet hit me. Myself and the other point man hit the dirt in a ditch on the left hand side of the road. As I looked up, I could see the German soldiers on the right side of the road on a high knoll; they had us pinned downed.

The point man behind me asked me if I could fire at them and he would cross the road and try to divert some of them away from me. As he crossed the road they fired upon him and hit him in the arm. I heard his rifle hit the macadam. He then ran through the farm house yard. I, too, ran across the road and into the same farm house. In the back yard there was a small storage shed filled with straw on the floor. I went into the shed with the idea of staying inside until dark and then sneak back to my line. As I looked around the shed, which was dug inside the high knoll, I noticed about half of the roof was missing. Everything became quiet for about fifteen minutes. Then, through the hole of the roof, a German Infantryman pointed a machine pistol at me at which time I surrendered. For five days, we were strafed by the British spitfires and shelled by the Americans. During the last two days of my captivity, I was semi-conscious. The Germans never left this battlefield. The Allies had the Cherbourg Peninsula cut off, I guess, and there was no escape route for them.

On the morning of June 27, I heard someone say, "Here's one of those sons of bitches." Then I heard them say, "Damn, he's one of ours." If I remember correctly, they were from the 4th Recon platoon. I sure was glad to see them. They then captured the Germans when I pointed out the machine gun position. The captured Germans carried me on a stretcher and mounted me on a jeep. I was headed back to a Battalion Aid Station. I hadn't had anything to eat for five days, and the doctor gave me some water, chewing gum and a shot of morphine. I was then transported to an Evacuation hospital on Utah Beach. From there, I went on a LST to Bournmouth, England and spent several months in the hospital recovering from a collapsed lung.

Bob, I hope if you print this that the soldier who was the second point man, if he is still alive, will contact me. I want to thank him for saving my life. If he did not take them off my back, I would not have made it back home. I can't remember his name after all these years.

Louis Kaplan, Baltimore, MD
Service Company, 12th Infantry Regiment

Lying In a Ditch

The Personnel Section left Bournemouth, England, for the port of embarkation on or about June 9, D+3. We arrived there the same day, but we ended up doing a lot of waiting. The next night, we boarded an LST and sailed across the English Channel to the Normandy Beach.

A strong wind prevented us from landing. During the night, standing on deck, we could see the flashes of fire from our artillery; it was firing from the beach at the enemy.

The next morning I marveled at the sight. I saw two long breakwaters made up of partially sunken ships. There were many ships with large barrage balloons flying over them, lined up in rows, waiting to land. I watched the tiny minesweepers moving in pairs between the rows of ships to snag mines dropped during the night, or which broke loose from their moorings. The minesweepers rode in pairs because there was a cable extending from one to the other. In the center of the cable was a contraption to snag mines.

After debarking the LST on a quarter-ton truck, my driver drove between white tapes where the area was cleared of mines. On either side were signs in German that read, "Achtung, Minen." We drove past the outskirts of St. Mére Eglise and stopped for the night within earshot of the screaming meemies. I was told that the concussion was so powerful that it broke the blood vessels of anyone near the point of impact and caused internal bleeding. I spent that night lying in a ditch on the side of the road. I was awakened later on when a battery of antiaircraft guns sent up a curtain of shells.

Donald Nolan, Lakewood, CA
Company G, 2nd Battalion, 22nd Infantry Regiment

Company Runner

I was on my first day as runner for Company G. Someone, probably the message center officer, pointed in the general direction and said, "Go." There was a sunken road, and on each side were fields with hedgerows. I was about a hundred and fifty yards from the Battalion CP, walking out in the field, when I heard a lot of commotion on the road. I looked through the hedges and was looking into the biggest German tank I ever saw. It was headed toward our CP on the road.

I ducked and headed back to the CP. There was Major Lum Edwards, standing in the hedgerow break, watching our antitank gun and half-track retreating down the road. What he didn't realize was that the gun was pointing the wrong way and was trying to get turned around. Major Edwards was sort of moaning that his own antitank gun was running away. When the gun finally got turned around, it put at least three .57mm rounds into the tank. I went back to my job and found G Company. That is also the day I met General Roosevelt.

Harold Blackwell, Mesa, AZ
Battery A, 377th Anti-Aircraft Artillery Battalion

With Teddy Roosevelt Jr. in the Hedgerows

377th AAA Bn and BG Teddy Roosevelt Support of
22nd Infantry in the Hedgerows

The following is a brief account of my contact with Brigadier General Teddy Roosevelt Jr., during the days before he received orders to take command of the 90th Infantry Division. At that time I was CO of Battery A of the 377th AAA Battalion, directly attached to the 4th Infantry Division.

The 4th Infantry Division was having a difficult time making progress through the hedgerows of Normandy. General Roosevelt, the Assistant Division Commander of the 4th Infantry Division was assigned the task of figuring out a way to take the hedgerows where the Germans were dug in. He got the idea of using antiaircraft weapons to assist the infantry, since it was almost impossible to get them out with the arms normally available to them.

I was assigned to work with the General, and in addition to my battery, I was given one platoon of four gun sections from Battery D of the 377th. From the very beginning, General Roosevelt and I hit it off real well. He was an outgoing, imaginative, enthusiastic commander. As I recall, we worked directly with Lieutenant Colonel Arthur Teague and his 3rd Battalion of the 22nd Infantry Regiment.

The tactics developed were to shell the hedgerows for about ten minutes with 40mm antiaircraft and .50-caliber machine guns. Under this intensive fire, the infantry advanced in a crawling position across the field. I had at my command, twelve 40mm guns, shooting two rounds per second, and six quad .50 machine guns with power mounts on half-tracks. We also mounted two of the 40mm guns on half-tracks. That way, we could pull up into position, fire immediately, and withdraw when no longer needed.

These tactics worked very well as our antiaircraft fire kept the Germans pinned down in their honeycombed hedgerows as our infantry advanced. When the infantry got close enough to use flamethrowers, hand grenades, and rifle power, they would shoot off a red signal and we would lift our AA fire and pull back until we were ready to get in place for the next hedgerow. This operation was successful, and we moved from hedgerow to hedgerow.

During this entire operation, in early July 1944, General Roosevelt was very much in command and provided the enthusiastic coordination necessary for the overall success of the operation.

I remember on one occasion, General Roosevelt came roaring up to my command post and called out to me, "God, Blackie, what are you trying to do, kill the whole German Army at one time?" Our AA firepower was more than General Roosevelt or the infantrymen were used to. They didn't realize we had such capability.

One afternoon, General Roosevelt made a special point of visiting my command post and told me that in the very near future, it looked like his next assignment was as Commanding General of an infantry division. The next day, he told me the orders had come through, that the CG of the 90th Infantry Division had been relieved and that he was going to their HQ that afternoon to meet the staff in preparation for taking over as CG. This was a promotion to Major General and an assignment he wanted very much. It was the last time I saw him.

Brigadier General Teddy Roosevelt Jr. was an inspirational leader. The next day, I heard that General Roosevelt died of a heart attack while at the 90th Division HQ. He was very common and always made you feel important. In the field, he usually wore only his green fatigues and the regulation knit stocking cap without his helmet on. Seldom did I ever even see his star of rank displayed other than a muddy red star on the front of his jeep. In my opinion, he was a great man, and one that I will always be proud to have served under, albeit for only a short time.

One outstanding remembrance of Brigadier General Roosevelt was when he told me about getting authorization to land with the first wave on D-Day. He said he was turned down by Major General Barton, 4th Infantry Division CG; Lieutenant General Collins, 7th Corps CG; and

General Bradley, 1st Army CG, so he said, "I went to see Ike (General Eisenhower) at his headquarters and was told by him that General Officers just didn't land with the first wave. "In disgust," he said, "I told Ike to let me use the phone, I'll call my cousin," (President Franklin D. Roosevelt).

Ike smiled and said, "OK, Teddy. You win."

Brigadier General Teddy Roosevelt Jr. did land with the first wave on D-Day, June 6, 1944, and was a great inspiration to the assault troops on that stormy morning on Utah Beach. The rest is history.

Darel Parker, Leipsic, OH
Company C, 1st Battalion, 12th Infantry Regiment

Journey Home

I joined the 4th Infantry Division at Camp Gordon Johnston in Florida. We moved from there to South Carolina, then to New Jersey and then to England. From England, we went to France, and then to Normandy on D-Day. The water was rough, but we made it and went on to cross the flooded areas. Some of the water there was six to seven feet deep, and with all the equipment we were carrying, it wasn't very easy. We then attacked on to Cherbourg and through the hedgerows. Then we went to Bloody Mortain, St. Lô, and on to Paris, which was a story in itself.

I was with the 4th and never away from Company C until November 10, at which time I was wounded in the Battle of the Hürtgen Forest. This started my journey home. I went back to a hospital in Paris and then to England. From England, I went back to the states and after a year in and out of hospitals, I was discharged.

Donald Nolan, Lakewood, CA
Company G, 2nd Battalion, 22nd Infantry Regiment

A Nosy Horse

We were in the hedgerow country of Normandy, fighting our way toward Cherbourg. I had my rifle sticking through a place in a hedgerow, and there were horses running around in the field with bullets flying everywhere. They were getting hit and were terrified. A horse came up and started to nuzzle my rifle. I stood up to throw a clod of dirt at him to get him out of there. I don't know how many bullets came flying by my ear about that time. A burp gun cut loose at me. I told myself, that horse is on his own from now on.

Jim Burnside, Richmond, VA
Company E, 2nd Battalion, 22nd Infantry Regiment

Gallant Paratrooper

I have a vivid memory of an incident that happened in the dim light of dawn on D-Day after our landing on Utah Beach. I had trouble finding some reference points that were given to us. I knew Company E of the 22nd was to advance inland to a macadam road, turn right, and attack toward the fortification of Azeville, but I couldn't find the damn road, only a plowed field. After walking in the field a couple of hundred feet, I suddenly realized what had happened. The Air Corps saturation bombing, intended to blow up underwater obstacles and barbed wire on the beach, had landed too far inland and completely covered the road for several hundred yards. Fortunately, the Navy landed us a mile or so too far to the left, otherwise we would have been under direct fire from the big guns in the Azeville pillbox.

Working cautiously up the road towards Azeville, I became aware of some movement on the road ahead. Holding our fire, we waited to see what was coming. To our astonishment, it was an oxcart with an ox pulling a full load of straw. Astride the ox was a wounded paratrooper who had dropped in the night before D-Day. He had a bandage on one arm and a blood soaked bandage on his forehead. In the cart were five or six of his wounded buddies. As they slowly passed us, looking for an aid station, the paratrooper raised his good arm, holding a Tommy gun. With a big grin he said, "Hi-Ho Silver, fellows." Thus, the gallantry and courage we were to see so often was always served so well by a keen sense of humor.

On a later date (I believe around St. Mére Eglise,) during a lull, Major Lum Edwards, our battalion commander, had cautiously worked his way to a shallow shell hole in the middle of a small field and squatted down to do his morning's duty. A shell landed in the same field. Lum squatted down a little deeper and pulled his helmet down a little further. Wham! Another shell hit a little closer. Lum—never rising up, holding his pants around his ankles in one hand and his helmet on with the other—did the most amazing duck waddle to safety in a nearby hedgerow, accompanied by our hysterical laughter.

'Nuff said. Isn't it amazing how our memories dull the horror of combat that was all around us and keeps the humorous events clear? Good soldiers were a necessity and how fortunate our outfit was, to always have some GI in our midst who saw the humor of things and got us laughing—breaking the almost unbearable tension and helping all to keep our sanity. God Bless them.

Carl Morris, Hertford, NC
Company I and HQ, 3rd Battalion, 8th Infantry Regiment

Wine Cellar

This story is just to show you how orders are often carried out to the letter in the field. Company I was prepared to make an attack late one evening, but was told not to do so until specific orders were given. In the meantime, they could see the Germans in the distance—in full action. It appeared that they were also preparing to make an attack. Our command post was notified of this situation, but we were still told to hold our fire. When the Germans began to move from their position in the direction of I Company, the CP was notified again. Again, Company I was told to hold their fire. Next, Company I reported that the Germans were walking all over us. The CP responded, "Shoot the bastards." Results…mission accomplished.

At one place, four or five of us got caught under shellfire near a church. For protection, we scrambled to get inside, which was the cellar. When the situation became quiet, we scouted around and came upon a French chateau nearby. Remember, this was grape country. Inside this place was also a cellar that contained racks and racks, fifteen tiers high. It was estimated that there was about sixty thousand bottles of champagne in that cellar. Soon, with a jeep and trailer, we loaded up some hundred and fifty bottles and took them back to our hideout in the church. Knowing that we might be there for several days, we settled down, waiting for ammo and rations. A GI came with supplies. He stayed and had a few drinks that evening. When he left, he was given a couple of bottles of champagne. About noon the next day, he was assumed missing. But later in the evening, he was found lying down on the ground near a small stream of water, passed out like a light. Fortunately, when they sobered him up, he was OK. It so happens that the officers found this out and when it became possible, they sent a large GI truck down there and loaded it up with wine for their big party.

Later, after being hurt scouting with my infantry company, I elected to join the wire section. This job was to help keep communication between the front line companies and the forward operation post. At one point while checking into the telephone wire for breaks, I spotted a body in a tree about fifty yards ahead. I chanced a shot to see what would happen. Nothing… I was a sharpshooter with a bunch of medals. Did I miss? I don't think so. Anyway, after four or five shots, still nothing happened. To my surprise, that German soldier was tied up in the tree, equipped with a telephone to relay information to his outfit. To my relief, he had been killed a little earlier by our artillery fire.

Louis Kaplan, Baltimore, MD
Service Company, 12th Infantry Regiment

Troop Replacement

I was the Regimental Classification Specialist of the 12th Infantry Regiment. My primary duty was to handle the details of assigning replacement soldiers for those killed, wounded, and or missing in action. Here is a description of the first time in Normandy that I had to go from the rear echelon location of the 12th Infantry personnel section, to a combat area, to handle the details of replacing soldiers. Captain Arthur A. Edmunds, the Regimental Personnel officer, alerted me to be ready to leave with him. The jeep driver was Glen Steensland, highly trained in night driving.

After leaving the rear echelon, we passed a lightly wooded area from which our artillery was firing at the enemy. We heard many "thunderclaps" but could not see the artillery pieces nor tell from which direction they were firing. Later on, after leaving the artillery far behind and as it was getting dark; we came to a crossroad in a desolate area. A military policeman climbed out of his deep foxhole near the crossroad and confirmed the proper road to take.

We arrived at the Regimental CP after dark. There, we were given directions for locating the convoy of replacement soldiers at a designated place on the road. We found the 4th Infantry Division classification specialists with their two-and-a-half-ton-trucks filled with replacement soldiers. They turned over to us the trucks with the soldiers assigned to the 12th Infantry Regiment.

Captain Edmunds guided the trucks to the 12th Infantry Service Company, located near the Regimental CP. Service Company soldiers outfitted the replacement troops with needed equipment and ammo. In the meantime, I was handed the Military Occupation Specialty Forms, one for each replacement. After studying the military skills of the replacements, I used my best judgment in assigning them to the companies that needed them. Quite often, we waited until the next morning before returning to the rear echelon.

James Drennan, Graniteville, SC
HQ, 42nd Field Artillery Battalion

Please Forgive...

Walking into the city of Montebourg on or about June 14, 1944, I felt complete sadness imprinted on my mind.

Dead mothers and fathers holding their dead children was a scene I was not ready to handle. Dead men from D-Day to the Battle of the Bulge have all but faded from my mind, but not the scene in the train or bus station. God, please forgive us.

Denver Sayre, Wildomar, CA
Battery C, 44th Field Artillery Battalion

Antiaircraft Fire

It was D+16, June 22, 1944. The 3rd Battalion, 22nd Infantry Regiment was assigned the task of advancing on the right flank on the drive to Cherbourg. I was with 3rd Battalion, 22nd Infantry, as usual. Our forward observer party from Battery C, 44th Field Artillery, consisted of a lieutenant and two radio operators. Robert Smith was with me. As the battalion advanced, they were suddenly subjected to a fierce concentration of antiaircraft fire, which we had never experienced in our sixteen days of combat. It was like a huge fireworks display with shells exploding in the trees and bushes and on the ground. Being pinned down and unable to advance, they called for artillery.

We were three frightened GIs, or at least I was.

This only made us angry and more determined to silence this terrible barrage.

Our Forward Observer had to crawl several hundred yards forward and we carried the heavy 610 radios with six-foot antennas through an exposed position to direct fire on the Moupertus airport. The Germans must have known where we were because we had plenty of fire sent in our direction. Needless to say, we were three frightened GIs, or at least I was. This only made us angry and more determined to silence this terrible barrage. We got a clear view and when the, "fire for effect" command went through, the airport seemed to explode; the shelling must have hit an ammo dump. That stopped the antiaircraft bombardment. It was one of those fluid situations. The enemy had infiltrated quite a large force behind us and we were cut off completely and surrounded for about two days.

We had some casualties during the shelling. There was one unlucky GI who had been wounded in the back. He kept telling us how deep the wound was and how he knew he was going to die. The medics patched him up, but he could not be evacuated because we were cut off. During the night, he was close enough that I could hear an occasional moan coming from his direction. The next morning, we discovered his prediction had come true—he had passed away.

Finally, there were several tanks that broke through to our position. We were very grateful that we were no longer surrounded, but the tanks did not stop firing soon enough and overran our position. We had several wounded by our own tanks. One poor fellow came by my position holding his hand which had been horribly mangled, yelling not because of pain, but because it was from friendly fire.

Some things you forget, but those two days left a lasting impression on me that I will never forget.

Louis Kaplan, Baltimore, MD
Service Company, 12th Infantry Regiment

Premonition Fulfilled

One night after 2300 hours, I was doing guard duty at the gate of the English army camp called "Higher Barracks," near the town of Exeter, on the English Channel coast. I permitted Private Harry Licht of Boston, to enter the gate after giving me the correct password for that day. He was returning to Higher Barracks after a visit to the nearby town of Exeter. Private Licht and I were both members of Service Company, 12th Infantry Regiment. We exchanged greetings and conversed with each other. During the course of the conversation, Private Licht told me that he had a premonition of death during the Normandy invasion. He told me that he was the jeep driver for Major Kenneth E. Lay, a most capable Regular Army officer, for whom he had the greatest respect and admiration. Private Licht told me that as long as he drove Major Lay in his jeep, he knew he was safe. But Harry said that one time when not required to transport Major Lay, he would be commanded by a newly arrived inexperienced officer to drive him to a Company Headquarters. The officer would direct him to make a wrong turn on the road with disastrous consequences. Not too long after D-Day, Private Harry Licht and an army officer were killed when their jeep was fired upon by the enemy.

Arthur Bart, Boynton Beach, FL
Company E, 2nd Battalion, 8th Infantry Regiment

Caught In a Trap

Joining the 4th Infantry Division as a replacement was the most frightening experience of my life, especially if you're only eighteen years old. Luckily, the GIs in my squad were very comforting and taught me quickly. Constant patrols and slow advances toward Cherbourg provided many hairy moments, but none scarier than the one that happened on June 25, the day that I was wounded.

Our company was the lead on the outskirts of Cherbourg when we found ourselves outflanked by a German unit and caught in a trap inside a hedgerow, which is not a very good place to be caught. The Germans tossed mortars systematically and slowly; the company was being wiped out. One mortar landed so close to me that my watch blew off my hand and five fillings came out of my teeth. My sergeant crawled over to me and told me to try to reach the rear echelon and secure much needed help. I took off my pack, and, with but a rifle in my hand, I dashed across the hedgerow towards the opening. I didn't make it. I ran at least twentyfive yards when a bullet tore through my arm and threw me to the ground. Knowing that I could bleed to death, I applied a makeshift tourniquet to my arm that temporarily stopped the bleeding. While I lay there sobbing, two GIs scuttled by and asked if I was able to move. I said, "I think so." Together we crawled to the opening, dashed across, and darted into a gully where we searched for an Aid station.

As we proceeded back to where we thought our rear echelon would be, we heard a tank coming down the road. Not knowing if it was German or American, we stayed hidden until we saw the White Star. I rose up, threw a rock with my good arm to get the driver's attention, and asked him for directions to the Aid Station. At the same time, I told him that my company was pinned down and needed help, desperately. Ultimately, the unit was relieved but suffered severely.

We finally found the aid station about a mile down the road. As a result of that action, I spent fifteen months in various hospitals until I was discharged. For this, I received the Purple Heart, the Bronze Star, and memories that I will never forget.

Franklin Shaw, Santa Fe, NM
Company F, 2nd Battalion, 22nd Infantry Regiment

Date of Rank

I caught up with the company on the morning of D+4, just after the disaster of the Château de Fontenay, to find that Harold Fulton, the company commander and one lieutenant had been killed. Two other lieutenants had been wounded and evacuated, amounting to a total of some ninety men lost. I reported to Jim Beam, whom I knew from the June 1 payroll. He was the XO. He looked at my collar and asked my date of rank. I thought, What kind of chicken outfit is this?

When I told him he said, "Damn, I rank you by six days. I had hoped you would take over this mess." I became XO and leader of the second platoon. I went up a hedgerow, found fourteen survivors, went back and secured fifteen replacements. I reorganized the platoon, putting half new, half old veterans in each squad, and moved out within the hour. I lost just one man in a firefight the next day. I myself, lasted until I was wounded while on patrol on D+6. Jim Beam, who was wounded and later lost a leg at St. Lô, became my lifelong friend.

My infantry career ended leading a squad. My next command, many years later, was a tank battalion with ninety-one M-48 tanks. It was quite a step up in firepower.

Richard A. Sover, Chicago, IL
Company I, 3rd Battalion, 12th Infantry Regiment

Cherbourg

Upon landing on Utah Beach in Normandy, France on June 6, 1944, we knew that our main objective was to free Cherbourg so it could be used as a port to receive supplies. I was a sergeant and a squad leader in the Weapons Platoon, 60mm Mortar Section. We broke to the seawall and landed in more water. The enemy opened all the water valves that the Normandy farmers used to irrigate their crops and inundated the area for about one and a half to two miles.

After lurking in the water for several hours, we finally hit dry land, reorganized, and proceeded forward on this dark, lonely road. About an hour later, we were halted and word got back to the weapons platoon to bring up the mortars. We had hit an enemy roadblock and we needed some small artillery to break it. All three squads of the mortar sections started to fire intermittent fire, and by 0200 hours, we broke up the roadblock. For the balance of the night, we heard a lot of moaning and groaning from the enemy, so we knew our mortars did some injury.

The following morning, June 7, we reorganized and once again started on the road where we saw road signs with an arrow showing, "Cherbourg." We marched on this road for about two hours when we bumped into a squad of paratroopers. After words were exchanged, the paratroopers started to return to the beach. I left the group, unbuckled my pack, and lay on the ground. All of a sudden, one of the paratroopers started to holler, "Take cover everyone—live grenade!" What he had tried to do was transfer a hand grenade from his jacket pocket to a pocket on his hip. In doing so, he pulled the pin in error. The grenade went off and injured his right thigh and right arm. A piece of the shrapnel buzzed my head and hit Scotty McNaughton. Scotty hollered, "I'm hit!" I immediately ran to him. He was lying on his stomach. I asked him where he was hit. He hollered, "My back." Upon careful examination, I found that the piece of shrapnel had hit him between his shovel handle and back where the handle was seared half way, and his back was cut about three inches. I broke open his sulfa packet, sprinkled sulfa on his back, taped a gauze packet to it and told him to go to the aid station behind us. In the meantime, I ran over to the trooper and the medic had him under control. I remember his last words before entering the ambulance, "I made my last jump." I hope he survived.

Once again, we proceeded to head for Cherbourg. On Sunday, June 25, we were nearing the city, according to the road signs. We proceeded cautiously. As we neared the English Channel, all hell broke loose. Artillery fire was hitting the road we were on. We spotted where the artillery was coming from. There was high ground to our left and we could see the flashes. I rolled off the road onto a ditch where someone had previously been digging. I slid into this ditch and stayed under cover until the firing stopped. Many Company I men were killed and injured on June 25, 1944. We made a direct attack on the enemy and secured Cherbourg around 0100 hours.

We reorganized and marched into Cherbourg and occupied many of the homes. The next morning, I took a patrol to see what damage we had done. We visited some of the concrete bunkers. The odor was awful. I did not stay in them very long. Our next visit was the "Atlantique Hotel," the General Headquarters of the enemy. Everyone was searching for souvenirs. I found an officer's trench knife with scabbard. It looked like a letter opener. I tied it under my left armpit.

178 ♦ War Stories: D-Day

We left Cherbourg on June 27, and headed toward St. Lô. On July 6, we were in a tough fight amongst the hedgerows. I had just dug a fox-hole when the ammunition truck came by and dropped off some mortar shells. I got out of my foxhole to distribute the shells to my ammunition carriers. All of a sudden, enemy artillery was shelling us. One shell hit close to me. It lifted me off the ground and I did a 360-degree turn and was slammed into the hedgerow. I must have been knocked out for a few minutes, for when I came to, I heard my platoon sergeant, Prewitt, hollering, "If there are any walking wounded, head for the ambulance." I noticed that I could not see from my left eye. Blood was rolling down my cheek. My arms were bleeding from shrapnel. As I stood up, I noticed holes in my jacket and I was bleeding from my chest. I was able to walk, so I told the platoon sergeant that I was going to the ambulance.

As I approached the ambulance I started to vomit, but the medic said all wounded soldiers did the same thing. All this time, I thought I had lost my left eye. I got in the ambulance and we went to an Aid Station. Immediately, the nurses and medics started to check my wounds. The first thing they did was to check my left eye and then they gave me the good news. The piece of shrapnel had lodged in my left eyelid and had caused bleeding, making it difficult to see. In checking further, they also found a piece of shrapnel in my right eyebrow, shrapnel in both arms, and across my chest.

My stay in the hospital was short-lived. I returned to Company I at the end of the Mortain battle, in time to enter Paris on August 25. Company I was the first of the American troops to come down the Champs Elysees, under the Eifel Tower, where we stopped at the Notre Dame Cathedral.

Little did I know when I joined the 4th Infantry Division in March, 1942, that forty years later, I would be elected President of the National 4th Infantry (Ivy) Division Association. Then on July 8, 2000, I was selected, along with Chaplain George Knapp, as one of the "Ivy Men of the Year 2000."

Martin L. King, (Deceased) Wills Point, TX
Company H, 2nd Battalion,
22nd Infantry Regiment

Hospital July 23, 1944

Through the providence of God, I came home lame, but believing. Of the things I will always remember and will always cherish are the thoughts and warmth in feelings of the others involved. I was hospitalized at this time in the 190th General Hospital in England. Our ward consisted of three rooms. One was the big ward with twenty or so beds, the second was my room, and the third was the latrine and bath area. Only two of us were able to use this facility. All of the beds were filled. One patient was a civilian named Smith. He was from California. He was an entertainer with a USO Group and had become ill. He was a magician with a trunk full of magic. He was a short, fat man with a big smile and wrinkled forehead. He and I were the only men capable of using the latrine.

It should go without saying that war is hell. It is rough on the home folks—it is sad—it is depressing, and yet, at the same time there are some lighter, happier, and gay moments. So, on July 23, 1944, they were ready for me when I returned to the ward after my final visit with my new eye from the dentist—that's right, a dentist had made my new eye to replace the one I had lost outside Cherbourg; they were expert at making wax impressions.

This ward was occupied by bedfast (confined to bed) men from the front. They had open wounds (being treated with sulfa drugs and penicillin for serious infections), and some had severed nerves in their legs and arms. Now, here is the memorable part for me. It is a resolution of the fun type. I was brought from my room by the nurse on the pretext of leading the singing of songs. I was led to a Warrant Officer's bed, whose name was Moses.

He read the following resolution: "Resolution unanimously adopted by the staff this 23rd day of July 1944. Be it resolved that Martin L. King, 1LT, U.S. Army, was wounded in Normandy, France on June 21, 1944, while heroically and honorably leading his platoon against an armed enemy of his country. Be it further resolved that 1LT King is an officer of uncompromising principal, undaunting courage, an asset of the highest type to his country and an irreplaceable member of the staff of our own General Moses. Be it further resolved that whereas said 1LT King did in unselfish devotion to duty, brave the wrath of nurses and ward boys in attempts to relieve distressed patients by delivering to the bedside of disabled and suffering fellow soldiers, numerous bed pans—(always with tissues and ducks, invariably emptying them by day and night. It is therefore further resolved that General Moses, by authority invested in him by his high rank, shall bestow upon 1LT King, the highest honor ever received by a member of the armed services."

At that time, the nurse produced a "duck urinal" and hung it around my neck on a loop of white gauze. When the whooping and such was over, I was humbled to say the least, almost to tears, as I had so many times answered their calls at bedside. To conclude, the magician gave us a show.

John Abraham, St. Ann, MO
Company M, 3rd Battalion, 8th Infantry Regiment

"Combat" Shower

On D-Day, I was a First Lieutenant who led my .30-caliber, water-cooled, machine gun platoon ashore in the first wave at 0630 hours, in support of the rifle companies.

Twenty-one days later, we had fought our way through the hedgerows to Cherbourg. Several days later, when everything was secure, I received word that I could take my men back down the peninsula for showers and clean clothing. We loaded on trucks and drove down to the Merderet River where the quartermaster had set up a large tent with showers inside, pumping water from the river. Needless to say, the men looked forward to enjoying a shower after three weeks of living in the same uniforms and no baths.

The following procedure was followed: The tent containing the showers was enclosed and on each side were flaps. Before entering, the men stacked their rifles, boots, helmets, and gun belts. As they entered, they disrobed, placing their dirty uniforms in piles. So, there were about fifty naked GIs standing in line waiting their turn.

All of a sudden, flying just above the trees, came an ME 109K. In pursuit was a "Spitfire," firing at the German aircraft and bullets were flying all around. The fifty or more GIs in their birthday suits were diving for any cover available. It was all over in seconds. There were no injuries and immediately everyone was laughing and scrambling back in line. All enjoyed their showers and after receiving those welcome clean underwear, socks, and fatigues, they retrieved their equipment, thankful that it all turned out all right.

I am sure there are many stories that veterans try to forget. This is one that we enjoy telling. Any happening that provides a little fun is worth remembering.

Joseph Kraynak, Lansdale, PA
HQ Battery, 29th Field Artillery Battalion

Keeping "The Pipers" Flying

Our next immediate objective after D-Day was to take the port of Cherbourg. This was scheduled to be accomplished in about a week. The fighting got rough, and it took about three weeks until we took the port. During these few weeks I was exposed to what is referred to as "combat," which was nothing like my idea of what combat would be. From the time of the invasion, it was one long day. I remember thinking how great it would be to fast forward my life about five years and get this one out of the way. It was only then that I really understood why one minute seemed like an hour. One of the aspects of combat is that there is no end of the day when you bathe, relax, or go to bed. There is no waking up to a new great day and no meals to look forward to. There is neither social life, nor any weekends to recharge your life for the week ahead. There are no plans for your own personal future. There is no medical help for the many minor sicknesses, no family, no toilet…nothing.

The cold winters add much more hardship, which one can feel only by having actually lived it back then. In addition to these miseries, you have the depressing thought that at any time it could be your last day on earth, or you could be wounded. One only had to pass by dead human beings to bring those thoughts to mind and realize how true they were. The thought of a million dollar wound entered my mind as it did the minds of many other soldiers. That was the kind of wound that was not very serious, but could get you out of the mess. I did witness this on a few occasions.

The next seven weeks or so, until we reached Paris, were days of constantly pressing forward. Our "Grasshopper Squadron" was constantly on the lookout for a field large enough for our Piper Cubs to land on and take off. It was always in range of the enemy artillery, and sometimes small arms fire. These fields dictated where we would bed down—either in foxholes or in any available shelter.

After D-Day, the paratroopers who landed in and around St. Mére Eglise left many dead and wounded from their drop on enemy territory in the dark of the night. I never experienced what this group went through, but there were parachutes just about everywhere you went. The chutes made excellent tents for us with some battlefield alterations. After those six weeks in combat, we felt very much like seasoned troops in comparison with our replacements. Most of our time was spent trying to keep the "Pipers" (Piper Cub airplanes) flying. This kept our artillery fire very effective.

Seeing wounded and dead was constantly a firm reminder of what could happen. After seeing a dead German soldier, I went through his equipment, which at the time, seemed like a very normal thing to do. I found, among other personal things, a letter and a photo of a young woman and a child. It was at that moment I stopped hating German soldiers and I realized his plight and call were no different from mine.

There was excitement throughout the ranks when we got word through the rumor grapevine that we were headed for Paris. I am sure it was a tough road for our infantry, but the artillery seemed to breeze through. One of the sights we saw when we got within the city limits was the parade of German collaborators. French girls had their heads shaved and some were made to parade naked for their collaboration with German soldiers.

After a few hours, when the city was completely in our hands, it was easy to break rules and loosen up. A few of us jeeped through the town, soaking up the welcome from the Parisians It was not long before we were invited into some private homes, given the hospitality of an old friend, with plenty of wine and cognac to celebrate. As our front moved on eastward, we would jeep back to Paris until it was too far to get back to the front. At this time, we were very confident of the allies total victory with not much resistance from the enemy.

While on the move, the Air Observation, which is what our small unit was called, was in constant search of fields from which we could fly the Pipers. The two-man planes were on call constantly from battalion headquarters to get into the air and direct the artillery on target. It was a very dangerous assignment. I remember several pilots and observers being shot down and killed by small arms from the enemy. The flight usually lasted about one hour if our position was close enough to observe the enemy and low enough not to be shot down by enemy fighter planes.

Directing fire presented the problem of being hit by our own artillery, since we were in a direct line between the Artillery and the enemy front lines. We later learned that the Germans, at the first sight of these toy planes, thought it was a joke. It was not long until they realized a strange coincidence: Whenever these "toys" were in the air, our guns were effective and accurate, so immediately they doubled their effort to knock us out of the air.

As pilots were killed or injured, the need for more pilots was crucial. I learned to fly off the record during our training, so once the Battalion Command knew this, they assigned me to fly the mail and communicate between units at the front. This was frightening to me, since I was not trained in navigation and it was easy to get lost. One wrong turn and you wound up in the German foothills.

Robert Williamson, Lakeland, FL
Company F, 2nd Battalion, 12th Infantry Regiment

Taking the Hedgerows

The next morning after D-Day it had stopped raining and we were moved into new foxholes. Across the road, we had no more than gotten there when the Germans started sending in artillery shells, mortars, and screaming meemies again. A lot of the replacements were killed, because by that time, they had the place zeroed in. They really did a lot of damage. We then stayed at this spot for a few days until we were in better condition to fight the Germans.

In a few days we took off across the countryside after "field-fighting" Germans. We took hedgerow after hedgerow and our men were being picked off one after another. They were dying. Some of our men were taken to a hospital, but would come back to fight again. Some were sent home, no longer able to fight.

In June we started for Cherbourg, and on June 25, 1944, my division, the 4th Infantry Division, took Cherbourg. After Cherbourg fell, the division prepared for a rest. We were then forced back into the battle when the Germans struck near Carentan, where the 4th Infantry Division relieved the 83rd Infantry Division. The 4th Infantry Division took an awful beating there. The Germans were dug in; they had foxholes in the ground that were at least six feet deep, and their tanks were also dug in. As we crossed a road, we ran into a hedgerow. One of the fellows looked over the hedgerow too many times in one place. The Germans were watching that place, sighted on it, and the second time he went up to look…bang; a German shot him right between the eyes. I lost a good buddy. We sure hated to lose him. He never did anything out of the way. It sure was a sight a fellow will never forget as long as he lives.

We got over one hedgerow and into the fields but our problem was to take the next hedgerow. We hit the ground after we got over the first hedgerow from the road and started firing at the next one. We got to our feet, one by one, firing as we went. We ran a little ways and hit the ground again, that is, those of us who were still able to fight.

My BAR man and I got up and a machine gun spit bullets all around us. I got out without getting hurt. My BAR man got it right through his helmet. The bullet just made a mark through his hair. He and I couldn't do it all by ourselves so we turned around and went up a different hedgerow. I was right behind my squad sarge, and a German stepped out and got my sarge and me. The German got my sarge around the neck and got me in the upper arm before I could get out of the path of the lead sailing through the air. I went to the hospital in England. When I got back to my company, there were a lot of new men there.

John H. Crowe, Covina, CA
20th Field Artillery Battalion

Accidental Fire

On June 24, 1944, the 12th Infantry Regiment was fighting its way toward the port city of Cherbourg, and was getting pretty close. I was a First Lieutenant with the 20th Field Artillery Battalion, a battalion of 155mm howitzers, available for assignment to any of the three regiments of the 4th Infantry Division as needed. On this day, I reported to Lieutenant Colonel John Merrill, the commanding officer of the 1st Battalion, 12th Infantry. They had just seized a second objective at 1540 hours and were consolidating their position, awaiting further orders.

I reported to the colonel in an apple orchard and he motioned me to join him in a search of the area. My memory of events is hazy here, but I do recall following the colonel, who was behind a bodyguard leading the way. We proceeded in a single file near the wall of a building and as we approached a corner of that building, the colonel motioned the point man to proceed around it. When the bodyguard did this, he drew machine gun fire from another building and one bullet struck him in the abdomen and passed through his body. Colonel Merrill helped the man back out of the line of fire and told me to take care of him. I did the best I could with the first aid kits we had, tiding him over until the medics arrived. I remember telling him that he appeared to have a clean wound since the bullet had passed completely through him without doing a tremendous amount of damage. If he was lucky, he had a million-dollar wound to save his life. It would take him out of the war.

At some point after this, as best I can recall, I discovered that my radio was inoperable. When I went forward to an infantry unit as a forward observer, I generally traveled in a jeep and was accompanied by the regular driver of that jeep, and a corporal or sergeant who served primarily as a radio operator. On this occasion, the radio operator was Corporal Wier. I sent the driver back to pick up a radio and Corporal Wier stayed with me to await his return. The 1st Battalion's new orders were to jump off at 2000 hours for a third objective. I don't remember much about my activities prior to the jump off time. I do recall meeting Lieutenant Manuel Herzog, an artillery liaison officer from the 12th Infantry's Cannon

Company, during that period. At 2010 hours, the battalion CP group moved out, marching along a road to be used by the battalion's support tanks. I was asked to join this group and would have been there except that I still had to wait for my jeep to arrive with the new radio.

A few minutes later I was standing by the side of the road with Corporal Wier when one of the tanks passed with its top open and the officer in charge riding in it. When he spotted me he said, "If you want to see some good gunnery, come on along." I explained that I had to wait there for my radio and the tank passed out of sight. I later heard that at 2020 hours, just a few minutes after I had spoken to the tanker, the Command Group had somehow come under the direct fire of his tank, accidentally. In this group were Lieutenant Colonel Merrill, Lieutenant Manuel Herzog, Lieutenant James E. Means, the Battalion S-4, two bodyguards, and five scouts. All but three of the party were killed. When my jeep arrived with the new radio, we proceeded along the road where this accident had occurred and passed the place of the accidental massacre with all of the bodies of those killed still there.

For the only time in my war experience, I did not look at these casualties because my imagination was sufficiently active to visualize myself among them. Corporal Wier said as we passed the carnage, "There's that colonel with the mustache." Colonel Merrill had a mustache.

This experience illustrates how pure chance can govern the fate of each of us, especially under circumstances of high risk.

Iz Goldstein, Monroe Township, NJ
HQ, 22nd Infantry Regiment

I Remember Ernie Pyle

Iz "Goldie" Goldstein was the first editor of Double Deucer, newsletter of the 22nd Infantry Regiment and an Ivy Leaves editor. This story was published in several magazines.

Dateline: France. D-Day Plus-One. (Just about twenty-four hours after the Utah Beach landing). In an area that was still inhabited by enemy tree snipers who were manufacturing Purple Heart candidates and featuring lush hedgerows that looked like they just took a mega dose of Miracle Gro, I met Ernie Pyle.

As a GI reporter for the 22nd Infantry Regiment, 4th Infantry Division, I was summoned to escort Mr. Pyle on a battlefield visit.

We had just come off the Utah Beach area, which came at you like an assailant or a vendor of dubious war wares. It even offered an inundated area featuring skeleton headed signs reading, "Achtung Minen!"

Ernie Pyle took the same route that every foot soldier took. The Mr. Pyle that I knew was a frail, humble, quiet man. A class act. Not talkative, a real Gary Cooper type—a gentleman. He injected relaxation to everyone he met. He carried a cheap spiral notebook, the same type that kids had in grammar school, to record his battlefield notes. The stories he filed were unvarnished accounts of dirt, death, and determination from the battlefield. The GIs in my outfit loved him.

During a quiet moment during our foxhole circuit, he questioned me about my family at home. He showed deep concern. He spoke about his wife, Jerry, and how worried he was about her. He was a hell of a reporter, with an ear for the laconic remark that explained everything. He had a way of just listening and putting himself in the other fellow's shoes.

His two prized possessions was an old wool cap that he wore on a head that did not have an abundance of hair. He even wore it when he slept. The other was a small Coleman stove. Everywhere that Ernie went, the stove was sure to go. His reporting was vivid—he was a journalist's journalist.

Goldie added: "The staff of the Double Deucer *had John Cheever, future Pulitzer Prize winner; Linn Streeter, creator of* Archie *cartoon; Joe O'Keefe of* The Washington Post, *and Bill Haggerty of* The Baltimore Sun."—*Bob Babcock*

Iz Goldstein, Monroe Township, NJ
HQ, 22nd Infantry Regiment

I Remember "Papa"

As wars go, this one was on schedule. Contributing our share of casualties to the successful Operation Overlord, those "Longest Day" French beaches were now hallowed ground and left to the scribes to duly record the historical event. We moved on.

Our invading GIs now began to tour the Normandy countryside on their bellies, slithering from hedgerow to hedgerow and flushing out the enemy in a new type of one-on-one warfare. The years of tough infantry training proved useful in the manner in which our men were scoring personal victories.

People lined the roadside as our vehicles rushed through their towns in pursuit of the enemy. Our troops took this opportunity to shower them with dextrose-maltose tablets. In return, the liberated French citizens mysteriously produced little American flags which they joyously waved as they shouted, "Vive le American." We relished that moment.

As our battle-seasoned combat team kept subjecting the enemy to well-orchestrated conquering jobs (while collecting medals and awards), visions of Parisian victory celebrations danced in my head.

Suddenly, as if someone called time out, we were ordered to dig in. Our new battlefield address was Mortain (Falaise Gap).

Assigned as Regimental GI correspondent, I was called from the safety of my foxhole to serve as guide for one more war correspondent. Ernest Hemingway was visiting our Regiment, which was then engaged in combat action.

Approaching Mr. Hemingway, I stared at a suspicious bulge in the pocket of his field jacket. "Papa" noted the question in my eyes. With a grin, almost lost in his bushy whiskers, he pulled out a grenade from his pocket and said, "Just in case!" Ernest Hemingway, who spent most of his time in the field with the troops and lived the same hardships and dangers, had seen as much of the war as most fighting men. He witnessed the same tragedies and always traveled to battlefields well equipped with both firearms and firewater. Upon returning to Regimental headquarters from the battle area where we both hit the ground countless times to escape the incoming 88s, we stopped at Hemingway's jeep. His driver automatically produced a dented canteen. The famous writer unscrewed the cap and passed the canteen to me. I took a drink. Then it struck. I shook for a moment, my head throbbed, my eyes popped and my ears felt as though they were falling off. It took me a moment to get over the effects of the drink. It had the power of a punishing punch thrown by a heavyweight champion. The gulp that I had taken from the canteen was pure, unadulterated Calvados—regular fare for Papa.

A short time later, after Mr. Hemingway left to return to division headquarters, all hell broke loose.

Mounting a counter offensive, the enemy gathered all the artillery they could muster and unleashed one of the most devastating barrages of the war. Activity concentrated on our position. The area was later named, "Purple Heart Hill."

During this action, I was badly wounded. For many long months, I endured several operations and stays in military hospitals.

Ernest Hemingway did not forget me. Upon his next visit to my Regiment he inquired of my whereabouts. Learning that I had been wounded, he would always ask about my well-being on his subsequent trips.

After the war, we continued our correspondence. His Christmas cards always included a personal message. One year he sent me a $200 check with a note, "Buy booze for the boys."

Yes, I remember Papa. And, Papa remembered me.

Milton D. Crippin, Danville, IL
Company B, 1st Battalion, 22nd Infantry Regiment

Raining Steel

Somewhere in France during July, I rested against a tree and went to sleep. I was awakened by the sound of thunder and heard hail stones hitting the ground. I was about to get away from that tree so as not to get hit by lightning when I realized the thunder was artillery and the hailstones were steel. I really hugged that tree until I could recover enough to get cover.

I was wounded July 31, and went to a hospital in England, then returned to duty. I went the usual route: Pheasy Farm, to South Hampton, to Camp Lucky Strike in Normandy. There, I discovered I was to be sent to an armored unit. Having seen what happened to the tankers when the tank was hit, I had no desire to join them, so, I took off and made my way to the company somewhere around Belgium. I thought I was in big trouble, but they needed men, so I lucked out.

After the war, I was at Fort Lewis when the 4th Infantry Division was there, but knew no one. I was at Fort Carson when the 4th Infantry Division was there, and again, I knew no one. The first time I found anyone was at the Nashville reunion. There I found three men. One is now dead, the other two I visit as often as we can get together.

Clarence Brown, Buchanan, NY
4th Signal Company

Spearhead Division

On July 25, 1944, our 4th Infantry Division spearheaded the break-through at St. Lô for Patton's Armor. Just two weeks before, we had handled the calls to try to get oxygen for Brigadier General Teddy Roosevelt Jr., who later died in the field next to where our switchboards were set up. He died of a heart attack.

John C. Clark, Spring Hope, NC
HQ, 29th Field Artillery Battalion

Trapped

One day in the St. Lô area, McGrady and I were looking for an obser-vation post when we came upon a stream with an old mill. I went over to the mill where I could climb up and see. I left McGrady the 610 radio, and I took the walkie-talkie.

I was headed to the fourth floor of the mill when McGrady called and told me he could hear vehicles. I could see German trucks in the distance by that time, so I rushed down and used old bags to cover any tracks I had made in the flour. I also closed the trap door that I'd left open. Then I crawled up a ladder to the top of a wooden flour bin, where I stayed for three days.

I had one D-chocolate bar and some water in my canteen. I tried not to drink much water, for I didn't want to urinate much, and when I did, I spread it around as much as possible so it would not run down where they could see it.

There were about twenty-five or thirty Germans there; I figured a whole platoon. They checked out the mill. I was glad I had covered my tracks. I was almost afraid to move, and I was afraid to sleep for fear I would snore. I was on the third floor, and they stayed on the first floor or outside, but I didn't want to take any chances that they would hear me.

They left about dark on the third day, so I walked across the stream and headed back to the infantry's headquarters. I called ahead so I would not be shot as an enemy, and found that I had already been turned in as missing-in-action, and Mom and Dad had already been sent a telegram.

This is just another of the many times that the Lord looked after me.

John C. Clark, Spring Hope, NC
HQ, 29th Field Artillery Battalion

Disaster at St. Lô

I will never forget our landing on Utah Red Beach on June 6, 1944. The smell of everything was unforgettable. I remember the difficulty in breathing as a result of all the burned powder from the bombing and the shelling. As impressive as that was, I remember more about our St. Lô experiences on the morning of July 25. Maybe I was too high strung to really appreciate what was happening on the beach.

We 29th Field Artillery forward observers were on point with Company B of the 8th Infantry Regiment that morning. Our objective was to lay a line of smoke shells along the St. Lô-Periers road as a marker to guide the planes on their bombing run. If memory serves me, it was a little after 0900 hours that we called for the smoke shells, and it was just a few minutes until we heard the sound of incoming planes.

There must have been several hundred fighter bombers that hit the smoke line from every direction for about a half hour. It looked as if they did a good job, but we wondered if this was all we were getting to soften up the line for the break out. Then we heard what sounded like a swarm of bees, but as the sound became louder, we realized it was hundreds of planes. It was one group of planes after another; they stretched as far as we could see. I had never seen so many planes at one time.

As the first bombers flew over us, the German 88's started to shoot at them and they got two or three before the Piper Cubs could report where they saw the gun flashes. After our artillery opened up, the 88's became quiet. I have no way of knowing how many planes were up there that day but it was an impressive sight.

As we watched them coming, we began to hear the bombing getting louder. Then we realized it was getting closer. The wind had come from the south and was blowing the smoke back over us. The planes were dropping their bombs on our positions. My driver, Jones, and I crawled under a tank and hoped we didn't get a direct hit. The bombs were so loud that all we could think to do was wrap our field jackets around our heads to help stop the noise. We put our arms up over our ears and found it helped to open our mouths when we heard some close ones coming in. We were in as safe a place as we could find so all we could do was sweat it out and hope they missed us. The bombing lasted maybe a half hour, but it seemed like forever.

After the bombing stopped, Jones and I came out from under the tank into an eerie quiet. The ground was covered with craters. The raw earth was everywhere. As we started to regroup, we were very fortunate to find our jeep would run, but the radios were out.

When we looked around for our squad, we found that our two new replacements, McGrady and McLeroy, had completely lost it. We tied their shoelaces together, wrapped their gun belts around their arms, and took them back to the command post. As for Jones and me, it was several days before we could even talk in a normal voice, rather than shouting at each other.

After we picked up some radios, we went back up to B Company, which was regrouping. A lot of them were wounded or in shock, so it was not a good situation. We heard later that we had over six hundred "friendly fire" casualties, including General McNair. As I look back over my war years, St. Lô stands out as the worst incident among many traumatic experiences.

Don Warner, Jr., Pharr, TX
Company A, 1st Battalion, 22nd Infantry Regiment

British Order of the Bath

According to records that I cannot put my finger on, members of the 22nd Infantry received twenty-five foreign decorations in WWII. There is still one pending for Lieutenant Colonel Lum Edwards: The British Order of the Bath. I was most fortunate to "liberate" a rough draft copy of the citation during my regimental tour serving under Colonel Edwards. You will notice that I removed the following inscriptions: TOP SECRET and FOR YOUR EYES ONLY, from this draft. If awarded, total foreign decorations will hit twenty-six, not including the Belgian Fourragier, which is both an individual as well as a unit award. The copy reads as follows:

"During the St. Lô breakthrough in late July 1944, Lum Edwards inherited a man by the name of Stone as his driver. As part of the combined Infantry-tank team spearheading the breakout through the German lines, Edwards, as Regimental S3, had very little to do and was assigned to the staff of General Rose of the 2nd Armored Division. He was to act as liaison between the 22nd Infantry and the 2nd Armored as needed. He had no idea that General Rose always acted as his own scout and was always where the action was the greatest. Lum had no choice but to accompany General Rose wherever he went on the battlefield. This meant that his driver, Stone, followed Lum Edwards.

"In so doing, in an open space in a barnyard, Stone noticed a horse or cow watering trough full of water. Stone then told Colonel Edwards that he thought the Colonel really needed a bath! Edwards was momentarily shocked to think that an enlisted man would make such a suggestion but knew that Stone was right. Edwards was also quick to point out that he religiously followed Colonel Buck Lanham's instructions on field hygiene, in that he shaved each day, washed his feet, his family jewels, and under his arms. Stone still insisted that the Colonel needed a bath and needed it real bad.

"Lum was shown the water trough out in the open barnyard. Lum told Stone that he didn't want to strip down in front of all the soldiers who had set up defensive positions in the stone buildings surrounding his bath trough and were watching his every move. Stone told Lum to go ahead, strip down, get in, soak, relax, and enjoy his bath because he really needed it. Lum, at last, followed Stone's instructions, stripped, and entered the green moss-filled water trough to enjoy the luxury of a bath. Stone told the others to look the other way while Lum reverted to his birthday suit and took the plunge. The men cheered and clapped. Stone told Lum to stay in, soak, and enjoy the bath—he and the other men would be on the lookout for Germans.

"About this time the Germans came out of a draw, in force, and attacked this location. Small arms fire covered the entire area, and it was nip and tuck for thirtyminutes with Lum pinned down inside the water trough. All during the period Stone kept calling to Lum to keep his head down and enjoy his soak, and that he was trying to arrange a counterattack to get him out. Throughout the counterattack, Lum could constantly hear Stone's voice telling him to enjoy his bath; they would get him out.

"When the water trough was recaptured and Lum surfaced, he was blue from exposure, covered with moss and trembling from cold although it was a hot July day. Stone spoke the first words following Lum's rescue, "Colonel, I know you enjoyed your soak, you really needed it."

Perhaps Lum Edwards should be recommended for the British Order of the Bath with moss cluster.

Orval H. Mullen, Bradenton, FL
HQ Company, 1st Battalion, 8th Infantry Regiment

"Commo" Man

We fought all the way to Cherbourg, which was not easy by any means. My job was to keep communications by laying wire to the outpost and the front line company. With all the traffic, the lines would get broken, or the Germans would get in and cut them at night and wait for someone to come in and repair them.

On July 7, before St. Lô, I was wounded in one of the worst shellings that I had ever seen. I was taken back to the beach hospital and the following day flew back to England where I spent the next several months. I was then sent back to HQ Company on December 21, just in time for the Battle of the Bulge, where I was wounded again. This time not badly. I just pulled the shrapnel out, put on a bandage, and went on.

The end came on May 8, 1944. We went on to Bamberg and Le Havre. After that, we were on to the Hermitage and back to the good old USA.

It would be good that no human would ever have to go through what the American troops went through in WWII and all wars. Let's hope that the "higherups" in these countries around the world will think before starting something like that again.

Billy Cater, Cambridge, OH
Service Company, 22nd Infantry Regiment

Commander of the Guard

D-Day, plus one night, I was awakened by the sound of hobnail boots going by my foxhole. From that night on, as the self-appointed duty officer of the guard for our company I was selecting the posts, assigning the guard, and also checking them on an irregular schedule. Occasionally (with some incoming rounds), it was necessary to convince the occupant of a nearby foxhole that it was OK to share it with me.

The replacements that had not been assigned to companies were not always ready to dig in. They slept on top of the ground, but after an incoming round or two, the shovels were busy.

One night, checking a post that had fired several rounds of rifle fire, I was told they had challenged two shapes approaching them, decided they were Germans, and fired. They were posted between two hedgerows about fifty feet from a main road. I told them not to fire low and I crawled out the hedgerow and up the ditch on the main road. There was a German soldier in the ditch. I made him understand to stand up and go back to the guard post. I crawled behind him, as I did not know how the guards would react. By this time, the company commander and others were there to search the prisoner.

There was an object in his pant leg I could not get to, so it was necessary to start taking off his clothes. I found a knife tied to a string, looped around his neck, and hanging just above his knee. It was quite a knife. Press a lever and a blade about five inches long would pop out. Folded at the other end was a spike, about five inches long, probably used by the Navy. He was wounded, so we sent him to the medics.

George Wilson, Grand Ledge, MI
Companies E and F, 2nd Battalion, 22nd Infantry Regiment

The Unfortunate Cow

George Wilson, author of If You Survive, *sent a story that is not included in his well-written book. – Bob Babcock*

In mid-July, 1944, our E Company cooks said they found a freshly killed cow. (Hit by enemy fire, they said.) They made good use of all the meat to feed the company and buried the hide and other waste. The next day the Company commander was confronted by a highly excited French farmer who wanted pay for his dead cow. He contended that our cooks had killed his cow. The farmer insisted that the remains be dug up and claimed the hide was from his cow. The captain insisted this cow had been killed by German artillery. The French farmer left, still very angry.

He came back later that day with a Major from the military government who spoke French and was able to calm down the poor man when he told him the American government would pay for his cow. The captain was afraid they would make him pay, but was told the government had a special fund to take care of such problems—"But don't let it happen again," he said.

Dr. Lewis L. Jacobson, Eagle River, WI
Company G, 2nd Battalion,
22nd Infantry Regiment

Farm Boy's Wisdom

At one point, our platoon was receiving incoming artillery rounds. Some of us took shelter in a rickety old barn containing three cows. I concluded this was not a particularly protective building. Therefore, being a farm boy, I crouched beneath the cow for about ten minutes until the artillery fire lifted. The last time I was that close to a cow was for milking duties.

Jack Fox, Jacksonville, FL
Medic, 1st Battalion, 8th Infantry Regiment

Ernie Pyle Praises the Medics

*Jack Fox was with the 1st Battalion, 8th Infantry when Ernie Pyle wrote this
article in July 1944*

"Forgotten Medics" Ernie Pyle

Praise for the medics has been unanimous ever since this war started.
And, just as proof of what they go through, take this one detachment
of battalion medics that I was with. There were thirty-one men and two
officers (Captain Strawn and Captain Accardo). And in one seven-week
period of combat in Normandy this summer lost nine men killed and ten
wounded. A total of nineteen out of thirtythree men—a casualty ratio of
nearly sixty percent in seven weeks. As one aid man said, 'probably they
have been excluded from the Combat Infantryman's Badge because they
are technically noncombatants and don't carry arms.' But he suggested
that if this was true, they could still be given a badge with some distinc-
tive medical marking on it to set them off from medical aid men who
don't work right in the lines.

"So, I would propose to Congress or the War Department, or whoev-
er handles such things, that the ruling be altered to include medical aid
men in battalion detachments and on forward. They are the ones who
work under fire. Medics attached to regiments and to hospitals farther
back do wonderful work, too, of course, and are sometimes under shellfire. But they are seldom right out on the battlefield. So, I think it would
be fair to include only the medics who work from battalion on forward. I
have an idea the original ruling on CIBs was made merely through a mis-
understanding, and that there would be no objection to correcting it."

B.P. "Hank"Henderson, Knoxville, TN
Medic, 22nd Infantry Regiment

Crazy French Women

During the St. Lô breakthrough, we were attached to the 2nd Armored Division. The men not riding the tanks were riding with a trucking outfit to keep up with the Regiment. The 22nd got into an area that they proclaimed a rest stop for us. One of our medics went on a scouting mission and came back and told us there was a large, clear stream of water not far away. A bunch of us grabbed soap and towels and took off to the stream. There were two foot bridges across the stream about seventy-five or eighty feet apart. After we all got in, naked as jay birds, some French women were coming down to the upper bridge, but instead of crossing it, they came down to where we were to cross and stood on the bridge watching us swimming in the water without any clothes on. Crazy French women.

Norman Webb, Mount Airy, NC
HQ, 1st Battalion, 12th Infantry Regiment

Along Came God

I made the landing on Utah Beach. I got a small wound just above my left knee. The medic put a bandage on my wound. He said it would be OK and when he rose up, the German's bullet got him. He died near the water. Again, I got another piece of shrapnel to my left hand…more blood. That also did not get in my record. This happened during the St. Lô breakthrough. It was almost more than I could stand, but along came God. He stepped in and everything was OK.

Tom Reid, Marietta, GA
Cannon Company, 22nd Infantry Regiment and Company I,
3rd Battalion, 22nd Infantry Regiment

The First Motorcycle Ride

The place was somewhere in Normandy. The time was late July 1944. The 22nd Infantry Regiment found itself in reserve (for once). Any period when the Regiment was not committed to action was devoted to training, but, after chow one evening, somebody in the company discovered an abandoned German motorcycle, complete with sidecar, on the entrance road to our bivouac area.

Someone soon checked it out, and found it had gas in the tank. It was still capable of running. After a few people had ridden it, I was offered a chance to ride. Although I had never been on a motorcycle before, I asked a few questions about operation (mostly on how to stop it), and took off down the road.

I went about a mile, got it turned around and started back. It was quite an achievement. I congratulated myself, but I spoke too soon. If you have been to France, you may remember that the telephone poles are made of concrete. They last a long time, but are mighty hard when you hit them. Coming back, I swerved to the right to dodge an oncoming truck. No one had told me that the accelerator on the right handle was adjacent to the brake handle, and the more I swerved to the right, the faster I was going.

The motorcycle hit one of those concrete telephone poles and the impact threw me forward to land astride the gas tank. The best way I can describe the results is, I didn't know for some time whether I could ever be a father or not. Some troops nearby extricated me and the motorcycle from the concrete telephone pole, got me to the medics, and I was evacuated to a field hospital where I stayed for a week. Although no bones were broken, I was in severe agony, as you can imagine. I couldn't walk. In fact, it was days before I could stand up. Parts of my anatomy had swollen to grapefruit size and the only treatment was "time," for everything to return to normal.

After a week in the hospital and a few days rest at the Regimental aid station, I was able to return to duty, although I was limping. Luckily, nothing was permanently damaged and I went on to have three children who have blessed me with six grandchildren. Indeed, I was able to go on and finish the war with the 22nd Infantry and later go to Korea, and even later serve twenty-one months in Vietnam with MACV.

The short title for this article is "The First Motorcycle Ride." Needless to say, it was my last motorcycle ride, too. Cecil Boswell, Cannon Company, from Gainesville, GA, was present and witnessed my untimely accident and at reunions, he still asks me if I still ride. I have news for you, Cecil: Not until hell freezes over.

Franklin Shaw, Santa Fe, NM
Company F, 2nd Battalion, 22nd Infantry Regiment

Purple Heart

On D+6 (June 12, 1944), while XO and 2nd Platoon Leader of Company F, I caught a fragment from a German 88. That started me through the medivac channel: litter, jeep, ambulance, field hospital on the beach for emergency surgery, DUKW out to an LST, evac-hospital in tents in England, general hospital at Bath, and a second general hospital in Salisbury. No baths yet.

Finally, a husky American "country-gal" nurse (we had British sisters, also) announced to the ward: "Bath time—I'll wash up as far as possible and down as far as possible, but you will have to wash 'possible.' " Needless to say, there was not much "possible" in that crowd.

While I am at it, here is another story from those times. We were the first casualties to reach the general hospital. The Colonel and his entire staff were out in front to greet us. The next day, he came to the ward with his entourage, read a formal citation for the Purple Heart, and pinned the medal on each of us. It was a nice ceremony. Some weeks later, a ward boy came through pushing one of those carts used to carry the doctors' and nurses' supplies. "Anyone here who hasn't gotten his Purple Heart?" he asked and tossed the little boxes on beds as he wheeled down the ward. Familiarity changes priorities.

Joseph Janelli, Visalia, CA
Company M, 3rd Battalion, 8th Infantry Regiment

A Personal War

I would like to tell you how much of a personal war it was. The things that happen to the individual soldier are comparatively minor to the totality of combat.

On the way to Cherbourg, we approached the airport just south of Montebourg. The typical deployment of a machine gun platoon was to support a rifle company. One-half of my men were moving forward on the left side, while the second section was on the right side. The terrain was open rolling country. I moved forward with the first section, not yet in contact with the enemy. I decided to cross over to the right section, and naturally did it at a lope. Halfway across I hear this "Wumph!" and screech. It came from a German 88mm antiaircraft gun, which was part of the defense of the airport. The gun had lowered its barrel from the typical vertical position to snipe at me! That first shot changed my lope into an all-out run. The gunner was determined to stop me, and two more wumphs and screeches later I hit the dirt as I got to my second section. I hate to admit it, but necessity made me lower my trousers, pull my trench knife, and cut off my shorts. Yes, they were full. Being sniped at by an 88 was a scary experience. My platoon had two casualties during that battle to take the airport. It was at this time that orders came for the 8th Infantry Regiment to turn to the west and head for the coast to block German reinforcements from getting to Cherbourg. The other two regiments kept moving north, and finally, after other outfits moved up from the invasion beaches, they rejoined the division.

We were in the hedgerows of Normandy. The enemy that we kept from moving north had started to dig in. Each field, which varied in size from two to ten acres, was at least a daily battle. Several days later, I scrambled to the top of a four-foot high hedgerow, when a German popped up from his slit trench on the other side, rifle with bayonet attached and lunged at me. I had my carbine at the ready, and we were so close that the bayonet hit the little finger of my left hand. I swung toward him and pulled the trigger three times. He had fired one shot from his bolt-action rifle as his bayonet hit me, but that was his last one. Later, our medic put a band-aid on the finger, recorded the incident, and that got me my first Purple Heart.

A second personal event in the hedgerows campaign came after we had been relieved by one of Patton's armored divisions. They were in their first firefight, being blooded (getting combat experience), and were subjected to a counterattack, losing all the ground we had gained. The 4th Infantry Division was put back into action to retake the lost ground. It was a bloody attack—the Germans didn't like the idea of losing the ground they had taken. We did the job and were close to our original line. I told my platoon sergeant that we had been ordered to dig in on that line and that we would check the men to see how they were faring. We soon found out that the guns were low on ammunition and that re-supply would be delayed. On the way up to our position, we had passed one of Patton's tanks that had been abandoned by its crew after it had nosed down in the ditch next to the hedgerow.

Sergeant Langman and I went back to it to see if there was any machine gun ammunition still aboard. The M-4 tank also had .30-caliber machine guns, one of which was co-axially mounted to the right of its 75mm cannon in the turret. We knew that there were four or five boxes of ammo under the two seats in the hull. Langman scrambled into the turret, unlatched the seat, stuck his head through the hatch, and said, "Yes, all five boxes are here." He handed them to me through the hatch, and I put them on the ground, saying to him, "Maybe we're lucky enough to find five more," and he replied, "I'll find out." I ducked under the gun and leaned against it, waiting for him to go and see.

Now, I must tell you about the M-4 tank's characteristics. It had an engine in the rear with a front-drive system. This required a large ring transmission and a differential mechanism between two seats. Langman reached up to grab the turret ring, accidentally hit the gun's solenoid button, and "Bang!" it went off. The muzzle blast knocked me to the ground—my glasses and helmet went flying. I checked myself out, rising up on my left leg. It was OK. Then I checked on my right leg; I was still OK—no blood or other problems. I thought, "Was the damn thing booby-trapped?" I found my glasses and looked up to see Langman in the turret, white as a sheet. I asked him, "Are you OK?"

He said, "How about you?"

I said, "OK. Let's get the ammo and get the hell back with it." We did. A couple of weeks later, while we were regrouping for the move to St. Lô, we described the event to our company commander while we stood in front of a similar M-4. Looking up to the turret, I turned white as a sheet. I finally realized that the button he hit was about five inches away from the button that fired the co-axial machine gun. I'll never know if that machine gun was loaded and ready, but either it wasn't or I was lucky that Langman hit the button he did.

Incidents like those made a believer out of you, and reminded you that you were very much alone. At the St. Lô staging area, the officers were told to give the "big picture" to the troops. One of the guys spoke up, saying, "I don't give a damn about the big picture. All I want to know is, Who's on my right and who's on my left?" Yes, combat, for infantry-men, is very personal. Yes, it's time I quit reminiscing and get on with writing about the war.

B.P. "Hank" Henderson, Knoxville, TN
Medic, 22nd Infantry Regiment

Automatic Artillery

When Cherbourg surrendered, we were around the underground air base. It surrendered after we used loudspeakers telling them that Cherbourg had already surrendered. A German Colonel came out and said they would come out the next morning in an orderly file. They came out four abreast. One small young lieutenant spoke to some of us and he said that he knew we were going to shoot him, but before we did, he would like to see that automatic artillery in action. He thought that the batteries firing in such close rhythm were automatic.

Bill Parfitt, Elmira, NY
Company G, 22nd Infantry Regiment and HQ, 4th Infantry Division

Anchovies Anyone?

Some of the little things that happened were the funniest of all. I re-member the huge underground storage places in Cherbourg that were stocked to the roofs with anchovies and tuna fish. I learned to love the tuna fish and still do if I can locate it packed in oil. That was top-grade eating. The anchovies I cannot go to this day. There were cases of this stuff in most of the vehicles until they were used up.

The bathing deals were always something else, too. It was always top secret when we were staying in some busted-up town and someone had located a coalfired water heater that was usable. Someone else would make up a list of names, and the news would go by word of mouth as to when your turn would be. I also remember the steel mirrors that most of us had.

Sigfred Nelson, Royal Oak, MI
Company I, 3rd Battalion, 8th Infantry Regiment

Out of the Fog

Another experience took place in dense fog while "Sig" was alone, at night, on outpost duty, with Germans everywhere. That was perhaps the most lonesome and terrifying feeling an infantryman could have. A shadow appeared in the fog, but no associated noise. What should be done—throw a grenade, or fire my rifle and disclose my position with a muzzle flash thereby alerting the entire unit? The image grew larger, the need for action more pressing. Off came the M-1 safety; the weapon was directed toward the intruder. The fog thinned a bit and, lo, before this frightened GI was the image of a horse wandering through the fields. Tension was eased, and all was quiet for the balance of guard duty.

B.P. "Hank" Henderson, Knoxville, TN
Medic, 22nd Infantry Regiment

"Detroit" Germans

Before we reached Cherbourg, during the fourth week of June 1944, Captain Marshan came up to me and said, "Hank, we have three wounded German soldiers down the highway, and we have been given orders to get them. Take your litter squad and these two (pointing to two men), about a hundred to a hundred fifty yards before you get to the curve in the road. Then bear off to the left and come in from the rear of the buildings, because the Germans have observation on the curve. Anything that comes down the road gets artillery at the curve."

We went off the road at about a hundred and fifty yards and came in from the rear of the buildings. The wounded Germans were in front of the buildings. We started to give them morphine, and they said, "Nix, nix," but we shot them with morphine anyway. We started to go back the way we came in. When we were leaving the buildings in the rear, we were bracketed with artillery shells. I could see them hitting the ground in front of me and to the left of me. There were twelve litter-bearers and three wounded German soldiers.

Now this is the hard part: Can you believe that none of us got a scratch out of that artillery? As we went on our way after the barrage lifted, the Germans began to speak English to us. It turned out that all three of them had lived in the United States and worked in the automobile plants. They went to Germany to visit relatives and were not allowed to return to the United States, but were put into the German army.

Sam Nelson, Ladson, SC
Company H, 2nd Battalion, 22nd Infantry Regiment

Danish Prisoner

While pushing toward Cherbourg, in June 1944, I came upon a trail leading toward the enemy. I saw a white flag waving on a branch and called for someone to come forth. A German, in uniform, came forth and handed me his pistol and a note, "I am Danish, not German." It was my first prisoner, but I thought it odd the way it happened since my father was born in Denmark.

Also, here is an after-the-war story from Sam:

I was living in Raleigh, NC and the metal in my right arm was giving me some trouble, so I made an appointment and went to the Winston-Salem VA hospital. While I was being examined, the doctor asked, "Do you recall seeing me before?" I said, "No." He then said that from records he had seen he was the doctor who had performed surgery on me in France in August 1944.

Francis W. Glaze Jr., Clearwater, FL
HQ, 8th Infantry Regiment

Military Police Training

A s I remember, Bed Check Charlie (BCC) was a twin-engine Henkel airplane and the engines were purposely out of synchronization. BCC came over at dusk almost every evening for reconnaissance—to draw fire and find gun positions, and to drop antipersonnel bombs on targets of opportunity. That night we were the "opportunity."

These APBs were the so-called "cluster bombs." That particular night the cluster was probably a mix of about one hundred small baseball-sized bomblets in a light metal housing. They had three different fuses that were activated on impact when a small central charge exploded, scattering the bomblets over an acre or so. Usually the fuses were assembled to sense impact, time delay, and motion—the rationale being that the "impact" bomblets would cause the primary casualties, the "time-delay" ones went off as medics and men came to help. The "motion-sensing" bombs were to keep you "loose" in case you thought they were duds and picked them up or kicked them to a side—"Boom!"

That particular night we had forty to fifty German prisoners in a barn near the Regimental CP. I never liked to keep prisoners overnight so I radioed 4th Infantry Division MPs to come and pick them up by truck. The MPs pulled in the area just as BCC was looking for action. We did not fire to give our position away, but someone on our flank did and alerted BCC to drop a cluster. Then, all hell broke loose.

The lead vehicle was a half-ton with four MPs in it. One of the impact bomblets hit the driver on the head. The two MPs sitting behind were mortally wounded. The driver was decapitated and the MP beside the driver was uninjured but scared "sh-tless." The lone survivor took off running and, to my knowledge, hasn't stopped running since.

To make matters worse, one of the bomblets ignited the hay in the barn, and the barn burned for hours—it seemed like days. BCC circled for a while and then finally went away. I radioed Division MP headquarters and asked for more MPs. Reluctantly, they arrived.

Our Company had five casualties. None were killed, but one was Warrant Officer Joe Powell, one of our old regulars. When he came back to us several weeks later, I never let him forget. He had more garrison time than I did, but I had more combat time than he did. At the time, I was twenty-one, going on one hundred, and he was a regular of twenty years. He realized that combat time was all that counted by our standards.

The next morning, I was "cruising" the area, and one of the "quiet ones," Hugh Jetton, asked me to come and look at his foxhole. I had been haranguing for covers for foxholes but met with typical GI resistance for weeks. Jetton showed me his cover—some boards with six inches of dirt on top. In the middle, on the top, was the neatest little "bomb" crater you ever saw. That was the first time he'd ever covered his foxhole, but now he was a believer. He converted the rest of the Company. They too, wanted to protect the "family jewels."

The Division MPs were very nervous after that. They preferred that we bring the prisoners back. Of course, as you could predict, there was, "no way, Jose."

…come and get a little combat experience."

Mark Channing, Orlando, FL
Company G, 2nd Battalion, 22nd Infantry Regiment

French Demoiselle

After fifty plus years, events once in sharp focus become blurred or forgotten. But you are pushing for a story, so here goes. By way of background, Lum Edwards pulled me out of Company G into the 2nd Battalion, 22nd Infantry Regiment Headquarters when he found out that I spoke fluent German and very good French. We were not doing any real interrogating, just quickies for possible tactical value before sending prisoners back to the rear.

Here's the first story.

I was still with Company G. It took place around D+9 and is a fine example of the concept that opportunities should not be wasted. We had just retaken Montebourg, for the fourth time I think, after a hell of a firefight lasting most of the day. It was late afternoon, and our platoon leader was missing. I was with the search party, and we found him rather quickly. He had a French demoiselle, with skirts hoisted, backed into a doorway, and they were having a good time. Being of the courteous generation, we naturally looked the other way and quickly left. The lieutenant's name will forever remain a secret with me—if I could remember it—which of course, I can't.

My second story isn't even a story. It is just an event that happened, at a guess, sometime around D+15.

General Barton produced the event and in the process, made one hell of an impression on a not quite nineteen-year-old kid—me. What he did was simply to have all of us (certainly the battalion and maybe even the entire 22nd Infantry Regiment), gather in an open field to give us a twenty-minute pep talk. He had P47s flying cover, or so he claimed. I thought then, "Boy, that is one crazy SOB." I haven't changed my mind in all these years. Maybe some of the guys can shed more light on this event, including the whys and wherefores.

Martin L. King, (Deceased) Wills Point, TX
Company H, 2nd Battalion, 22nd Infantry Regiment

"Spit" Bath

On June 22, 1944, I was caught up in a battle on the road just three days short of the Cherbourg victory. I received head wounds that sent me to a beach hospital. My head was bound, covered with bandage around and around, covering my eyes and all of the right side of my head, and I had a 24-day old beard.

So, here I am in the "gathering and examination tent," in pain, hungry, tired, and all that stuff, when a nurse and a ward boy came in and began to look me over. They tried to shave me (for a closer exam) with cold-watered lather and a safety razor. I gave them the extent of my vocabulary, and they stopped. Then at one point the nurse and attendant began to remove my filthy clothing. The nurse gave me a rundown on what to expect and asked if I minded a "spit bath." I said, "Well, I'm sure it's time 'cause everything I've got needs cleaning and scratching—and I don't care which comes first."

Marvin A. Simpson, (Deceased) Baton Rouge, LA
Company D, 4th Medical Battalion

Gas Attack

In late July 1944 we were stationed near St. Lô when all hell broke loose. A gas attack, the last thing expected, occurred during the night, and we scrambled for our gas masks. After about one hour, the all clear was given—it had been a false alarm. What a relief. Early that morning, wave after wave of Allied aircraft flew directly overhead, which was the start of the St. Lô breakthrough. They were so low we could see the bomb bay doors open and the bombs falling. Unfortunately, some of the bombs were released too soon, killing and maiming some of our own troops. The Germans surrendered or retreated and we were on our way, almost nonstop, to Paris.

Peter Triolo, Pueblo, CO
HQ, 1st Battalion, 12th Infantry Regiment

On to Cherbourg

Cherbourg had a harbor that the Navy and D-Day troops used to resupply the DDay operation. The 4th Infantry Division was part of the American forces that captured the city of Cherbourg on June 25, 1944. The harbor at Cherbourg was protected by an outer island fort, about one thousand yards out. The Navy refused to come in and occupy the harbor because their guns couldn't neutralize the outer fort's protective fire.

The 4th Infantry Division was asked to go out and capture or neutralize the fort.

The Air Corps started with 500-pound bombs, with no results. On the second operation they dropped 1,000-pound bombs. It did not damage the main fort, but it did destroy anything that could burn on the top. Fortunately, during the raids, they wounded the commander of the fort and some of his officers. They also destroyed the radio, causing them to lose contact with German headquarters. The survivors requested medical help. Colonel Jackson of the 1st Battalion refused their request unless they surrendered. It was finally negotiated that they would surrender the fort.

The harbor was mined with metal-reacting mechanical mines. We found a harbormaster to take a patrol that included myself, another lieutenant, my Germanspeaking sergeant, and about fifteen men from the rifle company to the island fort. We sailed out to the fort in a wooden sailboat.

The fort was formed like a half moon with gun placements on each end and one in the center. These placements were protected by sliding steel doors eight inches thick. The fort was built of concrete. As I recall, the base of the fort at the water line was over fifteen-feet thick. You would never believe what was in that fort besides the three big guns. A modern eight-bed hospital, canned food, water, and desserts to last one hundred and fifty men for months.

Upon arriving at the fort, we formed all the Germans on top of the fort wall above the center gun location, with a machine gun crew on both sides. The next day, we were informed that boats would be coming to take us off the island. The army sent out "Army Duck" trucks made of steel that could travel on water or land. When the Germans saw the steel constructed Ducks and were ordered to go down the stairwell to load these boats, they refused and kept yelling, "Mines! Mines!" We had our German sergeant inform them either they load or we leave them there dead. We fired a burst of bullets from the machine guns over their heads. Our passengers got a lot more willing, and down the stairwell they headed and started loading.

Upon reaching land, my driver, Shanks, was there waiting for me with a truck. He informed me that the Regiment had pulled out that morning and he was our ride back.

John Worthman, (Deceased) Medic, 22nd Infantry Regiment

An Aid Man's View of War

The dead and dying in the streets were an appalling sight, but particularly behind all the hedgerows. So was the smell. On the edge of the very narrow road from Cherbourg were many of the reinforcements. They, and most of their bicycles, were in the ditches. So now we bicycled.

Those were busy times. Around the clock we were treating wounded, carrying them, and moving them to the aid station. You slept in a slit trench and ate all you could. I routinely had two breakfasts, two lunches and two dinners of C-rations, often one or two D-bars. They were heavy chocolate bars loaded with vitamins and what all.

We moved slowly toward Cherbourg, toward the obstinate enemy. Finally, on about D+9, we captured the city, but the port had been ruined by the Germans before they left. Now, we had two days' rest, and for the first time since D-1, I took off my boots. The socks were shreds, and my feet were full of fungus. Two days later, with new socks and boots, we moved down the peninsula toward Carentan. On the way, at a depot near Utah, I found a crate of paratrooper's boots and got two pairs of size 8-E; the best foot gear I had ever worn.

Now, came more of the hedgerows. The Germans had time to organize the artillery and bring up Mark V and VI tanks. The infantry of both sides were behind the hedgerows with only a narrow field between. Tanks were vulnerable when they exposed their bottoms when climbing a hedgerow, and the artillery was too erratic. It was mortar, rifle, and machine gun time. I was an aid man with Company E and found out how much a platoon depended on aid men, if only for morale. I had a better look at the Normans also. They continued their farming unless the fighting was in their immediate vicinity, and they were genuinely happy to see us. A boy of about twelve years carried a large pewter tray piled up with fried chicken covered with a white cloth. He walked down a lane toward our platoon, seemed to ignore the sporadic small arms fire, and offered us chicken. Good? It was the best. We had two months' pay in our pockets in francs, and we would put a paper note on his tray and take a piece of chicken. It was "funny money" to us, but when we later figured its value, we think he made out with about two hundred dollars. We treated and evacuated any civilian wounded, and we respected their stubbornness and courage.

The fighting was very fierce and unrelenting. The smells became worse, the sights of mutilation and death more terrible, but strangely, we began to live with them and accept them as one would an undesirable background noise. I became a corporal about this time, as much as anything due to the attrition rate in aid-men in Normandy. Our regiment had eighty percent of its aid-men lost in Normandy. If you remained

212 ⬥ War Stories: D-Day

alive, unhurt, and not captured, you were almost bound to be promoted. The attrition rate was great. Riflemen were replaced so regularly that the remaining soldiers began to think, morbidly, that their turn was near. We learned to sleep in the rain, never undressing except when rotated to the rear, and eating everything in sight.

Finally, the fighting neared the St. Lô-Periers road. We were preparing to open the base of the peninsula and let General Patton and his troops pour out. The hedgerows were ours. The 22nd Infantry Regiment was now combat-experienced and a very good infantry unit, although casualties had been high. Through June and July there had been 2,664 wounded and 675 killed. Most of this was up to, and through, the breakout of the Third Army. We had assimilated too many replacements too fast but had maintained our effectiveness. I was happy and a little surprised to be promoted to sergeant.

George Knapp, Westchester, IL
Chaplain, HQ, 12th Infantry Regiment

A Chaplain's View of War

After a few months in England, the 4th Infantry Division made the amphibious landing as invading assault troops on Utah Beach on D-Day, June 6, 1944. Because of severe weather the invasion was postponed a day, so we bounced around in the English Channel on that day of waiting. Many soldiers were seasick. I was a bit sick but never missed a meal of those delicious C-rations on the ship. On the morning of June 6 we went down the side of the ship on the rope ladders to the landing craft bouncing wildly on the rough sea. Virginia wonders how I made it down with my Field Altar Communion set in one hand and a personal effects bag in the other. Anyhow, I made it, and the landing craft luckily made it to the beach, and the ramp went down on that sandy beach.

Some assault waves had preceded us, so we witnessed burning vehicles, bomb craters, wounded, dead, and dying soldiers, and other devastations of war. Our goal was to keep moving. It was a numbing shock for me to see the destruction of material and the dead and dying. As a pastor, I had officiated at a number of funerals. All of my life, I had seen the deceased all dressed up, with nice caskets, flowers etc. This was different. In my memory, I can see the paratroopers hanging in the trees of the wooded areas just in from the beach. They had dropped sometime after midnight, and in the darkness their parachutes had became entangled in the tall trees. They had been shot and killed by the enemy as they hung there. I also saw gliders that had landed among the trees, resulting in death or injury to the occupants. One glider was carrying four soldiers with a jeep behind them. When it crashed into a large tree not far above the ground, the jeep broke loose from its moorings, crashing into and killing the men. We had to keep moving, and there was nothing we could do for the men, except breathe a prayer, so we kept on moving. The dead men, by the way, looked as if they had just fallen asleep and were sitting there.

Speaking of trees, two medics and I used a tree trunk that first night to sit around and catch a bit of rest. I was still carrying my field altar and "ditty-bag." My jeep and trailer, with my chaplain's assistant, had landed via a different craft. For days, I had no opportunity to use my jeep trailer as it was commandeered in carrying the wounded.

At first, the three chaplains of the 12th Infantry Regiment stayed with our individual battalions. I was the 3rd Battalion chaplain. After a week or so, orders came from the Division Chaplain that the Commanding General wanted his chaplains to serve at the Regimental Aid Station, but not right at the front lines amidst the fighting. The General said, "I only have fifteen chaplains and if you are killed or wounded, there is no one to replace you." Some served a bit behind the front lines.

The 12th Infantry Regiment did lose one chaplain, killed instantly by enemy shrapnel while he was in the Regimental Command tent. Other chaplains were replaced due to injury, illness, etc.

I received a minor enemy shrapnel injury and was awarded the Purple Heart. I guess my fellow soldiers thought I did a good job, as I was also awarded the Bronze Star. It was not easy, even though I had volunteered for the chaplaincy. After about a week in combat, it almost got the best of me. After hearing a young company commander talk of getting orders to move out again and how exhausted his men were, it hit me emotionally. I just walked across to the other side of the field, lay down and had a good cry. I then said to myself, "Enough is enough. I volunteered for this job, so let's get going."

As history recorded, the 4th Infantry Division had the highest rate of casualties of any outfit that fought in Europe. We had two hundred casualties a day. Some died before they could be evacuated. Besides our prayers and words of comfort and encouragement, we helped the wounded by giving a drink of water, etc. If their hands were wounded, we helped them enjoy a few drags on a cigarette.

Clyde R. Stodghill, Cuyahoga Falls, OH
Company G, 2nd Battalion, 12th Infantry Regiment

Loneliness on a Battlefield

On the days when I carried the radio, it was hard to keep in touch with our latest company commander, although I was always supposed to stay nearby. He frequently told me to wait in a certain place and then would wander off somewhere.

For all practical purposes that meant the radio was useless. I attributed his determination to keep me at a distance to two things: First, he did not want anyone keeping tabs on his actions when the company was in the attack because he tended to linger behind. Second, he believed the stories about the radio drawing artillery and mortar fire and the antennae pinpointing the location of the key men.

He told me to wait beside a hedgerow one dark and cloudy evening when most of Company G was engaged in a firefight up ahead. The two forward platoons had advanced the length of a field and then turned right, apparently led that way by the Germans. The captain should have been with them. Instead, we were following along with the reserve platoon in the first field, staying close to the hedgerow on the right when he told me to wait there.

I kneeled and watched as the others reached the end of the field fifty yards away, then made the turn at a break in the hedgerow and were gone. An hour of daylight remained, but dark clouds that seemed low enough to reach out and touch had chased away all color so that only blacks and grays remained.

Twilight—the loneliest hour of the day for those away from home, the time when a light glowing in a window should mean friendly faces awaiting, a home-cooked supper, and later, a warm and comfortable bed.

Such thoughts were fleeting, impossible dreams that were best pushed aside. Now a glow in a window meant a building was afire. Supper, if it came at all, would be from a box of cold K-rations. The damp hard ground would provide the only bed—an empty world where comfort was a memory and killing was the norm. That is all that was left.

No feeling of loneliness can equal that of being alone on a battlefield. Soon the firing ceased ahead, and a silence more menacing than any gunfire added to the isolation. No bird chirped in the foliage overhead, no little animal rustled about in the undergrowth. They had sought shelter, leaving me as the lone living creature, in the open.

As the minutes ticked away, I grew apprehensive. Were infiltrators with knives and guns on the prowl? Among the hedgerows, enemy raiding parties and patrols were constantly searching for victims. What could I do if half a dozen Germans suddenly appeared?

Should I wait there, following the orders of an incompetent commander, or, should I go ahead and hope to find the company where men with guns were concealed, knowing that to men wary of any movement, I was at risk of being shot by either friend or foe?

The decision was made for me when a man appeared at the far end of the field and beckoned me forward. Elated over not having been forgotten, I ran toward the place where the soldier, who now had vanished again, had stood motioning for me.

I made the turn without slowing down and found myself in a long farm track no more than ten yards wide with hedgerows on each side. Forty yards ahead, a man was waving me on. The same man, I assumed, and I ran on. I had covered half the distance between us when he raised his rifle, grinning as he did so, and only then did I see he was wearing a German helmet. In the gathering darkness, his uniform looked no different from my own.

He had me dead to rights. There was nothing I could do but make a futile dive toward the ground. When a man has his weapon aimed at you and yours is not pointed at him, it's all over but the squeezing of the trigger.

But rather than coming from his rifle, the shot was fired from off to my left. A stunned look came over the German's face as he turned halfway around, the muzzle of his rifle turning with him and drooping toward the ground. He stood that way for several seconds, then slumped to his knees for a moment before slowly falling forward as if he had suddenly grown weary and needed to rest.

As I rose up on my knees, then to my feet, a Company G man came over to me. He guided me to a field on the left where the company was deployed. I asked who had fired the shot, and he told me it was Nick Scala. It seemed he had been watching the German all along, wondering what he was up to until I had come charging around the corner.

I don't know how Nick Scala, who later received a battlefield commission (but at that time was the machine gun section sergeant), scored on the rifle range. There is a vast difference, however, between hitting a paper target and hitting a man when there will be no opportunity for a second shot. At the latter, Nick had few, if any, peers. I was glad that he was such a deadly shot when it counted, but I wished he hadn't waited quite so long to fire. That was Nick's way, though.

Our less-than-competent captain had to have been responsible for the way in which the company was deployed along both sides of the same hedgerow. It made no sense whatsoever. Men were digging in on the opposite side, but on mine, we had taken over slit trenches abandoned by the Germans. That meant we lacked the protection of a hedgerow if Germans returned from the direction in which they had departed. They often did so.

My hole had belonged to an officer. He had left his "dress" cap behind; the kind that had a leather bill and rose to a high peak in front. Below the peak was the SS Death's head insignia. It would have made a fine souvenir, one that in coming years would have been worth a lot of money. I had no way of taking it with me, of course. An infantryman in combat has enough of a load to carry without gathering keepsakes.

A helmet also lay beside the hole. Unless he had fought bareheaded, the officer had been wounded or killed and then carried away by his men. Had he still been on his feet, it was highly unlikely that he would have left his cap behind.

In my exuberance over being back with other men rather than off by myself, and at having watched as Scala killed the German, I did a stupid thing. Acting the fool, I put the German helmet on my head and stood up so that everyone could appreciate my display of ignorance. That came to an abrupt ending when a shot was fired from the other side of the hedgerow. The bullet passed close enough to my head to crack like a pair of boards being slapped together.

I turned and peered over the hedgerow and there was Nick Scala. His expression told me what he had thought of my performance. After staring at me for a moment he said, "Don't fool around." I never did again.

Clyde R. Stodghill, Cuyahoga Falls, OH
Company G, 2nd Battalion, 12th Infantry Regiment

Along the Carentan Road

The two-lane, blacktop highway running south from Carentan to Périers, slopes gently upward until it reaches the village of Sainteny, midway between the two towns. The rise is all but imperceptible, but it is the high ground, so to military leaders it was the Sainteny Hill, and therefore had to be taken.

A short distance west of the road was a vast marsh. The Germans, leaving a narrow passageway in between, flooded both it and the ground to the east. For this reason some historians call the fighting there the "Battle of the Isthmus."

The land between the flooded areas is laced with small, irregularly shaped fields surrounded on all sides by high dirt hedgerows ten feet thick at the bottom, two to four feet at the top. Centuries old, these hedgerows are crowned by trees and underbrush whose roots make them all but impenetrable. Because of them, other historians favor the term "Battle of the Hedgerows."

Farm trails with hedgerows on each side run between some of the fields, creating sunken roads made dark and forbidding even by daylight. The area is dotted by settlements that are little more than a few buildings at a crossroad. Apple orchards are near some farmyards, and the farms are often situated at a place where two of the dirt roads meet.

A Frenchman pronounces the name of the village SAHN-tuh-nay. American infantrymen who had never heard of it, let alone heard the pronunciation say, "Saint Any."

Little has changed over the centuries in the land near the village. In peacetime, it is a place of tranquil beauty cooled by ocean breezes in the summer, warmed by them in winter. A hiker can set out from Carentan in the morning, have lunch at Sainteny, and then arrive in Periers in time for a shower and a drink before dinner. Not in July of 1944, however.

Signs now call it the "Route Americaine," but the Carentan Road was not the place to be a rifleman during that deadly summer.

In its first real action the 83rd Division, which had gained high marks in training, jumped off from a position just south of Carentan before dawn on the Fourth of July. A tremendous barrage preceding the attack was laid down by artillery and guns from offshore ships. From the start, it was a disaster. At our assembly area near Appeville, we heard reports of the fighting from panicky support troops of the 83rd. We were unaware of it, but late in the day Colonel Friedrich Von Der Heydte, commander of the German 6th Parachute Regiment, returned captured medics under a flag of truce, along with a note saying he was sure the 83rd needed them more than he did, and expressing the hope that if the situation were ever reversed, he would be extended the same courtesy.

As we set out to join the action on the wet, dreary morning of July 5, we heard that some men of the 83rd had shot Germans attempting to surrender while holding safe conduct passes. The Germans retaliated at night by having tanks with beacon lights move from hedgerow to hedgerow while riflemen disposed of the offenders.

The 12th Infantry, vanguard of the 4th Infantry Division in entering the battle, spent the night a short distance behind the front before taking over the ground west of the highway in the morning. Shortly before dark, Captain Jason C. Hardee, commander of Company G, gathered us in a semicircle and reminded us that there would be no drinking on the line, although the opportunity rarely arose. Then he said, "We've all heard stories about prisoners being shot. What you do in that respect is up to you, but if a man fights me fair and square, field for field, hedgerow for hedgerow, and then gets in a tough spot, I'm going to treat him the way I'd want to be treated in the same circumstances."

Captain Hardee would be mortally wounded the next day, but his words were heeded. With rare exceptions, prisoners were well treated by the men of Company G. With the captain as he spoke were Platoon Sergeant Bob Everidge and Squad Leader Jimmy Hewston. They also would die within a month.

Dawn broke quietly on July 6, and bright sunlight quickly burned off the morning mist. Without the usual sounds of war, there was little to warn us of what lay ahead. After leaving our blanket rolls near the kitchen truck, we assembled on the road beside our field.

As company radioman for the day, I was to stay close to Captain Hardee. I took advantage of this to sneak a look at a map he was studying. A short distance ahead was the Carentan Road—just north of a few dots on the map called Le Verimesnil. The name meant nothing to me, nor did anything else on the map.

The day was so pleasant that when we reached the highway I was wishing we could go on hiking for hours, but we had gone only a short distance when I could see the men ahead turning into a field on the right. Here and there, men clad in olive drab dress uniforms lay dead. It was surprising that anyone would wear a color so easily visible in the lush green countryside.

Other men from the 83rd lay in slit trenches. "This is the outfit I should be in," called Platoon Sergeant Eddie Wolfe. "Nine o'clock and they're still in the sack." "Better take a closer look, Eddie," said Joe Medaros, a nineteen-year old rifleman, who, by chance, was from Wolfe's hometown, Taunton, Massachusetts.

That led me to take a closer look. What I saw left me stunned. These men were not sleeping—they were dead—each with his bayonet protruding from his back. How could such a thing have happened? Did sentries fall asleep, or had they failed to resist when marauders came in the night?

We crossed several more fields with McDonald, a West Virginian who loved the music of the hills, quietly singing "Worried Mind." He was the second man ahead of me when he stepped on a mine, the kind we called a "castrater" because it spewed pellets like ball bearings straight upward. His helmet flew high in the air along with a shoe with a foot still inside of it.

Eddie Wolfe was the first to reach McDonald. He cradled Mac's head on one knee, but there was nothing he could do to ease the agonizing pain. Eddie looked up at those of us gathered around and said, "of all people, why did it have to be McDonald?" He didn't expect an answer, and, of course, there was none.

A unique variety of fear was experienced when someone nearby stepped on a mine. A giddy, lightheadedness that made it seem that your mind had left your body, and you were looking down from above. Where there was one mine, there could be more, so now your body, which would have to move again, had become something to fear, an enemy.

According to regulations, we shouldn't have stopped as we did. We quickly moved on to overtake the others and, as we did, so the ripping sound of a fast firing Spandau machine gun came from ahead. A second machine gun, rifles, and burp guns quickly joined in the firing. The men out front had made contact; the fight was about to begin.

We ran now, crouching a little, and joined the others in deploying along a hedgerow facing an unusually broad field. It was a strange hedgerow, seemingly stripped of all foliage. The field ahead sloped gently downward to a conventional hedgerow topped by trees and underbrush about eighty or ninety yards away. It was there that the Germans waited.

By stopping I had become separated from Captain Hardee, and as I looked around, I seemed to be among strangers. Had the weight of the radio slowed me so much that I had been overtaken by Company E, which had been following? Before I had time to decide whether or not to go in search of the captain, an incident as bizarre as any I witnessed during the war occurred.

A lieutenant wearing a trench coat came walking along the top of the hedgerow. I knew from having caught a brief glimpse of him in Cherbourg, that a trench coat, something not seen before at the front, was the attire favored by General J. Lawton Collins, the VII Corps commander known as "Lightning Joe." This had to be a copycat—a staff officer from Corps Headquarters. Didn't the fool realize he was clearly visible to every German across the field? They didn't fire though, probably because they were interested in learning the reason for this suicidal behavior.

As he walked along, the officer kept repeating the same message: "Six tanks are going to cross this field, and the 2nd Battalion is going to follow them."

Had he said it a thousand times, the order would not have made sense. Two machine guns, perhaps more, were covering the field and with them were many men armed with rifles and machine pistols. What chance did we have of making it across?

In the coming days, we learned by brutal experience that Lightning Joe didn't understand the lesson that had been learned at the Somme in 1916: men cannot succeed by charging across an open field in the face of machine gun fire. In his book, Lightning Joe, Collins wrote that no commander worth his salt liked to order men to make a frontal attack, but sometimes it was necessary—and futile. Any private on the line could

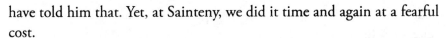

have told him that. Yet, at Sainteny, we did it time and again at a fearful cost.

In his book, Overlord, British military historian Max Hastings wrote: "If the German army was a superb fighting machine, a decisive factor in its ability to defend Normandy for so long and to such effect, was the superiority of almost all its weapons in quality, if not in quantity, to those of the Allied ground forces.

"What mattered was the weight of fire to saturate the battle area. For this, the Germans possessed the supreme weapons in their MG-34 and 42 machine guns—invariable known among the Allies as Spandaus—with their fabulous rate of fire drowning out the measured hammer of the British Bren or the American BAR. The MG-42's tearing, rasping twelve hundred rounds a minute, against the Bren's five hundred rounds a minute, proved deeply demoralizing to men advancing against it." Indeed it did, and with good reason.

I raised my head for another look at the field. A quick look, of course. A little to my left was a depression in the ground, one that ran nearly to the opposite hedgerow. Three or four large trees spaced well apart grew there. The shallow draw wasn't wide, perhaps ten yards, but could provide at least a semblance of cover. A number of dead cows also lay ahead, their legs extending grotesquely outward.

Where, I wondered, were our own officers? Major O'Malley or Captain Hardee could have devised a more sensible plan. They could not, however, countermand an order handed down by Collins. To be sure of that, he had sent one of his "hacks" to take charge.

The tanks, when they arrived, were not Shermans, just light tanks that looked as though they could be split asunder with a can opener or a pocketknife. They spread out on the right side of the field and lumbered along toward the Germans.

As they started out, the officer from VII Corps came running back along the hedgerow. Blood streamed down his face and drenched the front of his trench coat. This surely would have placed him in great favor with Lightning Joe. As he ran, he kept calling out, "Up and at 'em!" Not, "Follow me," because he had no intention of going along.

That other cry, the infantry battle cry, echoed all along the line. "Follow me, third platoon!" "First squad, follow me!" Follow me! Follow me! And we did, pushing up from the ground, heart in mouth, going over the hedgerow and running out into the open field. A hopeless endeavor… mass suicide.

The Germans had been waiting quietly, aiming a shot now and then to remind us they were there, but they opened fire as soon as we appeared. There were more of them than we were accustomed to facing. The loud and deadly fusillade blanketed the field.

I ran as I had learned to run by watching the Germans, rifle trailing at my side in my right hand, crouching as low as possible without sacrificing speed. Even with forty extra pounds of radio on my back, I was able to keep pace with those running at port arms, as Americans were taught to do. I headed slightly to the left toward that depression in the ground.

A German, overly eager to get at us, vaulted over the hedgerow ahead. A foolish move, leaving his covered position, but he was grinning as he came down with feet well apart and began traversing back and forth with an assault rifle. He had cast his helmet aside, revealing curly blond hair and was dressed in black—a tanker's uniform. A brave man, but not a wise or prudent one.

He had to be stopped. I joined several others in firing on the run. Someone's aim was true; the young German was hurled back against the hedgerow and then slumped to the ground in a sitting position… dead.

The six puny tanks were three-quarters of the way across the field when the Germans opened fire with 75 or 88-millimeter guns. There was no way of knowing if the fire came from other tanks or from self-propelled or stationary antitank guns. Whatever, there had to have been more than one because the shots followed each other as rapidly as a man could fire a semi-automatic rifle.

Five shots, five tanks knocked out. The sixth turned tail and ran. Men came out of the turrets of several of the tanks and then took off on the run. None made it far.

Men were dropping around me. There was no point in zigzagging; it could mean zigging or zagging into the path of a bullet as easily as dodging one. When I was close enough to the shallow draw, I dived head first for the protection it offered. Others were there ahead of me, some firing at the top of the German hedgerow to cover those still in the open field. Bob Everidge and several others I knew were there, so I crawled forward to join them. It was good to be among familiar faces again.

Bodies were lying in the field, and there were cries for help. Some who had fallen were moving a little and some lay still. Several of those who moved would jerk as aimed shots from German riflemen found their mark. Some men had taken shelter behind dead cows, but none dared rise up to fire. No one was still running toward the German hedgerow. The frontal attack had been doomed from the start, of course. Our ranks were considerably thinner and one German was dead; that was all that had been accomplished.

What happened next was a display of courage unlike anything we had seen before. A dozen or so Germans leaped over their hedgerow and headed for the knocked out tanks. Several dropped to their hands and knees and crawled the last few yards.

With sweat streaming down your forehead and blurring your vision, it was impossible to use the rear sight of an M-1 rifle for a well-aimed shot, but like a number of others, I fired as best I could. No one was successful; all the Germans climbed onto the tanks and dropped down through the open turret hatches.

We could only watch in disbelief as the turrets began rotating. They stopped when the guns were aimed at us and then we had to duck down as they began firing. Apparently the Germans were members of tank crews because they certainly knew what to do.

Someone expressed everyone's feelings by asking a rhetorical question: "Who in hell are those guys over there?"

We would find out later in the day; we had just had our first look at the SS in action. Facing us was the 17th SS Panzer Grenadier Division. In the days that followed we would also meet what remained of the 6th Parachute Regiment, and there were a number of times when tanks from the 2nd Panzer Division, das Reich, would come forward to strike, and then quickly vanish again.

The 17th SS Panzer Grenadier Division was one of the few elite units still available to the Germans. Its men had been training together since the previous October, so their spirit and determination was not like that of the watered-down divisions of 1944 that had been severely weakened during the brutal fighting on the Russian front.

Unlike the black-clad SS units at concentration camps, men other than tankers in the Waffen SS, the combat branch of Heinrich Himmler's organization wore field gray uniforms like those of the Wehrmacht. The quality seemed superior, however. On a black band near the cuff of their tunics, SS men had the name of their division written in silver lettering. More often than not, the SS grenadiers wore camouflage blouses over their tunics.

The 17th SS was named for a robber baron of the Middle Ages, Goetz Von Berlichingen. Their namesake had lost a hand in battle so he fashioned one of iron as a replacement. The 17th SS also was known by that name, the Iron Fist Division, and the fist was on their patch. That they had chosen such a character as their hero said a great deal about the men of the 17th SS Panzer Grenadier Division.

In the bloody days that lay ahead, days when the number of casualties was staggering and replacements arrived in huge numbers, the SS Panzer Grenadiers proved to be a group of men not easily forgotten.

Clyde R. Stodghill, Cuyahoga Falls, OH
Company G, 2nd Battalion,
12th Infantry Regiment

The Liberation of Hambye

Following the bombing and breakthrough at St. Lô, our battalion, perhaps the entire 12th Infantry Regiment, was assigned the job of cleaning out pockets of Germans left behind during the rapid advance. We hiked from place to place, frequently covering the same ground two or more times. Sometimes there were Germans waiting and a firefight ensued, but as often as not, they had either departed or had not been there in the first place.

It was a grueling assignment that allowed little time for rest or sleep and left us in a state of weariness beyond mere exhaustion. We kept going only because we did not want to fall out and let others down. There was little energy for talking, and I was among the many who repeated over and over to myself, "Just one more step, just one more step…"

I don't know how long commanders in the rear felt we could keep on that way. Certainly, we were past the point of being an effective fighting force. One day we passed a crossroad where military policemen held out candy bars for us to take, but no one within my range of vision had enough spare energy to take one.

After one entire night of hiking in circles, we dug in to take turns sleeping. Some had two hours; the lucky ones had three. In the afternoon we formed up on a road, but not the one we had arrived on. This one sloped gently downward to a little town about a mile ahead. Had the sun been shining, we would have been shaded by the many large trees where we had assembled, but the sky was dark and threatening, bringing thoughts of yet another soaking.

As we awaited the word to move out, one of the newer men in Bob Everidge's platoon suddenly keeled over and lay writhing on the ground. No one knew what to do for someone in the throes of an epileptic seizure, so we just stood watching. An aid man came forward, but seizures had not been covered in his training.

The lone comment came from Everidge: "I wonder if I could get out of here if I rolled around on the ground like that?"

The words were shockingly out of character. Not because they lacked sensitivity—very little of that could be found in any of us—but because it was the first time I had heard anything to indicate that Bob would have gotten out if he could. He never allowed any sign of fear to show in either his words or actions, always walking ramrod straight without bending in a "hedgerow stoop" as the rest of us did for protection. Was he nearing the end of his tether? No, I decided, not Bob Everidge. It was just that he was so damned tired.

Free of carrying the radio for a while, I went with Everidge's platoon when we moved out. One squad was on the point and the rest of us trailed about fifty yards behind as the advance party. The remainder of the company followed.

We were still some distance from the first buildings when a few civilians came out on the street ahead. This was unusual and therefore disconcerting. Germans were supposed to be in the town, and the presence of civilians was no guarantee that we wouldn't come under fire. If so, having non-combatants wandering about would complicate the situation. It was even possible that the Germans had driven them out on the street for that purpose.

As the minutes ticked away, more people poured forth from buildings. Others were hurrying along the street from the opposite direction, seemingly intent on greeting us. By the time the point squad reached the built-up area, the street was lined with people dressed in their Sunday best. Boys in black suits and young girls in white dresses carried flowers in their hands.

We passed a city limit sign reading "Hambye." Everidge and his squad leaders began the familiar, quiet chant: "Watch the windows, watch the windows. Observe to the left and the right, watch the windows." Over and over it was repeated, a reminder to men who knew what to do, but might forget for one fatal second.

Men on the left watched the points of danger on the right, and vice versa. It was done by looking more to the center of the street than directly at the buildings themselves, as peripheral vision would pick up movement that might go undetected if viewed from straight on.

The drill was forgotten, though, as we met the excited throng of smiling people, many of whom were clapping their hands and calling out a welcome. How could you watch the windows when small children were tugging at your clothes so you would bend down to let them entwine the stems of flowers in the camouflage netting on your helmet? Could anyone ignore the friendly overtures of freshlyscrubbed, laughing girls and boys? A few could, but not many.

What, I was wondering, must they think of this unsavory group of filthy, unshaven, odiferous men with hollow cheeks and glazed eyes sunk deep into their sockets? As best as I could tell, they didn't mind how we looked or smelled.

Soon, we were having to push our way through a solid mass of humanity. A young woman I passed just to my right said, "So, you've finally come!" I nodded my head, but by the time I realized she had been speaking English and turned to say more, she was lost in the crowd.

When we reached the cobblestone town square with buildings on all four sides, every foot of space was occupied. It was impossible to continue on. Everyone was facing a building with a tiny balcony on which an ancient record player with a flared horn had been set up. The balcony seemed too small to hold anyone until a man stepped out and stood beside the record player.

Another followed him—a small and very old man I felt must be the town's last surviving veteran of the Franco-Prussian war three-quarters of a century earlier. He held a folded flag, which he shakily fastened to a staff. Then, as the red, white and blue French Tricolor was unfurled in Hambye for the first time in more than four years, the strains of "Le Marseillaise" blared forth from the record player.

Every civilian, the majority with tears streaming down their cheeks, joined in singing what must surely be the most stirring of all anthems. In seven adventurous decades, I have experienced nothing quite so moving, so emotional, as those few minutes on the town square in Hambye. Several weeks later, we joined the French 2nd Armored Division in being the first troops to fight their way into Paris. It was exciting, of course, but failed to match the deep emotional impact of the liberation of Hambye.

Soon after the ceremony ended, a unit of the 2nd Armored Division, living up to its "Hell on Wheels" name, roared through Hambye on a road with a sign pointing to Villebaudon. Later, the sound of a major battle became audible in the distance.

We spent the night on the outskirts of Hambye, overjoyed at not having to spend another on the move. But as the night wore on, the sound of battle grew steadily nearer, and brilliant flashes lit the sky to the east. We did not know it, but the Germans were beginning to form a new line of defense that in the coming days would involve us in brutal battles at St. Pois and Mortain.

We left Hambye as the crisp night air was giving way to Sunday morning sunshine. A church bell sounded the call for early mass, but except for the presence of an elderly woman dressed in black, the streets were empty. I wondered if the fighting would reach the town, making the previous day's celebration meaningless. We could contribute little to a major tank battle of course, yet at least some of us felt guilty about leaving in the way that we were after having received such a joyous welcome.

Clyde R. Stodghill, Cuyahoga Falls, OH
Company G, 2nd Battalion,
12th Infantry Regiment

The "Iron" Major

On the fairly quiet Sunday morning of July 16, 1944, Major Richard J. O'Malley, commanding officer of the 2nd Battalion, 12th Infantry Regiment was killed by an enemy rifleman. Major O'Malley's worth can hardly be measured. His every action had been stamped by fearlessness, and he was undoubtedly one of the foremost combat officers of the Regiment. His men worshipped him. He had given them the inspiration that had carried the 2nd Battalion to its great successes, and, in turn, the welfare of his men was always uppermost in his mind. General Barton paid a final tribute to this gallant leader by ordering three volleys to be fired into the enemy lines by the massed artillery and mortars of the 4th Infantry Division—the only such occasion of the entire war. (Credited to the History of the 12th Infantry Regiment.)

The word that Major O'Malley had been killed was passed from man to man in disbelieving whispers, as if by repeating the words quietly they might turn into just another false rumor. The "Iron Major" dead—could it be true? Although death was all around us, it had seemed that the major was somehow immune, a man apart from the norm. To know that he had died left each of us more vulnerable. Words could not make it real to some of us—we had to see for ourselves. A friend and I were drawn to the place where he had fallen in Company E's sector as surely as metal shavings are drawn by a magnetic force. Neither of us cared that we had left our position without authority.

A medical jeep with racks for holding a litter had come up to the front. It was the first and only time I saw that happen. The United States Army was slow in removing the dead from a battlefield, but the corpse of a major could not be left lying on the ground for all to see.

Major O'Malley's body rested on a litter covered by an olive drab blanket. We arrived as the litter was placed on the racks of the jeep. The medics returned to a group of officers standing silently ten feet away. It was then that the only unexplainable incident of a long lifetime occurred. Although no one was close by and the wind was not blowing, the side of the blanket fluttered upward, remaining that way for a few seconds without support.

My friend said, "Look! The major's trying to get up." Knowing the kind of man Major O'Malley had been, his words seemed perfectly natural at the time, so I nodded in agreement. The only logical explanation that comes to mind is that the exhaust from the jeep's motor, which was running, had been responsible.

During my later years as a newspaperman, I came in contact with many men of stature: leading politicians, industrialists, entertainers, famous athletes, and coaches. Major O'Malley stands alone among them as a figure bigger than life, a man who towered above the pack.

Richard J. O'Malley was a ruggedly handsome man with a voice that could crack timber, a man whose every movement was brisk, decisive and authoritative. He was not the sort of leader who had a word of encouragement or kindly comment for everyone, nor did he lead by fear. It was his presence alone that inspired, and unlike many battalion commanders, he was always present or somewhere close by. He did not lead from a command post in the rear; he led from the Line of Departure. Many were the times when he could be heard calling, "Up and at 'em, 2nd Battalion, follow me!" We did so with apprehension, but without hesitation.

While we didn't fear Major O'Malley as a bully, we did fear committing an act that would arouse his anger, or above all, his contempt. Proving unworthy of his respect was unthinkable. To an eighteen-year old rifleman he was an awesome figure, a giant of a man. He was, as stated in the regimental history, a man worthy of worship.

O'Malley was a captain when he assumed command of the 2nd Battalion on the day in June when Lieutenant Colonel Dominick Montelbano was killed near Montebourg. He should have led a regiment, division, or corps. Many far less capable men did so. He had been our commander for only 33 days. In Normandy, that was the equivalent of a lifetime. Just as it came to seem that you had been there forever, it seemed that he had always been your leader and would continue to lead the battalion long after you were gone.

But now he was dead. Memories were alive, however, and would always remain fresh in my mind: the day when I didn't know what to do and was stammering on the radio so he came on and ordered me, an eighteen-year old private, to appoint a company commander; a dark afternoon when he grabbed canteens to find out if they held wine or cognac; the expression on his face as he looked down at a lieutenant who had shot himself in the foot; hearing him call, "Follow Me!" as he led an attack. Although he was a deadly serious man, I recall two occasions when he made us laugh.

The first came when we were lying in the sun on a slope that rose gently to where the major was attempting to interrogate a German. The man listened in bewilderment as the major grew louder and angrier. A GI I had not seen before and never saw again came walking over to them from our left. He wasn't wearing a helmet and was armed with only a pistol. He put a .45-caliber pistol to the man's head and shot him. After that, he went unhurriedly back to wherever it was he had come from.

Major O'Malley was speechless. He looked from one to another of us as if someone might be able to explain this extraordinary occurrence. Then, his expression changed to one of fury. He stalked off to the right saying, "I'll be damned! A man can't even interrogate a prisoner without some GI walking up and shooting him!" It required great effort to contain our laughter until the major was out of hearing range.

On another day we were spread out along both sides of a shady back road, waiting to go forward to where E or F Company was engaged in a desultory firefight. Sunlight filtered through the trees, and we sat there enjoying the short rest amid pleasant surroundings. Suddenly a German bounded over the hedgerow about twenty feet to my right, ran across the road without looking in either direction, and peered over the opposite hedgerow, apparently hoping to see friends.

The incident came to mind eight years later as my Company sat along another back road in Louisiana. A gray fox, oblivious of our presence, ran among a hundred armed men to investigate the noise being made by cooks loading metal cans onto a truck at the far end of a field across the road. He suddenly became aware of us. Like a cartoon character, he leaped high in the air, completed a full turn before coming down, and then took off at full speed.

The German was less fortunate, although we just sat there watching until from thirty yards to our left Major O'Malley cried, "Shoot that man! Shoot that man!" He began firing his pistol, but his wild shots were scattered all along the road, so we dived for cover. Realizing his mistake, the German ran back to the center of the road, then stood there in amazed desperation as the major ran toward him, continuing to fire, still shouting, "Shoot that man!"

A BAR man, probably in self-defense from the wild shooting, rose up and fired a burst that sent the luckless German sprawling on his back. After Major O'Malley turned and went back to the place where he had been, we started laughing. A rifle squad leader, Curly Walsh, sat shaking his head, and still laughing a little said, "I'll tell you what, I was a helluva lot more scared of the major with his .45 than I ever was of any Jerry."

In later years, at Ivy Division reunions, those of us from the 2nd Battalion often talked of the major. Cliff Burke, who served under him when O'Malley was commander of Company H in the States, told how he would drive around various camps and nearby towns in a red Packard convertible—an automobile well suited to the major.

Half a century after he died, I talked with Major O'Malley's grandson, Richard Roy of Atlanta, who was seeking information on his grandfather's death. I told him about an E Company private I knew who had been shot by the same sniper just before he killed the major. During a reunion, the man explained how he shifted position just as the sniper squeezed the trigger. As a result, he was hit in the shoulder, not the head or throat. After the major was killed by the second shot, the wounded man watched from the ground as other men killed the young sniper concealed in a tree.

Richard Roy said the major's brother, a captain with the 2nd Armored's advanced party, was killed on D-Day. Forty-one years after the Normandy campaign, my wife and I walked along the rows of white crosses and Stars of David in the cemetery above Omaha Beach. We were looking for graves of 4th Infantry Division men so when she said, "Here's one," I went over to where she was standing.

For a moment I remained there unmoving, stunned at reading the inscription: "Richard J. O'Malley, Major, 12th Infantry Regiment." We had found the Iron Major.

An hour later, we stopped at a German cemetery a few miles away. Two busloads of German students were renewing the gold lettering on crosses of black. We paused at the first we came to and read the brief inscription:

GEORGE DROST, 19
JULY 16, 1944

Too much of a coincidence of course, that this could have been the German sniper. And yet, as the regimental history states, it was a fairly quiet day on the Sainteny front.

Patricia O'Malley, Dallas, Georgia
Daughter of Major Richard James O'Malley, USA.

*In December 2000, Patrica O'Malley posted the following note to the
4th Infantry Division Association web page at www.4thinfantry.org.
— Bob Babcock*

My father, Major Richard James O'Malley, was Commander of the
2nd Battalion, 12th Infantry Regiment, 4th Infantry Division in
WWII. He was killed among the hedgerows in France on July 16, 1944.
I was one year old. I have tried to learn all about him that I can and
would like to hear from anyone who knew him.

Recently, I made my first visit to his grave in France at the American
Cemetery. It was a very emotional experience for me. I wrote my feelings
about the trip and would like to share it with anyone who identifies with
my feelings. May God bless you all for your service to our great nation
and for all the sacrifices that have been made.

I arrived at the American Cemetery at Normandy, France, with excitement and eager anticipation. All of my life I had waited for this moment.
And, here I was. I could scarcely believe it. I entered the office at the
cemetery and asked the location of my father's grave. When the director
found that I was the next of kin, she closed the office and escorted me.
After a short walk we stood before my father's grave. At last, I was there.
I fought to contain my tears. Then, as if by magic, I heard broadcast over
the loudspeakers, taps being played, followed by "volleys" being fired.
The sounds echoed loudly across the ten thousand graves and out across
the sea. I could no longer contain my tears, and I cried. The woman left
me so I could have time alone. I cried deeply for many reasons. I cried
for the joy of being there and the sadness of my father's death. I cried for
all the times I needed a father and never had one. I cried for all the words
I had wanted to say and wanted to hear but had not. I cried and cried.
And, when I was through, I just stayed there. I talked to my father and
told him I loved him. I talked to him as if he were alive. I put my hand on
the cold marble cross and held onto it as if it would make me somehow
be holding onto him. And I knew that under the grass and dirt lay my
father's bones. Part of my father was really here. He was real.

I spent the afternoon at the cemetery walking around and looking at the monuments and all the other graves. All of the men had their own stories, their own wives, and children. I sat on a bench and looked out over the ocean. I heard the cry of the gulls and the sounds of the wind. Normandy Beach looked so peaceful now. But it was holy ground. Though I couldn't see the bodies or the blood of the battle, they were there. And though I couldn't hear the cries of the wounded or the sounds of the battle, they were there, too. And they will always be there. And so, we have erected monuments and constructed museums and historical placards all along the battle zones. These sites will forever be hallowed.

I had always wondered why my family left my father so far across the sea. Previous to my visit, I thought that was a wrong decision. But now that I have been there, it seems right. It seems right that my father, who always led his men in battle, would not desert them even in death. As I walked through the cemetery, I saw his men buried all around him. I knew that he was where he should be. He lay a fallen hero in a foreign land, high atop the cliffs of Normandy. I said good-bye to my father and I thanked God that I was able to come. I said a prayer for him and for all the men who gave their lives that we might be free.

—Patricia O'Malley, Daughter of Major Richard James O'Malley, USA

Clyde R. Stodghill, Cuyahoga Falls, OH
Company G, 2nd Battalion,
12th Infantry Regiment

Unclaimed Bed Rolls

They were stacked high along a stone wall, across a side street from the Pasteur Hospital, an even one hundred-fifty of them resembling oversized, khaki-colored sausages. These were the casualty rolls, a mute testament to the savage fighting on the road to Cherbourg.

No one had returned to claim them when the rest of us walked along the rows of blanket rolls laid out in military precision on the ground, each man seeking his own among the many that in appearance were markedly similar. When everyone had picked up a roll containing all his possessions other than those on his back, we stood off to one side waiting to be told what to do.

Then, as was always the case, those remaining on the ground underwent a transformation. They had been blanket rolls; now they were casualty rolls. With the new name came a new look, one that spoke of infinite loneliness, lost hope, shattered dreams.

Someone had to open these pathetic reminders of lives that a short time before had been robust. The GI equipment had to be separated from the personal belongings and then formed into piles: shoes here, pants there; a different stack for every item issued by the army. Small cardboard boxes awaited what was left. Bundles of letters in feminine handwriting, photographs of smiling girls, sometimes ones of young children could be found in these personal stacks of belongings. A fallen man's memories of another time and another world. Shaving gear, a candy bar, a paperback book, a spare pair of eyeglasses, a harmonica, the sparse possessions that made every roll unique, gave it the stamp of individuality, the mark of the man who had not returned to claim it.

The last thing a rifleman did before starting back down the road to the battle was make up his blanket roll. He laid his shelter-half (buttoned together with another, it made a pup tent) on the ground and then placed his two wool blankets on top, folded so as to leave a foot of canvas exposed on each side. Then came personal belongings, spare clothing, an extra pair of boots, tent pole and pegs, mess kit, minus the spoon that went with him to the front.

Once everything was in place, the exposed sides of the shelter half were folded over then rolled up tightly and one end was secured by making a loop of his tent rope. Then the rope was tied near the other end, leaving enough slack so the finished blanket roll was ready to be tossed onto a pile near the kitchen truck where it would stay until he returned... or it became a casualty roll.

The routine was the same regardless of weather. If a roll was made up in the rain, everything inside was still damp when it was picked up again. A man's blanket roll soon took on the musty smell of a long-neglected gym bag.

The cooks were responsible for the rolls until the company came off the line for a night or even an hour during a move from one sector to another. When the cooks heated up a meal of 10-in-1 rations on one of those brief pauses, retrieving a mess kit from a blanket roll hardly seemed worth the effort.

Before our arrival, the cooks laid out the rolls in long rows. Room was left for walking between them and the names were facing upward. Weary and silent, we would amble along, each man searching for his own roll. Now and then someone would call out the name of a friend. That man would walk over, retrieve his roll and then help the friend find his own. It was a strange feeling, seeing the names of men in your own company displayed that way and finding the majority of them unfamiliar. At the beginning, it hadn't been that way for the company's original men, but it quickly became an organization of men who, for the most part, were strangers to one another.

In Normandy, the unclaimed rolls more often than not outnumbered those that had been picked up. At times, the neat rows were hardly disturbed, just a gap here and another there. I often looked at the haggard faces around me and wondered how many would be there the next time, or how many times any man could hope to be among those taking part in the grim ritual. My thoughts would drift back to the day when I had last tossed my roll on the pile at the kitchen truck and watched as others did the same. Where were they now, all those men who had not returned to claim their rolls? At times, I knew. More often, I did not, because so many were merely a face without a name to accompany it, or just names I had never heard and sometimes faces I had never seen.

In Cherbourg, the unpleasant job of opening the one hundred-fifty casualty rolls fell to Mike Spinelli and me, a pair of eighteen-year old riflemen from Northeastern Ohio. It was a job no one wanted, one that would spoil an otherwise sunny and pleasant day of two young soldiers who would rather have been doing almost anything else.

This was not the first time that Company G casualty rolls had been opened. Near Montebourg, about seventy-five others had been processed—roughly two hundred twenty-five in three weeks of combat, more than the number of Company G men in the third wave to hit Utah Beach on D-Day.

Donald Lewis, the weapons platoon sergeant, was in charge of the detail. He handed Mike a clipboard with several sheets of paper containing typewritten names and serial numbers. Following each name was one of three sets of letters: KIA, WIA, MIA... killed, wounded, or missing in action. The many names followed by KIA told how bitter those three weeks of battle had been for the 12th Infantry Regiment. Numerous others were listed as MIA—men buried under the dirt, hurled by exploding shells and as yet unfound, a few vaporized when a shell hit at their feet.

After giving us the few instructions we needed, Sergeant Lewis said he would be in a small room opening off an alley at the far end of the wall. He told us to bring the roll of a man he named back to him without opening it.

So we set to work, Mike and I. Each of us took a roll, put a check beside the name on the list and then sorted the contents. It proved to be a time-consuming job that lasted most of the day.

Mike was a small man with a serious face that seldom changed expression. He wasn't much of a talker. When he did make a comment, it usually was a sardonic one pertaining to the situation. His type was never seen in any of the inane war movies that always seemed to feature a noisy Italian. Aside from ancestry, Mike was the antithesis of that sort.

On the stock of his rifle he had carved "Lillian," an act that anywhere but in combat would have earned him a trip to the stockade. Knowing his taciturn nature, I felt certain that somewhere back in Cleveland was a girl called Lillian who was completely unaware that she had captured Mike's heart.

On the stock of his rifle he had carved "Lillian," an act that anywhere but in combat would have earned him a trip to the stockade.

He had a voracious appetite, but I never heard him complain when food was scarce. One day the cook who doubled as baker made doughnuts that were sent up to us at the front. The man had baked enough for a full company, and we were far short of being that. A great many were left over so Mike ate more than twenty of them. One day while in the rear, we were served canned pears, a treat beyond imagining for men starving for fruit and vegetables. A vat full of juice remained, so both Mike and I drank one canteen cupful of it after another. During the coming hours, a price had to be paid for our indulgence. It was worth it.

We had been working a short time when Mike came over to me with a sick expression on his face. "Look at this," he said, holding out a pocket-sized Bible open at the flyleaf. On it was written: "To Alton C. Bright from Mother. Read it and be good."

This was too much for Mike's sensitive nature. It didn't do a lot for my morale, either.

The advice had not been heeded; the gilt edged pages had never been separated. I called to Eddie Wolfe, our platoon sergeant who was passing by, and showed it to him. He told us that Al Bright had been a staff sergeant, a rifle squad leader from Paris, Tennessee. He was the first man killed in Company G. Eddie said that as the ramp dropped on his landing craft and he was preparing to lead his men ashore, a bullet caught him in the forehead.

When we were told that it was time for a lunch of 10-in-1 rations, Mike said he wasn't hungry. That was unheard of for him. I didn't have much appetite myself, so we went on working.

Sergeant Lewis came by to check on us. We had placed personal items for shipment home in a number of the little boxes so Lewis looked them over. He was not happy. From one he took a bundle of letters and tossed them at my feet. "Look at the return addresses," he said. All were from girls in England or living in towns near camps where the 4th Infantry Division had been stationed in the States.

"Going to send those back to his wife, are you?" said Lewis. "That should make her feel damn good." From another box, he took a pair of eyeglasses, holding them out to me by a thumb and one finger. "Do you think his mother and father will want these for something to remember him by? Anyway, they're GI issue."

He had a few more caustic comments before going back to the alley. His message was received. When the job was finished, there wasn't a single item in any of the boxes. As the day wore on, French civilians gathered to watch. After years of having to do without, seeing all those shoes and the piles of clothing was a moving experience for them. A man of fifty-five or sixty approached me, smiling and holding out a black fountain pen. Pointing to the word "Berlin" stamped on it, he kept repeating, "Boche, Boche." He wanted me to take the pen, hoping that in return I would give him something from the stacks that had accumulated along the wall. As far as I was concerned, the people could have had it all, but I had no say in the matter. Reluctantly, I took the pen, feeling guilty about doing so, and more than fifty years later I still have it.

The crowd kept growing until men and women were almost on top of us and we had little room to work. I went to the room in the alley and explained the situation to Sergeant Lewis. He came out and waved them back, but they soon were pressing forward again so he sent word for one of his machine gun squads to set up their gun at the corner. Most of the crowd dispersed then, but a few civilians remained watching us from the other side of the street, including the man who had given me the pen and his wife.

The pair slowly moved closer, finally halting at the center of the narrow street. A few minutes later four GIs from some newly arrived rear echelon outfit came by. They were a crude lot, the coarse type of men who were far too plentiful and gave all Americans a bad name.

The most repulsive of the group stopped beside the French man and his wife, grinning and making lewd remarks that the man could not understand. He believed they were being friendly so he and his wife kept smiling and nodding as the GI said, "Who's the old whore with you?" and other things of that sort.

His companions thought this was hilarious. What they didn't know was that Nick Scala, the machine gun section sergeant, was approaching from behind to check on his men. When he took in what was going on, he scared them out of their skins by shouting, "Ten shun!" from a foot away.

Scala shooed off the remaining civilians, then ordered the men to line up against the wall across the street. Turning to his machine gunner, he called, "Load!"

A .30-caliber light machine gun did not have a safety, so when not firing, the gun was kept on half load. This was done by feeding the belt of ammunition into the gun while pulling back on the operating handle a single time. This did not line up a round for firing, which was accomplished by pulling the operating handle back a second time to the "load" position.

The worthless foursome lined up against the wall shaking with terror. I was anticipating the command "Fire!" with pleasure. Instead of giving it, Scala ordered the interlopers out of the Company G area and told them never to return because the next time he saw them they would die.

They took off on the dead run. More than one, I would have bet, had to go back to wherever they came from to change shorts. It was the one bright moment of a bleak, depressing day.

When in late afternoon we came to the roll that Sergeant Lewis wanted to open himself, I took it back to him. A little later a question came up, and I returned to the alley. When I opened the door of the small room I saw the contents of his friend's roll spread out on the floor. Lewis sat bent over them, hands covering his face. I quietly closed the door and went back to where Mike was working. The question, whatever it had been, no longer seemed important.

Tom Reid, Marietta, GA
Cannon Company, 22nd Infantry Regiment and Company I,
3rd Battalion, 22nd Infantry Regiment

Forward Observer

The time: late August 1944. The place: a stable outside Paris. The circumstances: a forward observer and his two-man team seek cover from enemy small arms and mortar fire.

In August 1944, I was a forward observer with the 22nd Infantry Regiment's Cannon Company. This company had six, short-barreled 105mm howitzers designed to give the rifle companies some close fire support without calling on the supporting artillery battalion.

On paper, I was the platoon leader of the 3rd platoon, Cannon Company, 22nd Infantry Regiment. But in actual day-to-day operations, I was the forward observer attached to 3rd Battalion, 22nd Infantry Regiment. Upon reporting to the battalion, I was attached to one of the rifle companies making the main attack. My team consisted of two men, one to carry the SCR300 radio, and one to carry an extra battery. In those days, the battery was about the size of a large toaster and had an operating life of eight to ten hours of uninterrupted communication.

On this particular day the platoon I was attached to took cover in a large horse stable until the advance could be resumed. Soon the order came down to hold where we were until some adjacent unit seized a critical road junction. The minutes turned into hours, and the platoon leader posted a guard at each end of the stable and told his men to get some rest.

Seeing other men lie down to rest, my team and I followed suit. I don't know how long I slept, but I awoke with a start when I realized that my two-man team and I were the only people in the stable. The entire rifle platoon was gone. Panic was beginning to set in as I quickly roused my two men, and we rushed to the door to look out.

Troops were moving along the road outside the stable, and I dashed out to ask what unit they were from. It wasn't our platoon or company. In fact, they were from another battalion. Where was our platoon? Our company to which we had been attached? No one knew. Some said they thought the 3rd Battalion was up ahead in the "approach march." Others thought they were in this direction or that.

Where was my company to which I had been assigned? In the event the company commander or platoon leader needed supporting fires from Cannon Company and I was nowhere to be found, this would be serious. I would technically be AWOL even though I was desperately trying to find out the location of the company so I could rejoin them without delay.

We asked everybody on the road and finally found out that 3rd Battalion and my assigned company was somewhere forward.

We hurried along on foot, doubling past other units until at last we came upon men from 3rd Battalion, the rifle company, and the platoon to which I had been assigned, waiting on the side of the road. The total time we had been out of touch had been less than an hour, but it seemed like an eternity with the consequences of not being where we should be weighing heavily on my mind.

There we were, back with the company where we should have been all along. I was sweating a little bit, but greatly relieved that no one had noticed our absence.

The question of why the platoon had moved out without awakening us bothered me until I asked one of the riflemen why. He replied, "you weren't part of our platoon," thereby expressing one of the basic tenets of organization, the belief that one should adhere to loyalty to one's immediate family—the squad, the platoon, the company. No one else mattered.

I understood it, but the fear for that hour was real and left a lasting impression on my future military career and me.

In any event I was soon to be involved in something much larger in scope because two days later the order came for the entire 4th Infantry Division to mount up and become the first U.S. unit to enter Paris. That would take my mind off almost anything.

Paul Brunelle, Avon, MA
Company G, 2nd Battalion, 8th Infantry Regiment

Good Advice

From the book Company G, 2nd Battalion, 8th Infantry Regiment, 4th Infantry Division by Shirley Devine. Used here with her permission.

In early August 1944, I was assigned to the 4th Infantry Division. When I joined the Division, I was fresh out of training and one of the things they told us was that you never volunteer for anything. Well, I remember that when I was going to Company G, I was told that they needed some machine gunners and some mortar men—I guess to fill the companies that had received casualties at St. Lô. So, instead of listening to the advice that I was given in training, when they asked for mortar men, I immediately put up my hand. I didn't know one bubble from the other, but I was glad to say that I was a mortar man and had been trained to be a mortar man. Since most of what I did for the next few months entailed carrying ammunition, the fact that I didn't know much about mortars was no detriment at all.

We were at a place called St. Pois, out in the fields. We never really got to go inside of a city or town unless there was some "mopping up" to do. I remember that hill at St. Pois. We were dug in along a hedgerow. Some of the fellows were dug into the hedgerow, which was about six feet below the level of the field. Sergeant Conway came along as I was digging a slit trench and he told me that I had better dig a foxhole because they had reports that there were German tanks operating in the area. That advice proved to be very beneficial to me. It was just a little while later that some German soldiers in front of us and down the hill, started waving a white flag. I guess the American soldiers just threw caution to the winds and started exposing themselves. As they did, a white flare went up and we started getting shelled very heavily.

During that action, some German tanks did come up. The place that I was dug in was right on the edge of a wheat field. A couple of the shells landed very close to my foxhole. One of them exploded about twenty feet away. I had been having lunch when they approached. I ducked into the foxhole quickly and left my canteen and dish on top of the foxhole.

The nearness of the explosion threw dirt in my canteen and down on top of me. Thanks to the advice that I had received, I was not injured. Shrapnel from the same shot that exploded just a few feet from my foxhole went in between the two hedgerows where some of the guys were dug in. A young fellow who came in the day I did (his name was Whitehead,) was killed by a direct hit. There were others who were wounded too, because I could hear screams for help. The shelling didn't last all that long, but when it was over, we had received some casualties. I don't recall very many incidents like that.

I also recall another time when we were advancing and we had some American fighters over us. They were bombing and strafing the enemy. One or two of the bombs from a fighter broke loose and landed within our lines. I don't think we had any casualties from it, but it was unnerving to have our own fighterbombers dropping bombs within our own ranks.

Robert Gast, Warsaw, IN
Companies B and C, 1st Battalion, 12th Infantry Regiment

Welcome Aboard

I joined the 4th Infantry Division, 12th Infantry Regiment as a replacement officer just prior to the St. Lô breakthrough and the dash for Paris. The Commanding officer of Company B walked me to my new platoon, the 2nd rifle platoon of Company B. They sure looked like a rough bunch. They were sitting around drinking from a bottle something I later learned to be Calvados. One of the men took a big swig, filled his cigarette lighter, lit a cigarette, and then handed the bottle to me. I knew I had to take a drink, and I wasn't much of a drinker. I raised the bottle to my lips and took a big slug. Well, I coughed and choked until my helmet fell off. The men really got a big laugh, and it did kind of break the ice. I learned that they were really glad to have me aboard.

John K. Lester, Stone Ridge, NY
Battery B, 29th Field Artillery Battalion

"Still Had a War to Win"

I was a "jeep" driver for a forward observer party for Battery B, 29th Field Artillery. About two weeks after the initial invasion on June 6, 1944, I remember driving through Montebourg, in Normandy. The road that had to be used through the city came under constant sniper fire from the enemy. Once you started, there was no turning back. A jeep doesn't give you much protection. It was the road to Cherbourg, so you drove, you prayed, and thanked God when you got through the city. It was bad enough that you had to be worried about mines, enemy artillery, etc.; they had to throw in the snipers. Let me tell you, they were good at it. They had plenty of experience. I'd had about two weeks in combat, but I was learning fast.

The sunken roads between the hedgerows in Normandy were another dread for drivers. Along with all the above-mentioned hazards were hidden antitank guns, "zeroed-in" enemy artillery, dead cows, destroyed and burning vehicles, and on many occasions, bodies of those who were victims of war. Some of the dead were Americans. Seeing enemy dead didn't bother me. The sight of our own men was a different story. I remember one GI I thought I could help. I stopped to see, but he had been hit in the head by a shot from a sniper. He was propped against a tree. I cried when I saw a snapshot that I presumed to be his wife and two little girls. They looked to be about one and three years old. The picture was fastened inside his steel helmet liner. The shot up helmet was alongside him. Those steel helmets didn't stop sniper bullets. Something like that is hard to get out of your mind.

I remember one time when we were moving up in convoy, we were strafed by one of our own P47 fighter planes. By a stroke of good luck, he didn't cause much damage on his first pass. When he started the second pass, he was shot down by a GI who was operating a .50-caliber machine gun that was mounted on one of our two-and-a-half-ton-trucks. He really had him in his sights. He saved many of us that day. I remember him getting reamed out by a captain, for shooting down one of our own planes. We learned later that the plane was being flown by a German pilot. We also learned that, instead of a court martial, the GI was awarded a Bronze Star Medal for his excellent marksmanship.

On July 25, 1944, the 4th Infantry Division spear headed the St. Lô breakthrough. The 8th Infantry Regiment, supported by the 29th Field Artillery, was the attacking force. Over 2,000 heavy bombers flew over to bomb one thousand yards ahead of the infantry. I was at an observation post and could observe much of the activity. I hadn't seen as many planes since D-day. The first waves of bombers were on target, but the heavy cloud of smoke started drifting back over the infantry, and then the bombers started dropping their bombs on our own troops. Many of our infantry were killed, wounded, and stunned by this terrible error, but the attack went on as planned. I don't know how they did it under those conditions. They made it possible for the new 3rd Army to break out and start to roll over France. Some of the bombs that were dropped short landed close to our observation post. General Leslie J. McNair was killed by one such bomb not too far from my location. If I remember right, he was standing by a knocked-out German tank about one hundred yards from me. I saw at least four of our B-24 bombers fall out of the sky. Two of them were breaking apart as they fell. What an awesome sight. The Germans had put up plenty of antiaircraft fire.

Just outside Paris, France, in August 1944, my Forward Observer party, (three of us), had our first home-cooked meal. The area was under intermittent fire—nothing serious, just annoying. A boy of about twelve yelled at us to come into his home. We were a little apprehensive, but we parked the vehicle under cover and went in. What I saw amazed me. This boy knew more about the war than we did. He had large maps hanging on the wall and was trying to keep track of what was going on. The maps didn't help us, but he sure was proud of them. While he was telling us about his maps, his mother was fixing a meal. They didn't have much food, but wanted to share what they did have with us. I remember having chicken, potatoes, and green beans. It was a feast and of course, we had wine. It was an enjoyable hour or so, and a small reprieve from the war. For a change, I had something good to remember. When we left, we gave them whatever rations we could spare. All we had were K-rations and limited C-rations. The little chocolate bars were a big hit with the boy. I can still see him standing proudly by the maps he had made. They were happy people; the war was over for them.

We went on from there, to be among the first Americans to enter the city of Paris on August 25. We may have been there first, but we didn't get to stay in Paris very long. We moved out the very next morning, heading for Belgium and the road to Germany. I believe it was the 28th Infantry Division who got to parade and enjoy Paris. I know it wasn't us. We didn't have the proper dress for parades and celebrations. They needed fresh troops for that—not dirty, tired, out of place combat troops. Besides, we had to go on. We still had a war to win.

Peter Triolo, Pueblo, CO
HQ, 1st Battalion, 12th Infantry Regiment

Five War Stories

The following stories and events took place after the Battle of Mortain, on the road to Paris. My duties were basically to patrol and set up outposts. However, early each evening I would go back and locate Regimental Headquarters in order to make the Colonel's late evening trip to get combat orders for the next day. During the French operations, most of our combat took place from sunrise to sunset. My days were continuous activity: Daily patrols, scouting for the Colonel's meeting, and attending the operations meetings. We would finish the cycle at about 0200 or 0300 hours, just in time for the next day's officers' meeting. I kept this cycle going with limited opportunities for sleep.

1. Millionaire for a day

This morning we jumped off in the attack. The Germans had our front lines zeroed in. We received between fifty and sixty casualties in the first half hour. We pulled back to reorganize. The colonel called for me and several other officers. He said there must be a German outpost directing fire, because the shots were too accurate. Looking out over the front, we spotted a French farmhouse and buildings about a mile off our right front. Colonel Jackson said, "I bet that is what we are looking for." With a two-jeep patrol, we drove down to the farmyard. We talked to the French farmer and his wife. We could see they were nervous and scared. While checking out the barn in the hayloft we found a map and a radio. We had found our problem. We also found a small footlocker full of brand new French francs. We estimated it had to be close to a million dollars in thousand dollar packages. Corporal Shanks took a package of French francs and stuck it in the cushion on the driver's side of the jeep. The jeep cushions had a cheap zipper pocket where you could store things. When we arrived at headquarters, there was an officer from Regiment waiting for us.

He said, "Pete, give me the money." "I don't have any money," I replied.

He said, "Yes, you do." They had captured the two German officers. These two not only admitted to directing the artillery fire, but also continued to tell about the money that was in the barn. So, I was a millionaire only for the day.

2. The orange panels—a close call

This time, I was in the advanced CP with Colonel Jackson. The advanced CP was located about fifty feet behind the advanced fighting troops. We had Air Corps coverage. Two planes would fly overhead waiting for target assignments. All of a sudden, we heard one of the planes start to dive down on a target assignment. About a thousand feet above the ground the plane released a five hundred pound bomb and took off. Of course we all hit the ground, and I am sure we were all praying. The bomb hit about one hundred fifty feet from our location. Thank God, it was a dud. Colonel Jackson called the pilot on the radio to find out what was going on.

"We are friendly troops," he said.

The pilot said, "You are in front of the orange panels, so we took you for the enemy."

In the early days of the war, all the troops had orange panels that they would lay out so our pilots would know we were friendly troops. What had happened was the artillery unit about five thousand yards behind us had laid out their orange panels. As a result, the Air Corps thought we were the enemy out in front. This was a problem with many of the troops in the early days of the fighting. Finally a decision was made, I am sure

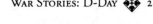

by Eisenhower, that only infantry troops would have the orange panels. All other troops turned in their panels, which eliminated the problem.

3. Tank Support

Another day in the advanced CP with Colonel Jackson, we were coming out of a wooded area ready to cross an open area. We received heavy machine gun and mortar fire from a wooded area about five hundred yards to our right front. As a rule, we had two tanks assigned to us every day to help us in combat. The tanks were about eight hundred yards behind us, with the reserve units. When I arrived there, I talked with the tank commander and informed him what the missions may be.

To get to the front lines, we had to go through about two hundred feet of a trail between two hedgerows. I told the tank commander that if the tank draws fire while we're on the trail to let me get into the tank for protection. Sure enough, about half way through the trail, German mortars started to fire on the tanks from that wooded area. I jumped on the tank to get in, but the commander had already closed up and wouldn't let me in. The only place left for me was under the tank. Well, to get out of the fire zone, the tank started to back up. To move backwards, the tank had to wiggle left and right as it moved back. Now I had to get out from under the tank or be crushed. I was left with the front lines being the safest place to go. I informed Colonel Jackson of what happened and that no tanks were coming up. Returning to the CP that night, we were informed the tanks did not stop at our CP but returned to their tank company area. We never saw that tank commander again, and that was lucky for him.

4. Ernie Pyle, here I come

On this day Colonel Jackson requested I set up an outpost with an anti-tank gun, a machine gun, and about ten men to protect the left flank. There was a main crossroad there, and we wanted to make sure that a German attack could not happen from those roads. Upon reaching the site, we found that there were three main roads, not two. On the top of the hill, about two hundred yards away, was a small village. I told my driver, Shanks, to take us up there and check it out.

To get to the village we had to take a sharp right turn. Our normal routine would be to get out and check before we made such a sharp turn. We hadn't seen German troops for a day or two, so I told Shanks to just go on in. Sure enough, sitting on the stoop of the first house were two Germans with their guns across their lap pointed in our direction. Even in their surprise at seeing us, they managed to fire a few rounds in our direction. Shanks and I went over the jeep backwards, leaving it as we took off back around the curve.

About half an hour later we took a small patrol up there and retrieved the jeep.

The Germans were gone. The two Germans ran straight into one of our companies and were captured. They told the officers interviewing them about the incident between them and two Americans on a jeep. Because of our stupidity, we were the joke of the area for the next few days. On returning home, I was told that this story was written by Ernie Pyle and was in the Minneapolis newspaper.

5. An especially memorable patrol

The morning before jumping off on the attack, Colonel Jackson asked me if I would fly over a bridge about two miles ahead of us in the artillery Piper Cub airplane to see if the bridge was safe. I didn't think that was the proper way to investigate the bridge, as I sure didn't want to fly in the Piper Cub. They could be shot down by a rifle. I'd rather take a patrol out there.

On the way back, the German patrol had set up a trap about a thousand yards before we reached our lines. They pinned down my patrol and me in about a fiveacre, hedgerow-fenced field. When the Germans set up a trap like this, they would usually set up two machine guns on separate corners of the hedgerows. They would set up the machine guns so one would fire shells as tracers about five feet off the ground, and the other gun would fire ammunition about three feet off the ground. One of my men said, "Lieutenant, I can see the guns, I can get them." Knowing their tactics, I told him to stay down. Being a young kid of eighteen or nineteen years old, he wanted to be a hero. He jumped up and was shot through the stomach.

I had to get my men out of this field quick. I told them to work their way back to one corner. Then I would count from one to five, and one man would jump out of the field and out of the trap. That left me with the young boy shot through the stomach. He died in my arms, so I left him there and got myself out of the trap. We went back to the CP and informed the Colonel that the bridge was OK.

William G. Cole, Tacoma, WA
Battery C, 29th Field Artillery Battalion

A Small Story about Winter Clothing and Its Source

I bought "tanker" clothing consisting of a lined jacket and "bib overall" trousers for the people in my forward observer party, and it was the smartest thing I did. Those clothes were not bulky; they closed tightly, didn't restrict movement when diving for cover, and were warm. To pay for the clothing I used money (francs) which I removed from the wallet of a German officer who surrendered to me the day of the breakout—the big bombing—July 25. He stepped out in front of me and said in English that his tank was out of gas. I got a Luger pistol from him, and one of my radio operators took his wristwatch after asking me if it was OK. There wasn't a chance that the officer could have kept his watch so we may as well take it. I announced when I took the money that I was going to buy winter clothing with it and that tanker clothes was what I had in mind.

I talked to Joe Gude for the first time that day and gave him the Luger pistol. I didn't have a convenient way to carry it, and we were busy. I figured that an infantry officer needed the pistol more than I did. On reflection, I believe Gude expressed envy at the trophy, and, in view of what those people had been through, I felt he deserved it. He was an outstanding officer who got three Silver Stars and two Purple Hearts. I wasn't making plans for getting back home anyway.

I was as good as my word. I ordered tanker clothes, which were for sale (maybe at the PX) and they arrived, I believe, before the winter got bitterly cold. At the time, Noah had been wounded and was not with the battery, so we kept his tanker suit on the jeep. Several people tried to buy his clothes. I always said that they were being saved for Noah. He was very glad to get them when he returned, but never said very much in gratitude. Bernie Mayer got a set of the clothes and loved them. Joe Gochenauer also got a set.

William G. Cole, Tacoma, WA
and Bernie Mayer, Linden, NJ
Battery C, 29th Field Artillery Battalion

A Shared Close Call

Anyone who spent time with the infantry experienced "near misses"—incidents when serious wounds or worse were avoided by very small margins of time or distance. It truly seemed that sometimes, "the bullet didn't have your name on it." It seems, in memory, that most of the near misses happened quickly and were over just as quickly, leaving only time for a quick move toward whatever cover could be found. But I am writing this to describe an experience shared by Bernie Mayer and myself, which was not so brief. I have put the narrative together using excerpts from letters exchanged between Bernie and me. It was the most terrifying few minutes I remember.—Bill Cole.

From Bernie's letter of 09-13-1993. Do you remember the time you and I were along with the infantry without the radio but with an EE8A phone and half a mile of wire? Martin was following behind, splicing the wire as we advanced. We were hit by a mortar barrage and I hit the ditch on the left; you were on the right. A carbine was pulled up alongside my head on the right side and the phone was near my helmet. A mortar shattered my carbine stock, and it hung only by the sling; the phone handset wire was in three pieces. Hockert couldn't believe I was holding the phone at the time; he never saw the carbine.

From Bill Cole's letter of 10-21-1993. The "close call" you describe when we were in roadside ditches during a mortar attack was the most terrifying thing I remember because what happened to me was very similar to what you describe as happening to you. It seemed like the mortar shells never stopped coming, and they were accurate—right on top of us. The Germans had adjusted the mortars on that little road and waited until we got there and let us have it. One round hit about eighteen inches from my left side, opposite my head and blew out my left eardrum—it has still not fully recovered. And that ditch I was in was very shallow, but just deep enough. Like you, stuff I was carrying got cut up. I had forgotten about the wire, but I remember I had a field telephone on my back, and it got shredded. My canteen got punctured. My jacket had holes in it. I was so scared I forgot the details of what happened to you and I'll bet you didn't remember the details of what happened to me. Why would I have a phone on my back and you have another one in your hand? We came close to getting chewed up that day. I believe this happened in early July when our division artillery was attached to the 90th Division and we were sent up front with a bunch of strange troops. I never felt so all alone. The situation was hot—lots of things happened that day, a horrible day for the infantry we were with. From Bernie's letter of 11-12-1993. Your memory of the close call we had involving the telephones was precise. The man in charge of that body of infantry was wrong, in my opinion, in refusing your offer to soften up his next objective with some artillery fire before going forward. You did come across the road to where I was in the shallow ditch. You asked me if I was all right. Then, after a two-second inspection of my person, we hauled it out of there. With no radio and only two phones that were not connected to the line, we were of practically no use whatsoever. We met Bill Martin who was laying the line from the jeep forward. He only had a roll of the thin little line with him, and he heard the "to do" up front so he waited for things to ease up a little before coming on.

The fact that you had the phone was proper for the Forward Observer. It would be connected for use and the lineman carried one to check the line for breaks or short circuits while backtracking the wire.

Bill Cole finishes this story. In closing: I have no memory of anything that day following this incident, which I have previously described, perhaps too dramatically, as a near-death experience shared by Bernie and myself.

Francis W. Glaze Jr., Clearwater, FL
HQ, 8th Infantry Regiment

Ammo Resupply

The time was probably about June 10 or 11, 1944, and we were holding just outside Montebourg in Normandy. The 90th Division had built up behind us and started across the Cotentin Peninsula to seal it off before we started for Cherbourg.

We were under pressure from the Germans all along our front and especially in the 2nd Battalion area. They did not want to be trapped on the Peninsula, and we did not want them to break out.

During the day, I was sent forward from Regiment to determine the situation in front of the 2nd Battalion. My jeep was elsewhere, so I went forward with a commo man to visit Companies E and F. The commo man was looking for a wire break, as I remember. I couldn't find him when I was ready to go back, so I hitched a ride to the 8th Infantry Regiment CP.

Shortly after dark, the Germans attacked the 2nd Battalion sector. The line held, but the pressure built. Battalion said they could probably hold but that Company E was low on ammo. Captain "Squeak" Greenip, CO of Company E, told Regiment that I knew his location and asked that I bring as much ammo as a jeep and quarter-ton trailer could hold—by midnight! We loaded a good selection and took off for the "front," about four or five miles away. Time was short, so we used the main highway—a straight shot toward Montebourg. An 88 covered the road, but we felt that the dark gave us cover. About two hundred yards short of where I planned to turn off to Company E, we found that the road had been mined. The Germans had not had time to dig in the mines; they just sat on top of the roadway. There were about twenty Teller antitank mines!

I decided that it was too dangerous to go off road around the mines so I walked in front, checked for trip wires, and guided Salvaggio, my driver, as he straddled the mines. We got through. The two "shotguns" rejoined us on "tother" side. We continued for about two hundred yards and turned left into a field, stopped against a hedgerow, and went looking for Company E. We finally found them. The firefight was about one hundred yards to their front and slowing down a little. "Squeak" gave me a carrying party, and we went back to the jeep, picked up the ammo, and took it to the company.

About thirty minutes later we got back to the jeep, and Salvaggio was still there, but "as nervous as a whore in church." It seems that the Germans were digging in on the other side of the hedgerow to our front. They hadn't checked, and we didn't tell them. So, there we were—about fifty yards apart and separated only by darkness and a hedgerow!

It was after midnight. We shared Salvaggio's nervousness, so we pushed the jeep and trailer back to the road and down the road past the Teller mines.

It seemed like a good time to share our "nervousness" with the Germans, so we took two grenades apiece, and the four of us returned to the hedgerow. It was only about one hundred feet long, so we spread out evenly and on my signal, we each threw one grenade long, and two or three seconds later, threw one grenade short, just over the hedgerow! By the time the first grenades went off, we were in high gear and running like a "Big A—Bird" for the jeep. The Germans were so busy shooting in all directions that we had no problems resuming our trip back.

It was very dark, and we were worried about our own sentries, so we made cautious haste. Suddenly we "sensed" a group of people in the roadway jumping into the ditches on each side of the road. The driver stopped about fifty yards from the group. We assumed it was an ambush about to take place and that we had appeared so suddenly that we had surprised them. We couldn't go back, so I decided to "run it" and throw two grenades in each ditch as we went by. I had just told Salvaggio to "gun it" and he had started the run when we heard a baby cry. Luckily, I called out in time; only one man had to get the pin back in the grenade. We stopped and found about fifteen French women, children, and a grandfather who had slipped out of Montebourg before midnight and were trying to get to our lines before daylight.

We spent a moment reassuring them, and then one of the men and I walked with them. The jeep led by a couple hundred yards to alert the sentries we might pass. The sentries were expecting us but not a gaggle of people walking down the road. About a mile later we arrived safely at an MP guarded road junction and turned our charges over to them. The French never knew the danger they were in, but we four were so thankful we heard the baby cry that we were downright maudlin.

Jack Cunningham, Manteca, CA
Battery C, 29th Field Artillery Battalion

France: A Unique Way to a Chicken Dinner for the Battery

Somewhere in Normandy the battery had a three-or four-day rest period. Captain Jim Hurst, CO of Charlie Battery, 29th Field Artillery told me to get Sergeant Brown, our mess sergeant, and the two of us were to take his command car and go to some of the farms in the area. We were to get some chickens so the battery could have a good meal. For trade, we took cigarettes, chocolate ration bars, (which had a lot of stuff added to the chocolate), naphtha soap, and miscellaneous items. A piece of the chocolate bar took an hour to melt in your mouth, and the soap produced no suds but did a good job of cleaning. Naturally, the farmer and his wife were happy to see us. He wanted cigarettes—and time to have a few drinks. His wife wanted the chocolate, soap, and some of the knickknacks. He brought out a bottle of cognac or Calvados, and we negotiated. When this was complete, the wife and the children went out and collected the chickens and we sat there and had a few drinks. We put the curtains up on the command car, tied the legs of two or three chickens together and put them in the back seat.

During the day, we visited four or five farms, and at each the trading and sipping was about the same. We returned to the battery after dark with a load of chickens. Hurst came out and unhooked the curtains to look in the back seat. He was very unhappy. There were chicken droppings smeared all over the rear seat along with a mass of feathers. I wandered off and he told Sergeant Brown to get some men, remove the chickens, and clean up the car. The next day Hurst had calmed down, and the dinner was good—or at least better than C-rations.

Irving Smolens, Melrose, MA
Battery B, 29th Field Artillery Battalion

Reflections of an Artillery Crew Member

Our gun batteries were equipped with M-7 track vehicles in England. The M105mm howitzers were mounted on the M-7 with very minor modifications and very little additional training was needed other than for the driver and assistant driver, for this new and unique addition to the 29th Field Artillery Battalion. All of the other crew responsibilities remained essentially the same as if it were a "traildrawn" howitzer.

Some ammunition was carried in their tarpaper-covered cardboard containers on the firing deck of the M105. Ammo was also stored under the steel floorboards of the M-7 track vehicle. Additional ammo, along with all of our extra equipment, such as barracks bags and blankets, were carried in an attached trailer. The normal crew for a gun consisted of twelve men. Six men were designated as the "active" crew, and six were designated as "reserve." Only three men were actually needed to aim, load, and fire the gun once it was in position. The driver, assistant driver, and back-up gunner would act as ammunition handlers, unpacking shells and extracting extra powder charges from the brass semi-fixed shell casing. For example, if we were firing a #2 charge, they would remove the cotton bags containing charges #3 through #7, and hand it to the loader. If ammo supplies on the gun began to get low, they would pass additional stocks up to the firing crew.

During the invasion of Normandy, at Utah Beach, the batteries would fire from the deck of the LCTs, with the Battery Commander issuing the "fire" order. He received his orders from the Battalion Fire Direction Center, which was located on another ship along with the men of the Headquarters Battery. Our M-7s were loaded on the LCTs, two in front, and two in back, each with their active crew. The reserve crews were located on other boats. As the front guns performed firing missions, the back guns also performed firing missions, actually firing high trajectory over the front guns.

On the ground, once a fire mission was called, it took less than a minute to get into operational positions at the gun. We always had several rounds of HE (High Explosive) encased from their containers and ready to fire. We would wait for the fire commands to come to us over a phone line from the Executive Pit. The fire commands would include the type of ammo (HE, Armor Piercing, Phosphorous, Smoke, etc.), which powder charge to use (from #1 to #7), deflection, altitude, and elevation.

Once the commands were set, the tubes were rotated to the correct direction, and bubbles on the instruments were leveled. The loader (#2 Cannoneer), rammed the shell into the open breech and up into the tube. At that point, the #1 Cannoneer closed the breech block and grabbed the lanyard. The next command might just be a simple "Fire," to zero the gun in on the target. Once the target was zeroed in, the next command might be something like "Five rounds, Fire for effect." The entire operation would take a minute or less, depending on how long it took to get the commands from the Executive Officer.

Some of the worst fighting in the war took place in the hedgerows during the period June 26 to July 25, 1944. In the interim, prior to Cherbourg, A & C Batteries operated with six guns each. I think I must have been a member of one of those extra gun crews during at least part of that time. I didn't pay much attention to the battery to which I had been assigned as long as I was part of a gun crew and doing my job as #1 Cannoneer. Battery B was re-formed after Cherbourg was liberated.

As far as I can remember, all privates and PFCs pulled KP (Kitchen Police) and Guard Duty. The Noncoms pulled "Corporal" or "Sergeant-of-the-Guard" duties. Guard duty was handled in the established manner: two hours on and four hours off throughout the night. In truth, I can only remember two stints on guard duty: one in Luxembourg, during the Battle of the Bulge, and one in the Hürtgen Forest. I don't think there was a regular routine of standing guard duty. Logic tells me there must have been, but evidently I was not involved, so I just don't remember. I can only remember one KP duty. Most of the time we lived on field rations that we supplemented with items obtained for cigarettes, such as eggs, onions, and the occasional chicken. These things we cooked ourselves and cleaned up afterward. Once our attack bogged down we entered a static situation, or a slow-moving situation, where we occupied the same gun position for an extended period of time. The army provided us "fold-up" cots, along with pyramidal tents large enough to sleep the entire gun crew. We used these once it became evident that the Luftwaffe was a virtual non-factor and seldom got counter-battery fire. This was in sharp contrast to the fighting in Normandy, where we took great pains to dig foxholes or occupy foxholes that had been previously occupied.

We no longer dug in the guns. We pounded heavy steel angle irons to support thick logs around the gun pit. From September 1944 to May 1945 that would be our only protection from any shrapnel exploding in our vicinity. When we still had our M-7s, we would duck under the track chassis. In retrospect, these practices seem somewhat foolhardy, but all of us had adopted a fatalistic attitude, and it just wasn't worth our while, or the energy, to dig in. As long as the officers did not insist on us doing that, we were not going to do it.

There was one exception, however—in Hürtgen. We occupied fairly large, fairly deep bunkers covered with logs and turf. We also put tarpaulins over the turf to keep out the rain. During these relatively static periods, the field kitchen would be brought up, and hot meals would be served. It was during this period that I remember doing KP, and my only duty was to act as a server in the chow line. I believe the mess sergeant had his own crew who did all the other things such as heating water for washing and rinsing mess kits. There were no floors to wash, no potatoes to peel (dehydrated were used), so the only menial tasks were washing pots, pans, and utensils.

Each gun battery had a supply sergeant and crew, and they did a lot of things that the gun crews were not called on to do.

Between fire missions, we built smokeless fires using the tarpaper cardboard containers that the shells came in. We would start the fires with a small amount of gasoline and then feed the flames by throwing surplus powder charges into the fire. We would leave enough men to operate the gun, in case of a fire mission, and wander around the area contacting locals (except in Germany because of the no-fraternization edict) and looking for souvenirs. This last activity sometimes ended in tragedy, as when one of our men moved a dead German who had been boobytrapped. It resulted in his death and severely wounded his companion. I think he must have died from the concussion, because there was no blood in evidence, and his clothing was not in tatters or otherwise visibly torn.

Of course, there was the ubiquitous poker game, writing letters, personal hygiene, reading Stars and Stripes and Yank. On Skyline Drive, we even had a "Siegfried Cinema" set up for us. The movies provided were from the bottom of the Hollywood barrel, just like the cigarette brands

258 🔷 War Stories: D-Day

we got were mostly the leftovers from what had been first picked over by supply and other rear echelon troops. We also spent time preparing ammunition to be fired and, of course, taking care of maintenance on the guns, vehicles, and our own weapons and equipment.

Letters for home were delivered to the battery clerk, who passed them on to an officer who, among his other duties, was the designated censor. They were then sent on their way to the APO for transfer to the States. Letters and packages were delivered to us by the battery clerk, and we had mail call at least twice each week. One other thing I should mention is that we did not buckle our helmet straps under our chins. We buckled them behind the back of our helmet, so as not to die from the strangling affect of concussion from a close explosion. Also, our helmets were used for heating water for shaving and for washing socks and underwear.

In closing, let me say that compared to the riflemen and other front line soldiers, we had a relatively comfortable time of it. How most of those men survived the horrible living conditions of rain-filled foxholes and freezing, or near-freezing weather in addition to the terror that they must have felt when launching an attack against a well dug in and deployed enemy is hard even for me to fathom. Yes, I was in some danger for most of the war, especially on D-Day and the early stages of the Normandy Campaign. But my death, if it were to come, would most likely be unexpectedly from shrapnel from a mortar or artillery round, and not from small arms fire while attacking an enemy strong point.

Francis W. Glaze Jr., Clearwater, FL
HQ, 8th Infantry Regiment and Jack Capell, Portland, OR
HQ, 8th Infantry Regiment

A Near Miss on the CP

The following comes from an e-mail exchange between these two veterans.

Frank Glaze: Let's start with the bombings and subsequent breakthrough at St. Lô on July 24 and 25, 1944. To set the stage, the assault was to be made by three U.S. Divisions. From left to right, the 30th, 4th, and

9th Infantry Divisions. The 8th Infantry was the assault regiment for the 4th Infantry Division. The St. Lô Periers road was the front line between the Germans and the "Amis." For safety, we pulled the assault companies back five hundred yards to avoid "friendly bombs." On July 24, the bombing started on schedule, but after about thirty minutes or so, it was stopped. We found out later that bombs had fallen on the Regimental HQ to our left (30th Division), and General McNair had been killed.

I had established liaison with the adjacent Regiment of the 30th Infantry and the lieutenant, the driver, and jeep came back an hour or two later, still in shock and useless. But they were survivors of that mass U.S. Air Corps bombing. It took me a week to get their attention. As a result of this incident, we withdrew the assault companies another five hundred yards after dark. The incident you described occurred the next morning, before the "big" bombing started. The Regimental CP was in an apple orchard, and about two hundred yards behind a low ridgeline that paralleled the St. Lô Periers road. Apparently, a German tank had fired an 88 toward something on our side and missed. The shell cleared the ridgeline and "trajectored" down at about the same rate as the slope of the orchard. The shell "moaned" in through an open window of the CP, hit the floor next to Sisk's foot, took off the heel of his shoe, and then the leg of an officer—I don't remember his name—and then up through the wall, about four feet from the floor.

In the back room, a liaison officer was asleep on a cot against that same wall. The shell used up all its momentum getting through the wall so it came to rest on the officer's chest. The noise and the weight and warmth of the shell brought the poor soul wide awake and put him in instant shock! I was about three minutes late in getting to the scene, so I missed Colonel Rodwell's reaction, the fainting spell, and the first few minutes of "God d---!" I did get there in time to make sure both officers got medical attention and were evacuated. It was bad for morale to keep them around any longer than necessary. I remember sending Sisk over to Supply Sergeant Stein to get a new pair of shoes. I figured he'd earned them.

The shell used up all its momentum getting through the wall so it came to rest on the officer's chest. The noise and the weight and warmth of the shell brought the poor soul wide awake...

As I remember, the rest of the day got even more exciting. The bombing by three thousand Allied planes started about an hour later using the St. Lô road as the dividing line between "them" and us That was fine for the first few waves of planes, but then the dust rose so high it obscured the road and the wind was toward us. The 2nd Battalion was to make the assault (I think), and the forward Regimental CP was immediately behind the battalion CP. To make the story short, the last half of the bombing was on the 8th Infantry Regiment assault companies, the rest of the 2nd Battalion, the Regimental CP, and the units stretched out five hundred yards behind us.

That was one time that the 8th did not "jump off" on time. It was a real effort getting those shell-shocked GIs (and officers) moving. The only good thing that day was that the Germans were worse off than we were. We moved forward on July 25 and 26, and got through the major obstacles, but it wasn't until July 27 that we picked up any speed.

Jack Capell: I was very pleased to get your recollections of July 24-25, 1944. My memory coincides almost precisely with yours. You spoke of the ridge about two hundred yards ahead of the CP. My foxhole was on the summit of the ridge. The 88 shell came directly over my head, so close that I was jolted by the shock wave. I looked back to the CP to see a cloud of dust rising over it, but there was no explosion. I headed toward it, being concerned about anyone being hit. I was sure that Horace Sisk had been in the building. He saw me coming and came out to meet me. He showed me his shoe and told me he had been sitting on a chair cross-legged when the shell came through the open window and clipped off the edge of his heel. The shell hit the leg of an officer and went through the wall. He told how it came to rest on the chest of a sleeping officer who awoke and promptly fainted.Rodwell was just arriving back at the CP. The officer was revived but was in a severe state of shock. Sisk told me the name of the officer who lost his leg was "Mabry," a brother of George Mabry of our Regiment.

I remember being told that the attack was postponed because of our casualties from the bombing. Shortly afterward, the word came that we were going forward. According to Ernie Pyle in Brave Men, our Company B did not get the word to postpone, so moved forward. When Rodwell discovered this, he ordered everyone forward.

P.S. Ernie Pyle was with the 4th Infantry Division before, during, and after St. Lô. He walked with the "dogfaces" of all three Regiments. He was the only correspondent that walked with the line companies that we knew of.

Liberation of Paris
August 25, 1944

Ogne of the proudest days in the storied history of the 4th Infantry Division came on August 25, 1944 when the division was the first Allied troops to enter Paris. History gives credit for the liberation to the French 2nd Armored Division, but our men who were there that day know differently. The 12th Infantry Regiment led the way into Paris, followed by the rest of the 4th Infantry Division. Here are some of their stories.—Bob Babcock

Quote from General Omar Bradley from his book, *A Soldier's Story:*

"To hell with prestige," I finally told Allen, "tell the 4th to slam on in (to Paris), and take the liberation." Learning of these orders and fearing an affront to France, LeClerc's French 2nd Armored Division mounted their tanks and burned up their treads on the brick roads to enter Paris.

Peter Triolo, Pueblo, CO
HQ, 1st Battalion, 12th Infantry Regiment

Capturing Paris

Paris was declared an open city. That meant neither the Germans nor the Americans could bomb or destroy the city on the way in or on the way out. At the time, we did not know it, but it was estimated that 10,000 German soldiers were in civilian clothes in Paris to escape the war at the time we arrived there. The 4th Infantry Division, upon arriving in an area about ten miles outside of Paris, was told to park along the road and hold our position. The 12th Infantry Regiment was leading the 4th Infantry Division. We arrived in this position about August 22, 1944. We were told to wait there because the French troops were going to pass through in order to take the honor of capturing Paris. However, at every farmhouse along the road, the French soldiers stopped and partied. This went on for two or three days. The problem was, every night the Germans would send over one or two German aircraft to machine gun the 4th Infantry Division parked along the road.

The commanding officer of the 4th Infantry Division requested permission from General Bradley to go in and capture Paris. It was stupid for the 4th Infantry Division to sit there and be shot up by Germans every night. Evidently, General Eisenhower agreed. On the morning of August 25, he gave permission for the 4th Infantry Division to go into

Paris. Since the 12th Regiment was the head of the 4th Infantry Division column, and the 1st Battalion of the 12th was leading the column, I was up front. I was told by Colonel Jackson to take my French-speaking sergeant and a two-jeep patrol and lead the 4th Infantry Division into Paris. We stayed about four hundred feet in front of the column the whole time. So, I was unofficially the first American officer to enter Paris.

Peter Triolo, Pueblo, CO
HQ, 1st Battalion, 12th Infantry Regiment

Events in Paris Worth Talking About

1. Party Pooper.

After entering Paris, we were stationed in a large city park about three or four blocks square. In one corner was a little shopping center. We took over a large building that was like a meeting hall for battalion headquarters. On the second morning, Colonel Jackson called me into his office. He wanted me to find out what all of the activity going on across the street was about. I walked into the building and entered a room. On one side, there was a long bar with tables and chairs out in the open area. But overhead, above the bar, there was a balcony with stairs on both ends leading to five or six rooms. As it turned out, it was a whorehouse. The men, of course, were going in and out of there. Colonel Jackson closed it up and made it off limits. A lot of men were unhappy.

2. Feed the Children.

At meal times, we had a real serious problem. When the men would go to eat, fifty to one hundred children would stand around and watch the soldiers eat. This would embarrass the men, and they would give their food to the kids. Colonel Jackson put a guard around the kitchen. He gave the mess sergeant orders to feed the men first and whatever was left was to be given to the children. That solved part of the problem.

3. The Daily Routine.

My duty for the five days in Paris was to maintain a motorized patrol around the area for security. It was reported that there were over ten

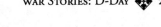

thousand German soldiers in civilian clothes still in Paris. They gave us no trouble—they were glad to get out of the war.

4. The Missed Parade, or, My soul for a Bath.

On the fourth day we had a big parade for the capture of Paris, strictly for publicity. I was supposed to march in it, but one of my officers talked to me. He said, "Pete, I got acquainted with the manager of the hotel. He gave me a room for two days so the officers could take showers and clean up." Well, you know where I was. I was up showering while everybody else was parading.

Carlton Stauffer, Charlton, NY
Company G, 2nd Battalion, 12th Infantry Regiment

Liberation of Paris

At 1900 hours, August 23, 1944, our 12th Regimental Combat Team consisting of the 12th Infantry Regiment, the 38th Cavalry Reconnaissance Squadron, the 42nd Field Artillery Battalion, Company B of the 634th Tank Destroyer Battalion, and Companies B and D of the 70th Tank Battalion, started a motor march, which was to be the most exciting experience I would have during my army career. The mission of our combat team was to seize and hold the bridges over the Seine River in the vicinity of Corbeil, which is approximately twenty-five miles southeast of Paris.

As it seemed to be in our usual pattern of things, the weather was dark and stormy. It was another night of skidding off the road into ditches with the usual few Nazi planes overhead. This motor march was in 6x6 trucks with as many fellows as could possibly fit into the cargo area jammed in. There were fold-down seats along each side, but most of us sat on the floor. To say we were miserable is a gross understatement, with the rain coming down in buckets all night long.

Every few hours we stopped to let the men stretch their legs and make the necessary nature calls. I remember one guy in the front part of the cargo space who had very little control and had to relieve himself several times during the night. Naturally, he used his helmet, the all-purpose accessory of the infantryman. As we were moving forward, he had to pass it back to have someone in the rear empty it so as not to blow into the side of the truck body. By morning, all of us were losing patience with the guy and about the only thing to relieve the tension was to curse at him.

As dawn appeared, matters became more tolerable. The rain finally subsided and we saw a new world—gently rolling terrain—the kind we felt would be tank country. Gone were the hedgerows of Normandy. War had moved quickly over this terrain, and there was less evidence of its devastation. As we passed through the small French towns, the townspeople lined the streets and greeted us with enthusiasm, holding flowers and wine up to us. It was only a taste of the celebration that awaited us in Paris.

We stopped at a little town named Orphin at about 1030 hours on the morning of August 24. We let ourselves dry out as we stretched our legs and got some rations. The vehicles were gassed up. We got the word that it would be the honor of the 12th Regimental Combat Team to be the first U.S. troops to enter Paris. We were to support the 2nd French Armored Division, which was given the political role of liberating Paris. To insure that nothing went awry, the Supreme Headquarters, Allied Expeditionary Forces assigned the responsibility to the 12th Infantry to insure a smooth liberation. We resumed our motor march some time during the afternoon of the 24th, and since we were in the suburbs of Paris, the celebrating was getting into high gear even then. Madly cheering French people wanted our convoy to slow down to give their hands, their flowers, their wine, and their sincere thanks to their liberators.

About 0800 hours on the morning of August 25, we began to move into the city of Paris. The details of an acceptable surrender with the Nazis are a matter of history, but we in our six-by-six's knew nothing of the plans. We all felt an exhilaration that would not be surpassed in the lives of any of us infantrymen. As we entered the Rue d'Itale, our tactical motor march became a huge victory parade, and our vehicles became covered with flowers. The pent-up emotions of four bitter years under the Nazi yoke suddenly burst into wild celebration, and the great French citizens made us feel that each of us was personally responsible for the liberation of these grateful people. We felt wonderful!

The men, women, and children surged against our trucks on all sides, making a four-mile travel to our positions hours long. There were cries of, "Merci! Merci! S'ank you, S'ank you Vive la Amerique!" Hands reached out just to touch the hands of an American soldier. Babies were held up to be kissed. Young girls were everywhere hugging and kissing the GIs. Old French men saluted. Young men vigorously shook hands and patted the GIs on the back.

Finally, late in the afternoon we took up our position for the night. I had the good fortune to be assigned to a chemistry building at a university on the west side of the Seine. We walked into the building and were met by a lady who was determined to make life just wonderful for us.

Captain Tallie Crocker, who was our company commander at that time, spread his blanket on the floor. Being an infantryman, he was always getting as close to the ground as possible. The lady immediately took his blankets and spread them out on a sort of couch that looked like an operating table. It was easier to let her do that than to explain anything. When she left, Captain Crocker put his blanket on the floor. At about this same time, we all heard loud machine gun fire outside the building. I went out with the captain to see what all of the noise was about. In the courtyard outside our building, a Frenchman of their 2nd Armored Division was in a jeep with a .50caliber machine gun firing away at the corner of a building in the court. Captain Crocker approached the Frenchman and asked what he was firing at. The Frenchman told him there were "Boche" in the building. Captain Crocker tried to convince him there were no Boche in the building. There was no meeting of minds. Finally, the Captain took the Frenchman on a "Boche hunt" through the building, proving once and for all—no Boche. Situation resolved! The girls came back to the jeep and we did more wild riding around Paris. When we went back into the chemistry building, Captain Crocker's blanket was back on the table.

That evening some of us went for a walk around town, hitting a few places for a celebration drink. The best part of the evening was to return to our chemistry building with its indoor plumbing.

At 0930 hours on the morning of August 26, Father Fries, our regimental chaplain, held Mass in the famous Notre Dame Cathedral, the first mass said after the liberation. Joe Dailey and I attended. It was a strange sight for Notre Dame to see us doughboys sitting at Mass with our rifles and battle gear. The problem confronting us at Mass and afterwards was to keep civilians away. There were ten civilians to one soldier. At last, the company commanders told the crowds that the soldiers were tired and needed sleep. Immediately, and with apologies, the civilians left our positions. That evening we were abruptly brought back to the reality of war when at 2330 hours, the Germans launched a heavy aerial bombing. Fortunately, all we encountered were the flashes and the booms—someone else at the distant part of Paris took it all.

Robert Gast, Warsaw, IN
Companies B and C, 1st Battalion, 12th Infantry Regiment

Fond Memories

Stories of our entry and stay in Paris are plentiful. I still have a hard time convincing people that women brought their babies to me—a twenty-one year old second lieutenant—to be blessed and kissed. There are four things that I remember the most about Paris: One, the children watching us eat, and we were not allowed to feed them. Two, the rumor that the 4th Infantry Division would stay in Paris and guard the bridges. Three, the day they bombed Paris I was officer of the day and riding about in a jeep.

When the siren sounded, the driver headed into a tunnel. It turned out to be a command post for the Free French Army. It was quite an experience. Four, the day we left Paris on foot. All of my men had stashed bottles of wine, loaves of bread, and jars of jam under their shirts. It was a very hot and humid day. The farther we walked, the hotter it got, and the more bread, jam, and wine ended up on the road.

George Knapp, Westchester, IL
Chaplain, HQ, 11th Infantry Regiment

Always First

One of the thrilling experiences was General Eisenhower selecting the 12th Infantry Regiment to be the only American unit to help in the liberation of Paris. Another "Top 25" experience was Cherbourg, Paris. As we entered, the Parisians came out to greet us by the hundreds. We were surrounded on the Champs Elysees. As chaplain, I had cigarettes from the Red Cross to give out to our men. I was passing them out to the Parisians, one at a time, when I accidentally showed an entire pack. Well, the people tore at the pack like a bunch of chickens, and all of the cigarettes were torn to shreds.

After one night in Paris, we had to move on towards Germany. Our Catholic Regimental Chaplain had the privilege of saying Mass to our Catholic men in Notre Dame Cathedral. The 4th Infantry Division was always the first—first on the beach; first into Paris; first into Germany.

Jim Roan, Fenton, MI
Company H, 12th Infantry Regiment

One Day in Paris

Regimental Headquarters was set up in a combination residential and business area in Paris. I rode shotgun with Lieutenant Ragland, and we entered the city the early morning of August 26, the day after the troops entered the city. There was a huge America flag flying under the Arc de Triomphe and more American flags flying throughout the city. The French civilian population used bicycles for transportation, and the street was full of them. The civilians were throwing kisses, trying to catch up with our jeep, and wanting to give us bottles of booze. Apparently, they were saving it for such a day. A very large French woman was standing on the curb of the 239 Arc de Triomphe yelling, "Where the hell have you guys been? We have been waiting for you!"

In the city we noted a number of French women getting their heads shaved by groups of Frenchmen with FFI arm bands. German troops were being marched as prisoners of war with a few GIs guarding them. We stopped at Notre Dame Cathedral, and an old man ushered us around. I stopped at a small souvenir shop nearby and purchased a ring that had the outline of the Eifel Tower engraved on its face. It immediately turned my finger green. We drove slowly among groups of civilians and turned down many bottles of various brands of booze. Ragland tried to follow a map, and we wound up on a side street close to the Arc De Triomphe in the city proper.

We parked the jeep at the curb and noted a young couple exiting an apartment building on the opposite side of the street, carrying a small child. They looked at us with a weird expression on their faces and slowly walked over to where we were parked. You have probably seen a number of newsreels of jeeps with large white stars printed on their hood and a small white star on each side, apparently a strange sight to Paris civilians. They walked over to us very cautiously and noted that we were speaking English and asked us, in broken English, who we were. We responded by saying that we are Americans. They started to cry and hugged and kissed us. We noted that a number of apartment dwellers started to exit various places, so we left before we were mobbed.

Lieutenant Ragland had to pick up and drop off various reports that only took a few minutes. We returned by driving close to the Eifel Tower, stopped, and tried to get the elevator ride to the top, but it was all locked up. We found our way back to the outfit. The Division was ordered to continue the war and only stayed in Paris one night, camped in a large park in tents. The civilians mobbed the area, and the GIs could not get any sleep. The Germans were regrouping in the suburban area and had to be dislodged before they could make a stand.

Paul Brunelle, Avon, MA
Company G, 2nd Battalion, 8th Infantry Regiment

The Tricolor Flies

From the book Company G, 2nd Battalion, 8th Infantry Regiment, 4th Infantry Division by Shirley Devine. Used here with her permission.

Entering Paris, I remember this little town of Longjumeau. I remember seeing the Eifel Tower in the distance. I had a pair of binoculars that somebody had loaned to me. I took the binoculars and looked up at the Eifel Tower, and there was the tricolor flying. The people in this little village had not seen the tricolor on top of the Eifel Tower since the occupation. As I handed the binoculars to the people, one by one, the emotion that they expressed was something that a person would never forget. They were just dumbfounded, and so happy that Paris was liberated. At least the area of the Eifel Tower had been liberated because there it was—the tricolor flying.

We were brought into Paris on two-and-a-half-ton-trucks and driven along a wooded park. I remember the people greeting us, and how happy they were to see us and to know that we were among the liberating troops.

One of the little things that I remember was going into a tiny French town one night. We were the first troops to enter, and the people were all outside singing the national anthem. It was quite moving. I was very young and I had never had a drink in my life. I think the first drink I ever had in my life was that green liqueur, Pernod. I had some, and said, "Well, I guess maybe I'm a man now, because I can drink something if I want to." However, I did not drink much of anything, even for the next few months of the war.

Bill Riiska, Winsted, CT
4th Reconnaissance Troop (Mechanized)

My Mustache for a Memory

To the best of my recollection I joined the 4th Infantry Division on D+2 near St. Mére Eglise. We moved into Arpajon, south of Paris and spent the night of August 23 there.

While in Arpajon, a Frenchman, Lladislaw (Woidek) Francuz, asked to join with us in fighting the Germans. He stayed with us more than three months when orders came that civilians could no longer stay with us. He came from Bretigny and rode in my jeep.

We moved into Paris some time before noon on I saw a shadow down at the corner and started to depress the trigger when a girl in short shorts and a blouse came waltzing around the corner.

August 25, from the south. I don't recall meeting any Germans at that time. I was fairly fluent in French by then, and when the captain's interpreter was busy and someone who spoke French was needed, I was often sent out.

We moved into Paris on the 25th and I recall meeting a French girl by the name of Audrey Cremer. I remember making two very exciting trips across Paris in a one-jeep parade with thousands of Parisians waving and cheering.

One trip was to deliver a message to the French Army, I'm sure that it was to General LeClerc and the French 2nd Armored Division. We found the tank outfit, and the message was delivered to the first ranking officer we found. I don't recall who was in my jeep, but I believe it was our platoon leader, Lieutenant George Gillon.

After we delivered the message, we found our way back to where the recon troop was located. It was like a parade when we were working our way back. I do remember that some of the Parisians were exacting retribution on the girls who were consorting with the Germans.

The second trip that I took was to bring up ammunition to one of our platoons. I also remember being posted near a park, observing a side street to the east and being told that no one but Germans would be coming up that street.

There was a .50 caliber machine gun mounted on our jeep, and I sat and watched down that street. Either it was extremely hot or I was very tense. I had my thumbs on the triggers of the machine gun ready to fire at anything I saw down the street.

I saw a shadow down at the corner and started to depress the trigger when a girl in short shorts and a blouse came waltzing around the corner. What a relief! I remember sitting on a corner under a street light, which I believe was lit, talking with Audrey Cremer. I made a date with her for the next night and she said, "Yes, but only under one condition." I had to shave off my mustache. I had a big handlebar mustache that I had been raising since we left the States in April.

We were sleeping that night in what seemed to be a garden house in back of a large estate. When we got up that morning, I shaved off my mustache. No sooner had I done that when our sergeant came by and yelled, "Pack up, mount up and move out." We left by the northeast, heading for Belgium, and I never returned to Paris.

As usual, those Americans most deserving of seeing Paris will be the last ones to see it, if they ever do. By that, I mean the fighting soldiers. Only one infantry regiment and one reconnaissance outfit of Americans actually liberated Paris, and they passed on through the city quickly and went on with the war.

Chester Frydryck, North Versailles, PA
Company M, 3rd Battalion, 22nd Infantry Regiment

Kisses from the Mademoiselles

From Utah Beach to St. Lô the landscape was devastation. Towns and villages were in flames and total destruction. Bodies, animal carcasses, and equipment destruction were everywhere. After the St. Lô breakthrough, the front advances were swifter. More destruction and bodies were encountered and columns of prisoners in greater numbers. Our outfit was in a sweep around the Falaise Pocket, heading for Paris.

As we were approaching Paris, there was a sense that the war may be ending. An airfield in the distant right was fully intact—destruction or annihilation wasn't evident. As we approached the suburbs, throngs of people lined the streets, cheering, waving French and U.S. flags, at times impeding our convoy, offering drinks as our convoy slowed. Many of our guys were greeted with kisses from the mademoiselles. Our convoy came to a halt in the Paris suburbs for several hours, offering an opportunity to mix with the French. Needless to say, some of our guys were quick to find the bars and gals. The excitement and activities were virtual pandemonium, an unforgettable event. I vividly recall a parade of dump trucks driven through the streets with French freedom fighters holding pistols to shaven heads of women who were supposedly German fraternizers.

Some French customs became evident to us when we had need for outdoor city rest rooms. They were unisex. As the celebrations continued, we began to move out to an area in town adjacent to a circus setup where we spent the night. We moved out the next day leaving behind a brief moment of civilization and the hopes and sense of the war ending. Continuing through France to Belgium, we had a beautiful view of the Swiss Alps, and on to the Siegfried Line. But the war and the devastation were far from over.

Lester Steele, Lexington, KY
Medical Detachment, 22nd Infantry Regiment

Wish I Could Have Spoken French

I do remember the day we went into Paris. Part of the time we were riding, and some of it in the outskirts was on foot. I remember a funny looking little Frenchman running up to me with a big hug and a kiss on the cheek that drew a lot of laughs from my fellow soldiers. I talked with a beautiful French girl on the edge of Paris. She gave me a glossy photo that I still have. Sure wish I could have spoken French!

I got a pretty good look at the Eifel Tower, and I think I can remember the Champs Elysees columns. We also made it into one bar, and I had a shot or two of some kind of cognac. While we were riding I remember that we were warned to still be on the lookout for snipers.

Oscar Romero, San Diego, CA
Company I, 3rd Battalion, 22nd Infantry Regiment

People Were Celebrating

Two things happened that day when we entered Paris that I still remember. Company I, 3rd Battalion, 22nd Infantry Regiment was in reserve, so we were riding two-and-a-half-ton-trucks, and our job was to clean up pockets of resistance by-passed by the spearheading troops. We had stopped because of a firefight ahead of us. We were ordered to dismount (what a mistake that was). People were celebrating and giving us wine, fruit, flowers, etc. We were short of officers after all the fighting since the breakthrough at St. Lô, so I was the platoon sergeant in charge of the first platoon. There weren't too many of us left, but when the word came to mount up to go, I had a hell of a time rounding up my men because everyone had joined in the celebration.

Anyhow, I finally rounded them all up except one. His squad leader and I went looking and found him in a bar, drunker than hell and waving his rifle in the air with a grenade launcher on the end of his barrel. He was singing the French national anthem when I hollered at him, "Let's go!" He accidentally pulled the trigger on his rifle and the sh-t hit the fan.

There were screams from the women, and everybody was covered with plaster and wood. We dragged him out, put him on the truck, and were on our way.

The next heroic thing we did that day was to liberate a bunch of women from a hotel that they told us was being used by the Germans as a prison. To this day, I still say this was a "cat-house" because among all these women were four American GIs who had been shot down over France and were being hidden by four of the ladies as their husbands—French berets and all. One of them came up to me and told me how glad they were to see us.

I said, "Are you ready to get back to your outfit?"

He said, "I think I'll wait for them to catch up with me." I said to myself, "What a beautiful way to fight a war!"

The next time I saw the real downtown Paris was in October 1944 when another sergeant and I were given a three-day pass from the Front before going into the Hürtgen Forest.

George Wilson, Grand Ledge, MI
Companies E and F, 2nd Battalion, 22nd Infantry Regiment

Friendly Smiles Were Everywhere

I was with the first U.S. troops to enter Paris. At the beginning, we were following tanks of the French 2nd Armored Division. They were feeling pretty excited about coming home. Some of the drivers should have been arrested for drunk driving. The tanks seemed to disappear as we reached the Champs Elysees. I was thrilled to see the huge crowds of excited people who jammed the streets from wall to wall. They gave us flowers, bread, cookies, wine, and anything you can imagine. My arm ached from handshakes. Friendly smiles were everywhere. Women threw us kisses, and some even climbed on trucks to give a few men a thrill.

Our next stop was at a suburb on the northeast edge of Paris. We didn't see any more French or German soldiers, only some very excited FFI groups hanging from cars and hanging guns from every window. We camped in the backyards and seemed to be welcome. We were told there were Germans in the area and one of our men was shot by a German. The next day, the French held a "kangaroo court" where five women were convicted of collaboration with the Germans. All five were found guilty. Shorn of all hair, they had to march down the street while the crowd threw eggs, tomatoes, and paper sacks filled with human waste at them. Shorn of all dignity, they were marked for a long time.

John F. Ruggles (Deceased), Phoenix, AZ
Executive Officer and Regimental Commander, 22nd Infantry Regiment

Major General (Retired) John F. Ruggles died on January 15, 1999. He was an Honorary President of the National 4th Infantry Division Association and Honorary Colonel of the 22nd Infantry Regiment. He also served us as a former president of the 22nd Infantry Regiment Society.—Bob Babcock

Those of Us Riding in Jeeps Were Really Mobbed

Bert Pokol was a very young soldier of Hungarian descent assigned as my jeep driver. He was a handsome young man with an eternal smile and eyes that danced. He never spoke of his father. His mother, if still living, was in Budapest. Hungarian-American friends back home in Perth Amboy, New Jersey, were the only ones to share his military burden with him. His English was very limited. As our acquaintance widened, our relationship become something approaching a fatherson relationship. Duties as jeep driver became secondary to Pokol's attention to my safety, welfare, and comfort. Food packages Pokol received from "home" were shared with me and others to augment our field rations. Pokol foraged vegetables from gardens all across France and Belgium to meet our needs. He did well, cooking on a small gasoline burner.

Thanks to the 12th Infantry Regiment's liberation effort, the 22nd Infantry Regiment moved through Paris motorized. It was a start-and-stop move as the streets were jammed with celebrating French citizens hugging and kissing soldiers they could reach. Those of us riding in jeeps were really mobbed. Steel helmets were not designed for wear in this kind of an encounter. Pokol, that handsome devil (with helmet abandoned), was having a hard time driving. He turned to me during a short break in the assault from beautiful French women and said, "Sir, you will get some of this if you get rid of that cigar," then he added, "and the helmet, too." He was right.

Bill Boice, Phoenix, AZ
Chaplain, 22nd Infantry Regiment

The Tomb of the Invalids

Shortly after midnight on August 25, 1944, Combat Team 22 was ordered to cross the Seine River. By noon the next day, the entire team was across the river and the liberation of Paris was accomplished— not by the French—as the news reported, but by the 4th Infantry Division. After the cheering and the impromptu parade was finished, David Mitchell, our Regimental American Red Cross Field Director, and I determined we would like to see the Tomb of the Invalids, better known as Napoleon's Tomb.

We tried to enter wrought iron gates at the front of the building, but they were securely locked. Occasional shots could still be heard from German sharpshooters isolated in buildings. We walked around the right of the building when a door opened in the heavy stone wall. An aged Frenchman in the uniform of a prior war stepped out of the building, saluted us as Americans, and asked, in halting English, if we would like to enter the building.

"Indeed, we would," we said.

Thus, Mitch and I were the first Americans to enter Napoleon's Tomb as the "City of Light" was being liberated. We stood by the great Rotunda, and our eyes went to the right where our guide pointed out the bronze tomb of Marshall Foch of World War I fame. His sarcophagus rests on the shoulders of six French soldiers. Then we looked across the rotunda and saw a huge mirror in front of which hung a great crucifix. But in a moment, we saw that it was not a mirror, but was a window through which we could see into a long chapel from whose ramparts hung the tattered and faded flags of the Napoleonic campaigns.

"Which is Napoleon's Tomb?" we asked. "Look down," instructed our guide.

We looked down. One full level beneath us, in the center of a mosaic circle, rested the imposing, bronze colored granite tomb of the Emperor.

Our guide continued, "When the memorial was being planned, the officials called for designs to be submitted. This was the one they preferred."

But a question was raised by some of the officials. "Why," they asked, "do you have visitors standing above the tomb around the rotunda and looking down on the Emperor?"

Napoleon's Tomb rests one full level beneath the rotunda. "I designed it," said the architect, "so that no one can stand in the presence of the Emperor without his head bowed."

"I designed it," said the architect, "so that no one can stand in the presence of the Emperor without his head bowed." It was a lesson of history that David Mitchell and I have not forgotten.

Tommy Harrison, Vero Beach, FL
HQ, 2nd Battalion, 22nd Infantry Regiment

The Day Paris Fell

The night before we were to take over and fight for the rest of Paris that was still in German hands, Colonel Lanham took about six of us to a cafe that Ernest Hemingway used to visit. Here it was night, and the six of us go to this cafe—and quite a place it was. Hemingway had left word that we would be there that night. The owner treated us like heroes and even opened up a wine cellar that he had hidden from the Germans. We had a great dinner and great wine. The owner said the Germans had been there the night before. We were the first Americans he had seen in years. Hemingway's French troops had opened up the area, clearing the Germans out.

The next day we were alerted to drive through the rest of Paris. We had a "point" out to warn us when and if we ran into any Germans. I remembered riding through Paris in a jeep. Parisians lined the streets, waving and yelling at us. It was like a ticker-tape parade down Wall Street. They told us the Germans had pulled out the night before. We were to go to a point where the suburbs started, set up a position and start cleaning out the area. Just as we set up in position, we were told to pack up and move

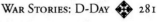

out—the Germans apparently had flown the coop. We alerted our troops and moved out. We got about ten miles outside of Paris when we sat up and sent out guards to keep us apprised of the German positions.

That was Paris. We (all except six of us) didn't get a chance to really get involved in Paris. As you know, we all are very proud that we were there, "the day that Paris fell."

David Rothbart, Pittsburgh, PA
Company E, 2nd Battalion, 22nd Infantry Regiment

Paris Jews in Hiding

I re-read what I had written in my World War II Army Journal. In the entry dated September 1, 1944, I wrote about Jews I spoke to in Yiddish who had just come out of hiding in Paris. Leo Gorelick and I visited them in the quarters that they still occupied—hideous rooms, with secret chambers in dilapidated tenements in the slums and back alleys of the city. There were quite a number of them. It just occurred to me now, fifty-four years later, that many French Christians had to know they were there and did not report them to the German authorities or their French agents. From time to time, I still hear a few Americans cynically question the integrity of the French while they were under German occupation. My observation today, that the Jews in hiding were not given away, convinces me that the French people, on the whole, other than the notorious Vichy French, truly knew and did what was right.

Weldon Frye, Columbia, SC
HQ, 22nd Infantry Regiment

Kissing Babies

Watching on television the thousands of happy, French citizens celebrating the World's Cup Soccer Championship in Paris brought back memories of when we entered that city in August 1944. The day that the 22nd Infantry Regiment entered Paris by way of the Champs Elysees, we were greeted by what I remember to be thousands of beautiful women in colorful dresses and different colored hair, riding bicycles.

Words cannot describe the happiness and appreciation shown by the people in Paris that day. They were crying; they were trying to hug, kiss, and love the 22nd Infantry to death. After being in hard and continuous fighting from D-Day until then, I can assure you that we loved and appreciated the way we were welcomed by these happy people.

As we moved slowly forward, we were surrounded by more and more people who just wanted to touch, hug, kiss, or share a toast. At times, we were picked up bodily and passed over the crowd so everyone could share in the excitement. We were passed into houses and offices full of people who just wanted to be part of the celebration. Of course, this meant kissing what seemed like thousands of babies. This scenario continued until late afternoon. I can't remember details (too many toasts) other than we were not allowed to remain in the city overnight. We moved on through and formed a defensive position outside the city in position to repel a counterattack if one occurred. If I remember correctly, the next morning, the famous 22nd Infantry members jumped off in their normal attack in pursuit of the enemy. As you know, we still had many more hard battles ahead.

B.P. "Hank" Henderson, Knoxville, TN
Medic, 22nd Infantry Regiment

Someone Found a Case of Champagne

We rode all night in a pouring rain. When we reached Paris the next morning we were quite wet, and we dried out in the hot sunshine. When we got into Paris we were stopped by huge crowds of people. They were hanging out of their windows, and the crowd was so thick that we could not get off our trucks to urinate. We had to take our liners out of our helmets and use it for a pot and pour it over the side of the truck.

Service Company pulled into a garage that was fenced in, and we were restricted to that area. Some of the men climbed up the gutters of a house that boxed the garage in. We stayed there two days. The second day some of us went about three or four blocks and visited a beautiful church. We moved out to the outskirts of Paris and stayed there two nights.

The first night someone found a case of champagne, and First Sergeant Hoit Chandler invited me to the champagne party. The next morning, we could hardly hold our heads up. After two days there, we moved a little farther out of Paris. That day I patched up three different men who had shot themselves in the hand with a German P-38 pistol. Not any of them were serious enough for them to be evacuated back to Paris. From there, we headed for the Belgium border.

Bill Parfitt, Elmira, NY
Company G, 22nd Infantry Regiment and HQ, 4th Infantry Division

Seeing General DeGaulle

We traveled in convoy along with the Free French and some of their tanks. It was amazing how often we stopped and, of course, the "ladies" would scramble up the sides of the tanks and disappear. We did remark that they must be packed pretty solid inside. I saw the first bikini I ever saw on a gal standing on the top of a high wooden fence surrounding a swimming pool. Along the way we were greeted by crowds of people offering bottles of wine and bundles of fresh vegetables. Even ripe tomatoes were "tossed" into our reach. Some were immediately eaten, and some were saved. We had an Italian lad with us by the name of Bennie Bertoline from Peekskill, New York, who was saving these vegetables like mad. As the convoy lurched along, some of the Free French tanks took on more passengers, and others just pulled off the road and stopped. We ended up at the Bois de Vincennes as the CP of the 4th Infantry Division HQ for the night. It was some kind of a public park that soon became a tent city with pup tents appearing all over the place.

Some of us were able to take a walk and ended up in crowds of people; all of them seemed to have a bottle of something with them. There is nothing to remind me of when we returned to Division HQ. I heard Bennie Bertoline call me and went over to his command car where he handed me his helmet. Inside was the most beautiful salad I think I have ever seen. He had added salt and pepper to the wine and had made a dressing that was poured over the vegetables the French had tossed us. Cucumbers were sliced, tomatoes were sliced, some carrots were added, and for lettuce, he used the leaves from maybe beets or greens. We sat and ate the helmetful, and drank wine and he made a second helmet full of "salad."

I remember little until the next morning when we were busy informing the entire unit Headquarters as to where we were going to set up
our next CP. It was funny to see strange heads emerge from some of the
pup tents or get out of trucks, etc. They were not in uniform and were
evidently female; they would look around and then start walking away.

This was also where we informed all of the units that we were moving
on and that another "clean" division was going to march in the victory
parade for General DeGaulle. We were too dirty, it seemed, and they
all had clean new uniforms. Somewhere in a book I have is the story on
DeGaulle insisting that President Roosevelt send his "best" troops to enter Paris with the Free French, so the 4th Infantry Division was chosen.
When we appeared and were dirty, unshaven, and not looking like fresh
new troops, they substituted the 28th Infantry Division that had all clean
new uniforms.

I think the greatest memory of this was in seeing General DeGaulle
among the frenzied French people as we came to a blocked street where
his parade was passing by. The funniest sight was the young "ladies"
climbing up and into the French tanks and the tanks pulling off the road.
The next funniest was seeing them getting out of GI pup tents just after
daylight and slowly walking away. Undoubtedly they had become tired
and had just stopped to take a nap!

David Roderick, Carlsbad, CA
Company H, 2nd Battalion, 22nd Infantry Regiment

Across the Seine in Three Hours

The breakthrough at St. Lô had been successful. We were proud we
could say that we had spearheaded the "breakthrough at St. Lô" for
the units poised to make the run for Paris. But the 4th Infantry Division never rested. We were ordered on the 23rd of August to make the
100-mile motor march to Ablis, France. The objective was to establish a
bridgehead over the Seine River, south of Paris. Our movement was fast
in spite of a torrential rainstorm throughout the night and all through
the next day.

We assembled near Corbeil to make the assault in small rubber boats
at 0300 hours on August 25. The first elements of the 3rd Battalion were

sunk by small arms fire and antiaircraft guns. The 2nd Battalion laid down a fierce artillery barrage and a platoon of Germans on the opposite shore surrendered. The battalion was across the Seine in three hours. The 1st and 3rd Battalions got a company across and the combined forces made quick work of the Germans, but we were not without casualties. George Cole of Company C, 4th Engineers, remembers lying on the ground after recovering from his boat being sunk. Bob Stockman came running by, and he told him to sit down with him. As he sat down, a German bullet went through his leg. George's good friend, William Bates, was killed there.

Combat Team 22 completed our part of the liberation by moving in jeeps and trucks into Paris. It was a joyous sight with the throngs of cheering people. Hugs, kisses, and wine were exchanged. This was the first and only time that the line troops had any time to mingle with the people of France. They yelled constantly, "Merci! Merci! Vive la Amerique!"

When I finally rode into the bivouac area, the city dump, at 1300 hours, I looked forward to acquainting myself with some rest and the gaiety of Paris. I was there less than an hour when I got word that my section of mortars would be a part of a scouting party to move out and make contact with the withdrawing Germans. On the way in, I passed the Arc de Triomphe and on the way out, I passed the Notre Dame Cathedral. Good-bye Paris!

Tom Reid, Marietta, GA
Cannon Company, 22nd Infantry Regiment and Company I,
3rd Battalion, 22nd Infantry Regiment

Overall, a Glorious Day

Paris, "Gay Paree," "City of Light… " By whatever name it is known, it has an inexorable pull on the human spirit, the traveler, the wanderer in us all.

After the bitter fighting in Normandy and the decisive breakout late in July, the 4th Infantry Division was in the vicinity of Chartres southwest of Paris. When the word came that the 4th would be the first to enter Paris, there was joy mixed with apprehension. Joy that the 22nd Infantry Regiment would soon be in Paris and apprehension that it might be denied us. In any event, it had a tremendous effect. No one wanted to leave the Regiment for any reason while this was contemplated. Word spread beyond the division and there were cases of men leaving the hospital without orders and making their way back to the Regiment. No one wanted to miss this once-in-a-lifetime opportunity.

The 22nd Infantry moved to positions at Corbeil, some twenty-five miles south of Paris, ready to move in, but no orders came. Instead, it was decided at higher echelons to let the French 2nd Armored Division be the first to enter Paris. There was no fighting in Paris; it had been declared an 'open city' in order to save it. For twenty-four hours, we watched the French limping along, towing some disabled vehicles, transporting others, and on the morning of August 25 they passed us and went into Paris to a joyful citizenry.

Soon the 22nd Infantry Regiment, motorized by the attachment of several quartermaster trucking companies, slowly wound its way through Paris. The only restraining order given was that no one could leave the vehicles. The day was glorious, the sun shined brightly, and crowds pushed forward until it seemed that all of France was welcoming us that day. People thrust bottles of wine into outstretched hands, threw flowers and notes at the troops, and crowded into the trucks. All in all, it was a most memorable experience. Soon, however, with the extra consumption of the wine, the order to remain in the vehicles was becoming harder to observe. This was where the steel helmet was given one more task to perform.

Still, the experience was unforgettable and lives with me to this day. The people lining the streets, the generosity of the French people, the noise, the excitement of being present at the Liberation of Paris—all of this was indelibly imprinted on a first lieutenant whose only command up to this time was an infantry platoon. The route through Paris was terminated by our arrival at a bivouac for the night at a walled enclosure. It was somewhere on the northern outskirts of Paris. The Regimental Commander had sent an advance party ahead to locate this compound. I've heard it said that, in fact, this was an insane asylum, and we merely used the grounds for the night. This I will leave for the historians to verify. The next morning we were off in hot pursuit of the retreating Wehrmacht, and soon found ourselves in Belgium. On September 11, 1944, the 22nd

Infantry Regiment became the first U.S. unit to enter German soil. But that is another story.

One final word. Whenever you see the oft printed picture of American troops massed fifty abreast marching down the Champs Elysees in Paris with the Arc de Triomphe in the background and billed as the liberation of Paris, brand it as a phony. That is the 28th Infantry Division some three or four days after the 4th Infantry Division had rolled through Paris that bright August day. Indeed, when this picture was published in the Stars and Stripes, the 22nd Infantry Regiment had already shaken the dust of France from its boots and would soon be in Germany.

Overall, a glorious day.

John C. Ausland (Deceased), La Crosse, WI
Headquarters Battery, 29th Field Artillery Battalion

In Paris, We Were the Finest of All

This article, written by John Ausland, appeared in the August 25, 1994 International Herald Tribune.

As August 25, 1944, dawned, the U.S. 4th Infantry Division found itself in a bivouac just south of Paris. Orville Schroeder, my communications sergeant, brought me out of a deep sleep by shaking me and saying, "Wake up, Captain Ausland. We are going to go take Paris."

A few hours later I found myself driving my jeep through throngs of civilians as we made our way to Choisy-le-Roi, a suburb of Paris. The mission of the 1st Battalion of the 8th Infantry Regiment, to which I was attached as artillery liaison officer, was to guard the bridge at Choisy. The 12th Infantry Regiment of the 4th Infantry Division reached the center of the city around noon. It joined up with the French 2nd Armored Division. Shortly after noon (after firing him to preserve his honor), General Dietrich von Cholitz, commander of the German forces, surrendered and was taken into custody by the French.

Soon after, in a letter dated August 29, 1944, I wrote this account of that day in Paris to my parents: "Well, this division has now been in on three of the most important phases of the French campaign: 1) the landings on D-Day, 2) the breakthrough on the St. LôPeriers road, and 3) now the freeing of Paris.

"This has been one of the most exciting times we have had since arriving in France. I won't go into the military details, but perhaps you would be interested in the purely nonmilitary points. We started into the city late one morning. The infantry battalion with which I traveled was one of the first to enter the city from its particular side of entry.

"It was a grand welcome the people gave. They lined the streets for mile after mile, thousands of them. All were shouting, "Vive l'Amerique," or, "Vive la France," literally wild with joy. We were the first Americans they had seen, the first sign of freedom after four years of domination.

"As we rode through the streets, the crowd would surge about us until it was impossible to move forward. People would crowd about and onto our vehicles. Women, men, and girls flung their arms around us, insistent on kissing us on both cheeks. Mothers held up their babies for us to kiss. We were literally showered with fruit of all kinds, wine, and flowers, until our vehicle resembled a garden.

"At street intersections, the crowd was so thick it was impossible to move forward, with the street solid with people as far as the eye could reach. We moved only with loud use of the horn and insistent urging. There were thousands of pretty girls, all dressed in their Sunday best. It seemed to me I'd never seen so many beautiful women. Until they spoke, one would think he was in America.

"At last we stopped and set up our headquarters in an ex-German Army building. The people crowed the gates to watch the Americans. It was impossible to work because of the kisses, handshaking and shouting. Our men were having a wonderful time.

"That night there was singing, drinking and dancing until the wee hours of the morning. The hardships of occupation were forgotten, though it was difficult to convince them that the Americans, unlike the Germans, would permit them to dance, collect in crowds and enjoy themselves.

"It was a big moment in the city's history, and the French were the ones to demonstrate it. For the moment at least, the Americans were the finest persons who ever existed.

Paris was liberated.

"It was a big moment in the city's history, and the French were the ones to demonstrate it. For the moment at least, the Americans were the finest persons who ever existed. Paris was liberated. "And, so, it has been for days as we move from one part of the city to the other—crowds, kisses, and celebration. A new kind of war. But the fighting will come again. There are many Germans between here and Berlin. They haven't given up and are not defeated.

"In another letter, I will tell you of the FFI, the French Forces of the Interior, and their fight to help free Paris. Also, of the "little war," I got into at the Place de la Concorde in the center of the city.

Love, John."

Jack Cunningham, Manteca, CA
Battery C, 29th Field Artillery Battalion

Surrounded by a Street Celebration

When we arrived in Paris, the streets were lined with the local people of all ages greeting us with wine and flowers. The motor column had stopped until places could be found for us to wait until orders to move on were given—which was going to be dependent on what was happening ahead of us.

Captain Jim Hurst, the CO of Charlie Battery, asked my forward observer party and me to follow him in my jeep as he went ahead to look for a suitable place to get the battery off the street. We found a big grassy, wooded park; he left my party and me there and returned to bring up the battery. My forward observer party that day consisted of Corporal Karam, radio operator; Corporal Turnier, driving the jeep; and Technician/5 Fitzgerald, if I remember correctly. We were standing on the street side of the stone wall that bordered the park when an elderly man, who spoke English, accompanied by a young man, came along the sidewalk. He asked us to visit his house nearby. We went there and met his wife and others. He left the room and came back with two bottles of Scotch whiskey that he had been saving for the liberation. By the time the battery arrived, we had undergone an attitude adjustment and felt as if the war was over. On our last day in Paris, which may have been August 27, I was with the infantry as they made a street-by-street advance through the northern edge of the city. Phase lines had been established on designated cross streets and no unit could move beyond a phase line until all were at that line. Sometimes we had to wait at a phase line while others were moving up. There were hundreds of French men and women with bottles of cognac and wine. When the time came for us to move again, it would take all of a half hour to find those who had wandered off and get them all together again.

That night we reached the outskirts of the city and kept going. My party rode in our jeep, but the infantry was on foot with some vehicles accompanying them. Somewhere along the road we gave a woman a lift, and she rode in the limited space in the rear of the jeep with Karam and Fitzgerald for several miles. We did not encounter any enemy opposition that night.

John Worthman, (Deceased) Medic, 22nd Infantry Regiment
They Waited a Long Time

As we neared Paris we were ordered to cross the Seine west of Paris and hold the far shore as a beachhead. This was done so the regiment could move rapidly into Paris if needed. French General Gerow's Second Armored Division was slated to liberate the city, a deal worked out between SHAEF, DeGaulle, and the Free French. We were to support them only if needed.

In the morning of August 25 we were ordered by radio to enter the city in support of the Free French. A few German tanks had been reluctant to leave the city but did so when our self-propelled artillery appeared. They probably held as long as possible according to orders to allow the other troops to get away as far as possible. By midmorning, there was no more firing, and we moved into the heart of the city on jeeps and trucks.

The Parisians had waited a long time for liberation from the German occupation. Each one seemed to have decided what he would do on that delirious day, and it usually involved a bottle of the best vintage available, which probably had been well hidden. The people cheered and laughed and cried and wanted to embrace us, give us a drink, feed us the newly ripe tomatoes, kiss us, and just try to believe we were really there and the Germans gone. We had little room for the vehicles to move through the press of people, and stops were frequent. I had many different kinds of wine. I had a swallow of several champagnes and a number of cognacs, armagnacs and other liquors before we arrived at our truck park. All officers and noncoms made sure no one had strayed away—they might go AWOL and get lost in Paris forever. We loaded up before evening, moved north of the city about fifteen miles, and camped. Had we stayed in Paris overnight, we would have lost too many men temporarily or permanently to the attractions of that ecstatic city. I kissed babies, children, young women, old women, and women in between. Men between eighteen and fifty were in very short supply until we arrived. When Paris now celebrates the 25th of August, the TV indicates that the French liberated Paris.

Epilogue

If you enjoyed reading the stories of these 4th Infantry Division veterans, there are plenty more, equally as gripping, in the second volume of this three-book series, *War Stories: Paris to V-E Day*. While the first two books of this series are focused exclusively on the 4th Infantry Division's experiences in WWII, the stories could just as easily have come from any of the dozens of divisions who fought to liberate Europe.

War Stories: Paris to V-E Day, available in both paperback and e-book from www.deedspublishing.com, continues the fight after Paris was liberated. While others celebrated the liberation in Paris, the 4ID continued the hot pursuit of the Germans across France, into Belgium, and were the first Allied force to breach the famed Siegfried Line and fight into Germany on September 11, 1944. After their fight against the pillboxes and bunkers of the Siegfried Line, the 4ID found itself in the bloodiest battle in their history—before or since. November and early December 1944 found them fighting through Germany's Hurtgen Forest, a battle that has been all but forgotten after it was overshadowed by the Battle of the Bulge. But the 4ID Soldiers who fought there will never forget it—a typical rifle company suffered 150% casualties in the Hurtgen Forest, yet the division's objective was accomplished.

In early December, a tired division, desperately needing rest and refitting, moved to the relative quiet of Luxembourg, only to be thrown into the largest battle of WWII—the Battle of the Bulge. General George Patton praised the division's performance for holding the southern shoulder of the Bulge and securing the capitol city of Luxembourg and the major supply lines running back into France.

Once the German surge into the Bulge was stopped, the 4ID was part of the counter-attack in January 1945, going back through the Siegfried Line, often using foxholes the 4ID Soldiers had dug in September 1944. Slugging it out through the coldest winter Europe had experienced in years, the 4ID fought through Prum and many other German towns as they continued pushing the Germans back across the Rhine River. By the time the war ended on May 8, 1945, the 4ID had suffered more casualties than any other American division in Europe, yet had accomplished every mission assigned to them.

To read more of the personal stories of those members of the "Greatest Generation," order your copy of *War Stories: Paris to V-E Day*, available now from www.deedspublishing.com.

About the Author

Bob Babcock has had a passion for the military and military history since he was a young boy growing up in Heavener, OK during the Korean War. He was fascinated by the troop trains and freight trains with military equipment passing through his home town. In high school, he wrote a term paper on D-Day, his first deep dive into military history.

A Vietnam veteran of the 4th Infantry Division, Bob became a member of the National 4th Infantry Division Association where he met and listened to stories of many 4ID WWII vets—those who made the history reported in this book. As a founding official partner of the Veterans History Project, Bob expanded his interest in all military history through interviews with hundreds of veterans of all ranks and all services, with a strong focus on preserving WWII veteran stories while they are still with us. In 2004, Bob led a tour of ten 4ID D-Day veterans to the 60th anniversary ceremony in Normandy, France. For two years, Bob was a Department of Defense historian, serving as the official historian of the active duty 4th Infantry Division, collecting the history from Iraq and Afghanistan as it happened and acting as the go to person on all other 4ID history.

A retired IBM executive, Bob has written six books and founded Deeds Publishing, a family owned and operated publishing company in Atlanta, GA. His spare time is spent working with veterans of all wars and preserving their stories for posterity. He is currently in his third term as President of the National 4th Infantry Division Association and continues in the 4ID historian job he has held for almost two decades.

Books by Robert O. Babcock

War Stories: Uath Beach to Pleiku

War Stories: D-Day to the Liberation of Paris

War Stories: Paris to V-E Day

War Stories: Vietnam 1966-1970

World War II WAC (with Helen Denton)

What Now, Lieutenant?

Operation Iraqi Freedom I: A Year in the Sunni Triangle

Operation Iraqi Freedom 07-09: Dispatches from Baghdad

You Don't Know Jack… Or Jerry

For more information, visit www.deedspublishing.com.

CPSIA information can be obtained at www.ICGtesting.com
Printed in the USA
LVOW12s1912240114

370906LV00002B/5/P